Beyond Pearl Harbor

MODERN WAR STUDIES

Beyond Pearl Harbor

A Pacific History

Edited by Beth Bailey
and
David Farber

University Press of Kansas

Published by the University Press of Kansas (Lawrence, Kansas 66045), which was organized by the Kansas Board of Regents and is operated and funded by Emporia State University, Fort Hays State University, Kansas State University, Pittsburg State University, the University of Kansas, and Wichita State University.

Library of Congress Cataloging-in-Publication Data

Names: Bailey, Beth L., 1957– editor. | Farber, David R., editor.
Title: Beyond Pearl Harbor : a Pacific history /
edited by Beth Bailey and David Farber.
Description: Lawrence, Kansas : University Press of Kansas, [2019] |
Series: Modern war studies | Includes bibliographical references and index.
Identifiers: LCCN 2019004055
ISBN 9780700628124 (cloth : alk. paper)
ISBN 9780700628131 (pbk. : alk. paper)
ISBN 9780700628148 (ebook)
Subjects: LCSH: World War, 1939–1945—Campaigns—Pacific Ocean. | Pearl Harbor (Hawaii), Attack on, 1941. | Pacific Area—Strategic aspects. | Japan—Foreign relations—Pacific Area. | Pacific Area—Foreign relations—Japan. | Pacific Area—Foreign relations—United States. | United States—Foreign relations—Pacific Area. | Japan—Foreign relations—United States. | United States—Foreign relations—Japan. | Japan—History, Military—1868–1945. | United States—History, Military—20th century.
Classification: LCC D767 .B495 2019 | DDC 940.54/26—dc23
LC record available at https://lccn.loc.gov/2019004055.

British Library Cataloguing-in-Publication Data is available.

Printed in the United States of America

10 9 8 7 6 5 4 3 2 1

The paper used in this publication is recycled and contains 30 percent postconsumer waste. It is acid free and meets the minimum requirements of the American National Standard for Permanence of Paper for Printed Library Materials Z39.48-1992.

Contents

Beyond Pearl Harbor

Introduction

December 7/8, 1941

Beth Bailey and David Farber

In the United States, December 7, 1941, is remembered as "a date which will live in infamy." The phrase, of course, is President Franklin D. Roosevelt's. And whether his words shaped the nation's perception or simply captured it, "infamy" is how Americans, both then and later, understood Japan's attack on Pearl Harbor—a dastardly, unprovoked surprise attack by a treacherous enemy on the United States.[1] And a majority of Americans, we wager, have no idea that Pearl Harbor was not Japan's sole target, or that Japan's coordinated attacks hit the imperial possessions of Western nations scattered across the broad reach of the Pacific Ocean.

Roosevelt did not think, at first, to characterize December 7, 1941, as a day of "infamy." In his first draft of the short speech he would deliver before a joint session of Congress on December 8, he wrote, "Yesterday, December 7, 1941, a date which will live in world history . . ." It was not so memorable a bit of phrase-making as the one that would resonate through the following decades. Nonetheless, as we argue in this book, it offered a more accurate summation of what happened that day, not only at Pearl Harbor but at the many other points of attack that occurred (on the Japanese side of the international date line) on December 8, 1941. World history *was* altered that day, as the new world war shattered the status quo antebellum of people and nations in what the United States called "the Pacific theater" and the Japanese came to call the "Pacific War."

In this collection of original chapters, we look again at the great cataclysm of that monumental day—December 7 from the American perspective; December 8 on the other side of the international date line—to assess its impact from an angle different than usual. While not ignoring the strategic military meaning of the attacks or the domestic political impact of the attacks on the major belligerents, we focus on how Japan's great—if short-lived—victories roiled the

Pacific world. Collectively, we analyze the impact of the attacks Japan launched that day—on O‘ahu, of course, but also on the Philippines, Malaya, Guam, Wake Island, Hong Kong, Singapore, and Thailand. These attacks and their aftermath, if seen as interconnected, expose broader historical patterns. They reveal the arc of imperialism, colonialism, and burgeoning nationalism in the Pacific world; they demonstrate the transformation of racial solidarities and racial identities within and across Pacific world societies; and they show how a variety of elite actors incorporated the attacks into new regimes of knowledge and expertise that challenged and displaced prior disciplinary hierarchies. In our analysis, the attacks of December 7/8 belong to a story of clashing empires and anticolonial visions. It is also a story told from multiple perspectives.

A brief caveat: given our focus on the events of December 7/8, 1941, the history we recount here, while international in scope, is also limited. We focused more on the "Pacific Rim powers" and their colonies than on the "oceanic history" of Pacific Islanders.[2] We tell the story of those Pacific Islanders and the arc of their historical journey pre- and post-December 7/8 either in relatively narrow terms or tangentially. This Pacific history is far from the last word on the meaning of the events of December 7/8, 1941, on the peoples of the Pacific.

More forthrightly, we do aim to rethink the narrative of "surprise attack" that has long dominated how Americans, at least, understood the events of December 7, 1941. The wave of Japanese attacks that occurred on December 7/8, 1941, were, in general, far from a surprise, though the specific targets were unexpected. Japan had made clear since 1931, when it seized Manchuria in northern China, that as an imperial power it intended to compete for dominance and resources against the other great colonial powers that operated in the Asian-Pacific world. And since Japan had begun a full-out war on the Republic of China in July 1937, the United States, Great Britain, France, the Netherlands, and other interested parties—sometimes in concert with the divided Chinese, occasionally in shifting alliances, and, more often, independently—had maneuvered to limit further Japanese aggression in the region.

By 1939, most—though not all—American policymakers had surmised that if the United States pushed hard enough against Japan's military aggression in Asia, specifically by embargoing exports of oil to resource-poor Japan, the Japanese would strike out against American and European colonial possessions in and around the Pacific. Certainly by 1940, people invested in the future of the Pacific world anticipated, if not world war, then a storm of belligerency heralded by Japan's regular declarations that the time had come for the "expulsion of Anglo-American influence" from Asia.[3] The successful attacks launched by the Japanese on their December 8, 1941, were far from inevitable, but neither were they a surprise to reasonably well-informed parties across the contested lands and seas of the Pacific realm. In fact, as historian and contributor to this volume Christopher Capozzola insists, the "politics of anticipation" more than the trope of surprise figured the viewpoint of people in much of the colonialized and already war-torn nations and territories of the Asia-Pacific region as they waited, in late 1941, for Japan's next moves.

By late 1941 the US government, with little public discussion, was preparing for war against Japan. Secretary of State Cordell Hall and Secretary of War Henry Stimson understood that the oil embargo and freezing of Japanese assets in the United States in retaliation for Japan's invasion of French Indochina had left the Japanese with few options. The US government followed its punitive measures against Japan by establishing a Far Eastern military command in the Philippines and began to rapidly build up military assets there. Additional military assistance was hurried to the Chinese by both the United States and Great Britain.

As Akira Iriye writes in his classic account of the war between the United States and Japan, *Power and Culture*, by the fall of 1941 the United States, Great Britain, the Chinese, and the Dutch had begun "to exchange information and coordinate their defenses in the Pacific."[4] And by November 1941, the Dutch government-in-exile in London (Germany had overrun the Netherlands in May 1940) knew that the Japanese had the rich oil fields of the Dutch East Indies targeted. Simultaneously, the British had watched with increasing concern as the Japanese massed troops in French Indochina with their likely target British Malaya.

Filipino and Indonesian nationalists, as well as other colonized peoples throughout the Asian-Pacific world, well clued in to Japan's determination to rid the region of the Western powers, had begun to ponder what a war between the United States and Japan would mean for their colonial status, their hopes of liberation from the West's colonial yoke, and their national, regional, and racial identities, even before the Japanese invaded their lands. In the months before December 7/8, 1941, the winds of war were already blowing hot. While war was far from inevitable, even in the late fall of 1941 Japanese leadership had begun to move decisively toward an attack on the Western powers, and the people and the nations of the region were preparing for what might come.

Still, when war came, few expected it to arrive exactly as it did. American military planners anticipated the *possibility* of an attack not on Hawai'i, but on the Philippines. And they believed they had a reasonable amount of time to prepare for such an eventuality. The British, throughout 1941, were focused elsewhere. Britain was being bled dry by Germany's successful submarine attacks on its merchant marine; in the first four months of 1941 alone, the Nazis had destroyed almost 2 million tons of shipping, sapping Great Britain's ability to fight.[5] Prime Minister Winston Churchill had declared the "Battle of the Atlantic" a life-or-death struggle, and he threw what resources he could muster into it. Great Britain's Asian-Pacific empire was, relatively speaking, an afterthought. Australians, long accustomed to the protection of the British Navy, understood what Great Britain's Atlantic focus meant for them: they were largely on their own, and thus dependent on establishing a new defense relationship with the untested and, until December 7, relatively uninterested, United States.[6]

In China, the attacks of December 8 changed everything. For the preceding four-and-a-half years, the Chinese had been fighting a desperate stand-alone war against Japan's technologically superior military. Fighting with little hope and overcoming powerful factional divides, the Chinese had avoided defeat and stalled Japan's drive to create a Japanese-controlled imperial regime in Asia. Upon hearing of Japan's attack on Pearl Harbor, Chinese leader Chiang Kai-shek immediately wrote Franklin Roosevelt, declaring that China and the United States were now united in a "common battle."[7] For China, Japanese belligerence was hardly news—800,000 Japanese troops had been brutalizing the Chinese people for years—but the attacks on America's imperial possessions were quite unexpected and wholly welcome.

The Japanese government launched the attacks of December 8 uncertain of the outcome but certain of the righteousness of its actions. The freezing of Japanese assets in the United States in July 1941, and the subsequent embargo launched in August by the United States, Great Britain, and the Dutch, nearly cut off Japan's oil supply and decimated its foreign trade. Japan faced what its leaders believed to be an impossible situation: give in to the ABCD (American, British, Chinese, and Dutch) encirclement, or resist Western domination of Asia and strike a blow for a sovereign Asia, led by Japan.

Japan chose to resist. Japan would not bow to Western ultimatums; it would reject the role of victim; and it would, instead, act in "self-defense" and "self-preservation." Japan would refuse to accept Anglo-American superiority. It would instead assert itself as a world power and champion of Asian self-determination.

The attacks of December 8 astounded even the most optimistic Japanese militarists. Japan had gambled and it had won. As historian Jeremy Yellen notes in his chapter, public satisfaction with the victories was electric, even as some, privately, feared the worst. If for Americans, December 7 would be "a date which would live in infamy," for many Japanese "the spirit of December 8" marked the zenith of Japan's imperial glory.

The Pacific War, of course, did not end as it had begun. Japan's wars in China, Southeast Asia, and throughout the Pacific drained its limited resources even as the military-industrial might of the United States continued to accelerate year after year—despite its own two-front war. And while the United States was slow to launch major offensives on either front, Atlantic or Pacific, the American-led war in the Pacific would become a juggernaut the Japanese had no means to defeat. The Japanese victories of December 8, 1941, led to the decimation of the Japanese homeland; Japan's war ended not with world power but with American atomic bombs.

Herein, however, we focus not on the end but on the surprising, world-history-altering beginnings of the Pacific War: the "surprise" attack on Pearl Harbor and the "anticipated" attacks throughout the Asian-Pacific colonial world.

To tell this tale, we brought together scholars whose expertise lies in the Pacific world and the colonial powers that claimed Pacific lands. These scholars hail from universities on four continents and represent six nations: Australia, China, Japan, the Netherlands, the United Kingdom, and the United States. Their expertise lies in the history of imperialism in the Pacific, and the United States, Japan, China, Australia, the Philippines, and the Netherlands and Dutch East Indies.

The chapters begin with the reactions of United States to Japan's initial attacks. This is in part because of chronology: Japan hit Pearl Harbor and the other targets on O'ahu first. It is also because this is the story best known, and thus the first that is necessary to disrupt and recast.

In Chapter 1, Beth Bailey and David Farber show that in the immediate aftermath of the Japanese attacks, Americans struggled to make sense of what had happened. Was Japan attacking America's empire? Its projections of power in the Pacific? The United States itself? Were Americans responsible for defending imperial colonies, including those of the British, or just their own? Quickly, however, that uncertainty disappeared. Led by its president, the United States obscured the role of empire—including its own—and the ongoing contests for power in the Pacific. In so doing, the nation repositioned the territory of Hawai'i in relation to the nation: rather than imperial possessions or defense outpost, despite their distance from the mainland the islands of Hawai'i were part of the United States. And when Hawai'i became the nation's fiftieth state, the United States would claim not a Pacific empire, but a Pacific nation.

Daniel Immerwahr, in "American Lives: Pearl Harbor and War in the US Empire" then assesses the boundaries of the US nation, approaching the Pacific War by considering belonging and its consequences. "American lives" have been lost, Franklin Delano Roosevelt told the country after the Pearl Harbor attack. But who was "American" and who wasn't could be a hotly contested matter. Were the Pacific territories part of the United States? Were their inhabitants "Americans"? Immerwahr argues that inhabitants of the US mainland by and large declined to identify the inhabitants of the Pacific territories as their countrymen. That understanding, moreover, shaped US military strategy, facilitating a "Europe-first" approach that privileged the protection of Britain over that of Guam and the

Philippines. It also shaped US battlefield tactics in the Pacific War by encouraging US soldiers to prioritize mainland lives over colonized lives, with disastrous consequences for the inhabitants of those Pacific lands.

Chapters 3 and 4 analyze the Japanese response to the successful attacks. In "Japan and the 'Spirit of December 8,'" Jeremy A. Yellen puts Japan's response into historical context. The Japanese military had been bogged down in China since 1937, and the nation had demanded significant sacrifices from its people in service of that undeclared but all-out war. But even though the broader Japanese public recognized Japan's material weaknesses vis-à-vis the United States and understood the huge gamble their nation took in launching war against the Anglo-American powers, he argues, the attack on Pearl Harbor, in particular, energized the Japanese public's patriotic ardor. The public mood was one of jubilation, not trepidation, and a wave of popular jingoism swept the nation in the months following the attacks of December 7/8.

Samuel Hideo Yamashita also considers the Japanese response, distinguishing between popular responses that were orchestrated by government (central, prefectural, and town and village) and those responses that were genuinely private, recorded in personal journals and diaries. Huge numbers of people participated in the government rallies staged by authorities in the days and weeks that followed the attack, and government-designed public rituals offered ordinary Japanese the chance to affirm their commitment to the war effort on a nearly daily basis. In such events, government representatives used the vocabulary developed during the ongoing Sino-Japanese war to mobilize the population, promising "certain victory." In their private writings, many Japanese citizens adopted such frameworks, writing with enthusiasm about the war; others betrayed grave reservations.

Japan had already been at war with China for years when it launched the ambitious attacks of December 7/8, but those attacks on other sites would alter China's experience of war, both militarily and domestically, and would reshape the nation's sense of its own engagement with the wider world.

In Chapter 5, "Identities and Alliances," Rana Mitter uses the writings of four wartime participants to show how concepts such as "the nation" and "Asia" were reshaped in the circumstances of a desperate war for survival. He argues that China began to develop a new global, postimperial, and sovereign identity in large part because of the country's forced engagement with the United States and the British Empire in the immediate aftermath of the attacks of December 8. This developing identity would help shape China's sense of mission, both in Asia and beyond, in the postwar order.

Nicole Elizabeth Barnes, in "Worldly Medicine in Wartime China," turns to the domestic impact of the attacks and their aftermath. As is well known, the United States' entrance into the war profoundly affected China's military battle against the Japanese. Barnes tells us another critically important story. In the immediate aftermath of the attacks of December 7/8, the United States began a massive effort to shore up China's medical infrastructure. Not only did this medical aid contribute to China's ability to patch up soldiers and continue the fight against the Japanese, it also allowed for a general reorganization of China's overall health system. This improved health-care system strengthened Chinese civilian morale and will to fight on.

In the years between the Wall Street crash of 1929 and Pearl Harbor, in which not only the Asia-Pacific region but also the world confronted the deepest and most multifaceted crisis of modern times, voices in Japan called increasingly for a "return to Asia" as a solution to imperial Japan's woes—as well as those of surrounding Asia. Although the Japanese voices were the loudest and most prominent, similar rhetoric appeared among anticolonial nationalist spokesmen in South and Southeast Asia.

In "Pearl Harbor and the Asian Cultural Turn," Ethan Mark argues that before the attacks of December 7/8, Southeast Asians rarely saw Japan as offering a serious alternative to Western-style modernity and nation-building. With those attacks and the series of dramatic Allied losses that followed closely in their wake, however, this situation changed dramatically—above all, in occupied Indonesia. For both Japanese and Indonesians, Japan's victories appeared to bring the two sides not only physically but also ideologically closer, prompting a new Japanese conviction in their cultural powers and an outpouring of Indonesian interest in Japan as an alternative model of modernity. In his chapter, Mark explores this "cultural turn to Asia" and its enduring postwar and postcolonial legacies across Asia.

Christopher Capozzola's chapter, "The Philippines and the Politics of Anticipation," focuses on the Philippines, which was also occupied by Japan during World War II. Capozzola makes two key arguments. First, he shows that from September 1940 forward US strategists, Philippine politicians, and ordinary Manileños alike had assumed that the Philippines would be the first target of a Japanese strike—thus undermining the usual narrative of "surprise" attacks. And within the Philippines, he argues, a "politics of anticipation" shaped not only military and civil defense, but questions of national sovereignty and executive power, as well as everyday life, with long-term consequences.

The attack on Pearl Harbor and on British imperial possessions was momentous for Australia. Although the nation had been at war since September 1939, Japan's entry into the conflict brought military action to its immediate Pacific region as the Japanese advanced through Southeast Asia in early 1942, taking Singapore on February 15 and bombing Darwin, with 250 casualties, just days later. With the British strategy to protect Australia dashed, Prime Minister John Curtin looked to America.

In "Pearl Harbor and Australia's War in the Pacific," Kate Darian-Smith treats the attacks as a "pivot point" for Australia during World War II. Darian-Smith argues that Australia's wartime experience transformed and modernized its society and economy. It also, she argues, reshaped the nation's diplomatic and security alliances with Britain and the US both in the short and the long term. In her discussion of the profound impact of the war on Australian society, she focuses on struggles over race, indigeneity, and Australian identity in the context of European colonialism, as well as the response to huge numbers of American service personnel who were based in the island nation.

The "attack on Pearl Harbor," even as the phrase itself obscures the multiple attacks and the imperial struggles underlying them, continues to play a role in contemporary debates and analyses. In the final chapter, "Tolerance, Reconciliation, and the Alliance of Hope," Yujin Yaguchi considers the continuing significance of the attacks in Japanese politics and society. Despite the international criticism of "Japanese amnesia" about World War II, the attack on Pearl Harbor is one of several wartime events that continues to receive extensive media coverage, not only on its major anniversaries but also when Japanese Prime Minister Shinzo Abe made an official visit to the site and met with President Barack Obama in December 2016. Yaguchi argues that in Japan, accounts of the attacks of December 7/8 focus on Pearl Harbor, which has become a symbol of the need for a continuing postwar alliance with the United States. This historical narrative, he notes, comes at the expense of a more dynamic and expansive historical memory that foregrounds the imperial complicity of the two nations in Asia and the Pacific.

NOTES

1. For a wonderfully written American-oriented account of the "day of infamy," see Steven M. Gillon, *Pearl Harbor* (New York: Basic Books, 2011).

2. In thinking about the historiographical distinction between "Pacific Rim" powers and Pacific Islanders we are influenced by Matt K. Matsuda, "The Pacific," *American Historical Review* 111, 3 (June 2006), 758–780.

3. Akira Iriye, *Across the Pacific* (New York: Harcourt, 1967), 207.

4. Akira Iriye, *Power and Culture* (Cambridge, MA: Harvard University Press, 1981), 29.

5. Richard Overy, *Why the Allies Won* (New York: Norton, 1995), 31.

6. See the insightful essay by the Australian Minister of External Affairs: Herbert Vere Evatt, "The Future of the Pacific," *Pacific Historical Review* 14, 2 (June 1945), 145–156.

7. Rana Mitter, *Forgotten Ally* (Boston: Houghton Mifflin, 2013), 236.

Prologue

The Attacks of December 7/8

Beth Bailey

On December 8 (December 7 on the other side of the international date line), 1941, Japanese military forces hit eight major targets across a 6,000-mile front. These carefully planned attacks, all but one on Western colonial possessions and military outposts in the Pacific, required Japan to move men and ships and planes across the vast distances of that ocean, positioning them for what—in a different era of communications technology, and accounting for local time zones and conditions—were near-simultaneous attacks.

Japan launched its campaign in the early hours of December 2, broadcasting a coded message to all Japanese military commands: "*Niitaka-yama nobore 1208.*" The coded instructions to climb Mount Niitaka on December 8 initiated the attacks, but Japanese forces were already in motion: aircraft carriers began their journey to the standby point 1,000 miles north of Hawai'i on November 26.

MALAYA

6:30 a.m. December 7 in O'ahu;
12:30 a.m. December 8 local time

Kota Bharu was the first site hit by the Japanese in their attacks of December 8. The city of Kota Bharu lies on the northeast coast of Malaya (now Malaysia). Malaya was then part of a British crown colony; it had a complex history of control, with the first colonial claims asserted by the Portuguese in the early sixteenth century, followed by contestations and alliances between local sultanates and the Dutch and then British. In 1941 Kota Bharu served as the base of operations for the British Royal Air Force (RAF) and the Royal Australian Air Force (RAAF) as well as for ground forces of the British Indian Army. Japan meant to neutralize this British military outpost but also to claim natural resources (most particularly rubber and tin) it deemed necessary to the war effort.

Japanese transport ships, escorted by a fleet including four destroyers, sailed from Japan's Hainan Island on December 4 and were then joined by Japanese troops from French Indochina. The ships were obscured by clouds and mist as they crossed the Gulf of Siam but were spotted by RAAF pilots on December 6. Bombardment—the first shots of the Pacific War—began at 12:30 a.m. on December 8, and landing vessels braved the rough seas soon thereafter.

The British Indian Army fought the Japanese invaders in fierce hand-to-hand combat; aircraft from an RAF squadron soon offered support. But Japan succeeded in landing three infantry battalions by morning, and their superior numbers forced Britain's troops to fall back. Japan gradually gained control of Malaya, occupying it for the remainder of the war. Following Japan's surrender the United Kingdom reasserted control, claiming Malaya as a protectorate, though it faced strong resistance. The nation declared independence on August 31, 1957.[1]

THAILAND
7:35 a.m. December 7 in O'ahu; 1:05 a.m. local time

Thailand was the only site attacked by the Japanese on December 7/8 that was not claimed by a Western power. Nonetheless, colonialism profoundly affected Thailand's role in the war. After Germany defeated France in 1940, Thailand saw an opportunity to reclaim territory it had lost to French control in 1893 (territory that currently is part of Cambodia and Laos) and went to war with French Indochina in January 1941. Japan, which had invaded a weakened French Indochina in September 1940, setting up military bases, brokered a peace. Thailand regained some territory, and Japan gained a secret promise from Thailand's increasingly autocratic prime minister that Thailand would allow Japan to launch attacks on Malaya and Burma from its territory (a promise that was later withdrawn).

As Japan extended its control in south Indochina in July 1941 it also became clear to Thailand that it could not depend on military support from Britain or the United States. At this point Thailand announced its neutrality, insisting nonetheless that it would resist any invasion of its lands. Japan was determined to attack Burma and Malaya through Thailand, whether by agreement or force, and planned for a multi-site invasion simultaneously with the attack on Malaya and Pearl Harbor.

The Japanese troops destined to invade Thailand, Malaya, Burma, and Singapore departed Hainan Island on December 4. At 11:00 p.m. local time on the night of December 7, Japan issued an ultimatum to Thailand, offering only two hours for response. The prime minister was unavailable; his cabinet made no decision.

Attacks began at 1:05 a.m. December 8, shortly after the deadline passed. Japanese troops traveled across the border from Indochina, flew from Indochina to strike an airfield near Bangkok, and landed at seven different sites along Thailand's gulf coast. Resistance ranged from strong to desultory to none; government sources report that 174 soldiers and police officers, along with 54 civilians, were killed. An armistice went into effect at noon, December 8. Within hours, Japanese aircraft from Indochina had moved to Thai airfields that gave them easier access to Malaya and Burma. Thailand formally allied itself with Japan on December 21 and declared war on the United States and Britain on January 25. (The United States did not reciprocate, considering Thailand occupied territory.) Throughout the war, a rival faction of the Thai government and population worked to support the Allies.

At war's end, the United States and Britain briefly occupied Thailand. Britain sought restitution, but its demands were partially countered by the United States, which saw Thailand as a potential ally in an unstable region. France, meanwhile, made clear it would prevent Thailand from joining the United Nations if it did not return the territory it had claimed in 1941.[2]

PEARL HARBOR/O'AHU
7:55 a.m. December 7 in O'ahu; 1:25 p.m. in Washington, DC

Pearl Harbor is the attack most remembered. The first wave of planes launched before dawn December 7 from Japanese aircraft carriers 230 miles north of O'ahu; a second wave followed soon thereafter. Approaching over Kahuku Point on the island's north shore, some circled leeward toward the battleships anchored at Pearl Harbor; others swept down the center of the island between the Ko'olau and Waianae mountain ranges, aiming for US Army, Navy, and Marine Corps air bases. The first bombs fell at 7:55 a.m.

Japan's war planners had determined that it was necessary to destroy the US Pacific Fleet, thus preventing it from contesting Japan's actions in Southeast Asia. Admiral Isoroku Yamamoto was confident that neither a conventional assault on Pearl Harbor or Japan's usual naval strategy of lying in wait closer to home could accomplish that goal—especially because, in this war plan, Japan needed naval resources for attacks on other targets. Yamamoto thus gambled on a surprise attack. Because so much depended on surprise, Japan's aircraft carriers traveled a route that avoided usual ocean traffic. Departing on November 26 from the Kuril Islands, they took a path far north of Midway and then turned south to Hawai'i.

It was only in May 1940 that the United States had moved its Pacific Fleet from its west coast to Pearl Harbor, on O'ahu's south shore; basing the fleet forward in the Pacific Ocean was meant to deter Japanese attacks on the colonial possessions of the British and Dutch in Southeast Asia. And though American war planners had discussed the possibility of a surprise attack on US military bases in Hawai'i, evidently no military leaders had truly believed it was possible.

Luckily for the United States, its Pacific aircraft carriers were not in Pearl Harbor that Sunday morning. But ships in Pearl Harbor were anchored in close proximity—a Japanese commander noted he'd never seen ships, "even in the deepest peace," anchored so close to one another—and planes were tightly clustered in nose-to-tail rows as a means to guard against sabotage. In two waves, Japanese attackers sank six battleships and damaged two more, plus three destroyers, three cruisers, and five other vessels. They destroyed or badly damaged at least 200 planes. And more than 2,400 people died in the attacks.[3] Shortly thereafter, two destroyers from the Japanese fleet bombarded the US Marine Corps base on Midway atoll in the Hawai'ian archipelago.

Although those who lived on the islands of Hawai'i worried about what was to come, the Japanese did not invade and Hawai'i served as a key defense outpost in the Pacific throughout the war. This US territory, which had been annexed by the United States in 1898 following the 1893 overthrow of the Hawai'ian monarchy, in 1959 became the fiftieth US state.

SINGAPORE
10:15 a.m. December 7 in O'ahu; 4:15 a.m. December 8 local time

Singapore was Britain's "Gibraltar of the East," key to the defense of its Asian empire. The island of Singapore, which lay at the tip of the Malay peninsula, was taken by the British from Dutch control in 1819. It remained under the Dutch East Indian Company's authority until 1858, when it became a crown colony administered under the British Raj in India.

After World War I, Britain intended to counter Japanese power in the region with a naval fleet of equal size. During the 1930s new threats in the Atlantic, followed by the outbreak of war, drew naval power away from Singapore. Nonetheless, British prime minister Winston Churchill sent two battleships to strengthen Singapore's defenses in October 1941.

Japan's military resources were also shaped by other demands. The planned attack on Hawai'i required all of Japan's available aircraft carriers, so the southern force would rely on land-based long-range bombers in southern Indo-China. Few American or British military leaders believed that Japan had such long-range capability.

The monsoon weather that obscured the approach of Japanese ships to Malaya had a less beneficial effect on the planes assigned to attack Singapore. Thirty-four planes set out from Saigon the night of December 7, but all were forced to turn back. Thirty-one made the next attempt; fourteen turned back and seventeen reached their target.

Radar picked up the planes en route, but Singapore's air raid headquarters was unstaffed. No sirens sounded, and Japanese planes found brightly illuminated streets and an unprepared population. Japanese planes attacked the harbor and naval base, as well as two airfields, though with minor effect. Most bombs fell on Singapore's Chinatown, killing 61 civilians and wounding 133.

The Japanese, focused first on pushing the British out of Malaya, did not conduct regular air raids on Singapore until the night of December 29. A full-scale invasion began on February 8, and Britain's forces surrendered on February 15. Seventy thousand men were taken prisoner by the Japanese; it was, according to Churchill, "the worst disaster and largest capitulation in British history."

Japan held Singapore for the remainder of the war. Following the war, Britain separated Singapore from British India and created it as a new crown colony in 1946; it became independent from the United Kingdom in 1963.

GUAM
11:57 a.m. December 7 in O'ahu; 8:27 a.m. December 8 local time

Forty minutes after the first bombs struck O'ahu, Japanese naval air forces on Saipan were ordered to attack the US territory of Guam. The United States had acquired Guam from Spain in the 1898 Spanish-American War, but Japan controlled the rest of the Marianas chain, which included Saipan. (Japan had captured the Marianas, Marshall, and Caroline Islands from Germany during World War I and had been given a League of Nations Mandate for them following the war.)

Japan saw Guam as a potential threat. But although Guam was a US military outpost, it was lightly defended: just a few hundred US sailors and marines plus the Chamorro Insular Force Guard. These forces counted among them only four .30-caliber machine guns and a range of small arms. In its war planning, Japan had greatly overestimated Guam's defensive capacity. Two days after December 8's air attacks, a 5,500-man regimental combat team, along with 400 marines, invaded the island. Guam surrendered that day—the first US land formally surrendered to the Japanese. It remained occupied by the Japanese until US forces recaptured it in July 1944.[4] Guam remains an unincorporated territory of the United States.[5]

WAKE ISLAND

1:30 p.m. December 7 in O'ahu; 11:58 a.m. December 8 local time

Wake Island is actually an atoll of three coral islets (one of which is named Wake), together comprising less than thirteen square miles. It lies approximately 2,000 miles west of Hawai'i, on the other side of the international date line. The United States claimed the unoccupied land in 1899, and Pan American Airways began using it as a refueling and rest stop for its new flying boat transpacific "Clipper" service in 1935.

With war on the horizon, American military planners saw Wake Island's importance as an advance defense outpost, offering reconnaissance of the Japanese-held Marshall Islands and a refueling base for aircraft bound for the Philippines. In January 1941 a consortium of civilian firms began to construct military facilities, including a 5,000-foot runway. An understrength garrison of 449 US Marines, along with a few dozen naval personnel, joined the 1,100 civilian contractors and the 45 Chamorro employees of Pan Am on the atoll.

Japan's tactical bombers, launched from Roi in the Marshall Islands, struck just before noon on December 8. The garrison knew about the attack on Pearl Harbor, but without radar and with heavy cloud cover, it was surprised by the attack. Most of its fighter planes were destroyed, and two-thirds of the aviation personnel were killed or wounded.

Air attacks continued in waves over the next two weeks. On December 11 a Japanese naval task force attempted to land troops on Wake Island's south shore. In an amazing feat, the Marines repulsed the attack, sinking two destroyers and forcing the ships to withdraw. A larger force arrived on December 23, and though the Marines (joined by many civilian contractors) fought ferociously in close infantry combat, Wake surrendered to the Japanese that day. The atoll remained in Japanese hands for the remainder of the war. To this day it is an unorganized US territory, occupied only by US military personnel and civilian contractors.[6]

HONG KONG

2:00 p.m. December 7 in O'ahu; 8:00 a.m. local time

The British crown colony of Hong Kong was acquired from China in stages. China ceded Hong Kong Island to the British following the First Opium War/ First Anglo-Chinese War in 1842; Kowloon peninsula followed in 1860. In 1898 Britain, seeking a defensive buffer, leased what were referred to as the "new territories"—approximately 200 islands surrounding Hong Kong island—from China for a term of ninety-nine years.

By 1940 the British saw Hong Kong as less central to its regional defense than Singapore but also understood the symbolic value of maintaining its military presence. Abandoning the crown colony off the shore of southern China, some argued, would signal that Britain was not committed to its Asian colonies or to China in its struggle against Japan.

In 1941 Hong Kong had a garrison of about 12,000 British, Canadian, Indian, and Scottish military personnel, along with Chinese volunteers in a civilian defense force—far too few men to defend against the Japanese foe. Japan had conquered Guangdong, the section of mainland China closest to Hong Kong, in 1938; by late 1941 it had moved four army divisions, plus supporting air and naval units, to Guangdong. Despite what many there and elsewhere saw as Japan's clear intention to invade, Hong Kong's colonial governor dismissed the possibility of war and drastically underestimated Japanese capability.

The attack began around 8:00 a.m. the morning of December 8, as bombers from the Japanese colony of Formosa (Taiwan) hit Hong Kong's Kai Tek airfield, destroying every one of the British forces' seven planes. A land invasion began the same day. British-controlled forces managed to repel an attempted landing on Hong Kong Island on December 15, but a second try on December 18 succeeded. Defenders continued to fight, but they were running low on ammunition. After Japan destroyed the island's water mains on December 24, they could no longer hold out. Hong Kong's forces surrendered unconditionally on Christmas Day.[7]

Hong Kong was held by the Japanese for the duration of the war. Following Japan's surrender, Great Britain resumed control. In 1984 the British and Chinese prime ministers signed an agreement that added Hong Kong Island and Kowloon to the ninety-nine-year lease agreement signed in 1898. Hong Kong and its surrounding territories were returned to Chinese control on July 1, 1997.

THE PHILIPPINES
5:55 p.m. December 7 in O'ahu; 12:25 p.m. December 8 local time

The Philippines, like Guam, had been claimed by the United States in 1898 following the Spanish-American War. Filipino nationalists, resisting the new colonial power, fought for independence, and a brutal war between Filipino and US forces lasted until 1902, with scattered resistance for another decade. In 1916 the United States began altering the legal status of the archipelago, and by 1935 the Philippines had become an autonomous commonwealth under US control with promise of independence in ten years. But the Philippines were also key to US military power in the Pacific, the site from which the United States planned to resist Japanese expansion.

Japan's plan of attack called for bombers to depart Formosa (now Taiwan) air bases around 2:30 a.m. on December 8 in order to arrive at their targets by 6:30 a.m., twenty-one minutes after sunrise; they expected US military forces to be on full alert, having been notified of the attack on Pearl Harbor. But things did not go as planned. The Japanese planes were held up by thick fog, delaying their departure. And US military commanders, though they had learned of the Pearl Harbor attack by 3 a.m. local time—within an hour of the Pearl Harbor attack's beginning—did not launch the attacks on Formosa dictated by US war plans or prepare for a Japanese air attack. (Lost, confused, and self-serving reports from that day make it difficult, if not impossible, to offer definitive proof for any potential explanation of their actions and inactions.)

Japan's attacking aircraft found the United States' Far East Air Force on the ground. At Clark Field, eighteen of the force's thirty-six B-17 "Flying Fortresses" were hit, along with many others; at Iba Field forty miles to the north, bombs fell on a full squadron of P-40s that had just returned from patrol. In the forty-five-minute attack, half of the Far East Air Force was destroyed.[8]

The Japanese ground invasion of Luzon began on December 10. The American-Filipino resistance was fierce, lasting longer than resistance to any other Japanese invasion, but these forces surrendered on May 8, 1942. The American reconquest of the Philippines began in October 1944 but was not yet completed when Japan surrendered in August 1945. The United States granted independence to the Philippines on July 4, 1946.

NOTES

1. Drawn from John Burton, *Fortnight of Infamy: The Collapse of Allied Airpower West of Pearl Harbor* (Annapolis, MD: Naval Institute Press, 2006); and Bert Kossen, et al., "'Seventy Minutes before Pearl Harbor': The Landing at Kota Bharu, Malaya, on December 7th 1941," www.dutcheastindies.webs.com/kota_bharu.html. This site, though not created by academically credentialed scholars, offers detailed and densely researched descriptions of military campaigns in the Dutch East Indies and Southeast Asia that are not available elsewhere.

2. David K. Wyatt, *Thailand: A Short History* (New Haven, CT: Yale University Press, 2003), 244–252; E. Bruce Reynolds, *Thailand's Secret War: OSS, SOE, and the Free Thai Underground during World War II* (Cambridge: Cambridge University Press, 2005), 6–8; Duncan Stern, "A Slice of Thai History," *Pattaya Mail*, March 28–April 3, 2003, www.pattayamail.com/504/columns.shtml.#hd6.

3. Ronald H. Spector, *Eagle against the Sun: The American War with Japan* (New York: Vintage Books, 1985), 1–7, 78–84.

4. Thomas Wilds, "The Japanese Seizure of Guam," *Marine Corps Gazette* (July 1955), https://www.mca-marines.org/gazette/japanese-seizure-guam.

5. An unincorporated territory is one that is controlled by the US government but whose residents have only those rights and privileges specifically granted them by Congress. Residents of Guam, like those of all US unincorporated territories other than Samoa, hold birthright citizenship.

6. Gregory J. W. Urwin, "Battle of Wake Island," britannica.com; William B. Hopkins, *The Pacific War: The Strategy, the Politics, and the Players* (Minneapolis: Zenith Press, 2010), 54; Jacob Neufeld, "The Japanese Octopus," in Bernard C. Nalty, ed., *The Pacific War: The Story of the Bitter Struggle in the Pacific Theatre of World War II* (London: Salamander Books, 1999); Spector, *Eagle against the Sun,* 102–106. For a full account, see Gregory J. W. Urwin, *Facing Fearful Odds: The Siege of Wake Island* (Lincoln: University of Nebraska Press, 1997).

7. Compiled from Terry Copp, "The Defence of Hong Kong, December 1941," *Canadian Military History* 10, 4 (2001), 5–20; Priscilla Mary Roberts, "Hong Kong, Battle of," in Spencer C. Tucker and Priscilla Mary Roberts, eds., *World War II: The Definitive Encyclopedia and Document Collection* (Santa Barbara, CA: ABC-CLIO, 2016), 804.

8. Compiled from Spector, *Eagle against the Sun*, 107–141; William H. Bartsch, *December 8, 1941: MacArthur's Pearl Harbor* (College Station: Texas A&M University Press, 2003), 266–409; Hopkins, *The Pacific War*, 46.

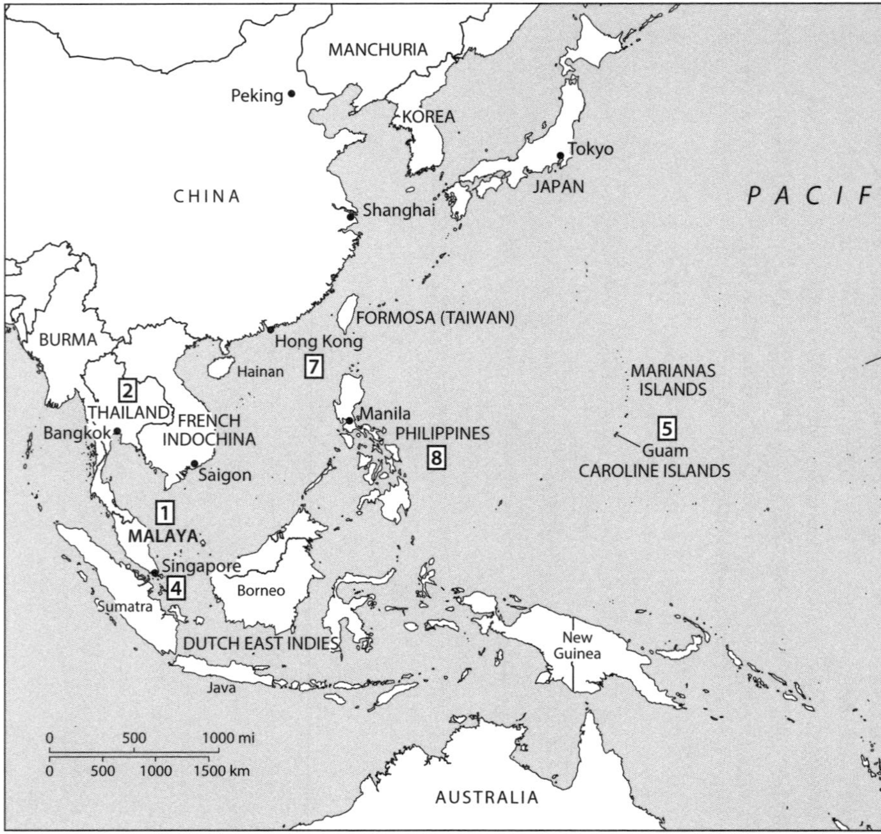

	Time on O'ahu (12/7)	Local Time (12/8)
1. Malaya	6:30 a.m.	12:30 a.m.
2. Thailand	7:35 a.m.	1:05 a.m.
3. O'ahu	7:55 a.m.	
4. Singapore	10:15 a.m.	4:15 a.m.
5. Guam	11:57 a.m.	8:27 a.m.
6. Wake Island	1:30 p.m.	12:00 p.m.
7. Hong Kong	2:00 p.m.	8:00 a.m.
8. Philippines	5:55 p.m.	12:25 p.m.

Japan's Attacks, December 7/8, 1941

CHAPTER 1

The Attack on Pearl Harbor... and Guam, Wake Island, the Philippines, Thailand, Malaya, Singapore, and Hong Kong

December 7/8, the Pacific World, American Empire, and the American Political Imaginary

Beth Bailey and David Farber

In the immediate aftermath of the Japanese attacks, Americans struggled to make sense of what had happened. Was Japan attacking America's empire? Its projections of power in the Pacific? The United States itself? Were Americans responsible for defending imperial colonies, including those of the British? Japan's attacks of December 7/8 caused Americans to ponder the meaning, making, and maintaining of their Pacific empire and the relationship of that empire to those of its allies and its enemies. They forced Americans to confront the physical, geopolitical, and emotional boundaries of their nation-state.

Within days of the attack, Americans began to distinguish between their need to restore empires and defend allies in the Pacific and their desire to protect "America"—a term open to debate on racial, geopolitical, and historical grounds. During those perilous and anxious opening days of America's war in the Pacific, American elites distanced themselves from the realities of their imperial power and authority in the Pacific, even as they narrowed the political and cultural ground between mainland Americans and the people of Hawai'i—who became more "American" as days passed. The attack on Hawai'i, American elites quickly came to argue, was an attack on "us," the American people, whereas the Japanese attacks on other American Pacific possessions were attacks not on American people or imperial territory but on America's military defenses. The postwar disposition of America's Pacific empire was portended in the days and weeks that followed Japan's "surprise" attacks in Asia and the Pacific.

Almost unimaginably, from a twenty-first-century perspective, nearly twenty-four hours went by before the president of the United States spoke to the American people about Japan's attacks. But before Roosevelt delivered the famous "Day of Infamy" speech to a joint session of Congress, the White House had begun to communicate news of the attacks and to shape their meaning for the American people.

FDR received news of the attack on Hawai'i by phone from Secretary of the Navy Frank Knox at 1:47 p.m. EST, Sunday afternoon, more than thirty minutes after Japanese bombers had first struck Pearl Harbor. Few White House staffers, junior or senior, were on hand when Roosevelt received Knox's call in the Oval Study, the intimate second-floor office where he normally worked. Roosevelt had, just half an hour earlier, concluded a meeting there with the Chinese ambassador to the United States. Following that meeting he had lunched informally with Harry Hopkins, his most trusted aide, and then busied himself looking over his stamp collection. Hopkins was at the president's side when Knox called; he heard FDR shout "No!" into the phone. Hopkins, after being filled in, was skeptical—"there must be some mistake." But Roosevelt had no doubts. His instinctive response was verified minutes later when Admiral Harold Stark, chief of naval operations, called to confirm that the attack was very real and that it was still in progress. Roosevelt phoned Secretary of War Henry Stimson and then Secretary of State Cordell Hull. He mobilized his personal staff. He also called the Chinese ambassador, the last person with whom he had met before receiving word of the attack: "The Japanese have bombed Pearl Harbor and Manila. . . . It is terrible, simply terrible."[1] The Japanese, of course, had been at war with China since 1937.

President Roosevelt, even before his senior staff and advisors gathered, phoned his press secretary Steve Early and personally dictated, for immediate release, a terse statement: "The Japanese have attacked Pearl Harbor from the air and all naval and military activities on the island of Ohau, the principal American base in the Hawaiian Islands."[2] This first official White House communication emphasized the military nature of the attack and informed Americans—as few knew—

of the militarized status of "the island of Oahu," which it identified not as the home of nearly 230,000 American citizens but as "the principal American base in the Hawaiian Islands." Only in May 1940 had the US Pacific Fleet moved its headquarters from San Pedro, California, to Pearl Harbor.[3]

Press Secretary Early released this first official statement by conference call to the three major American news services. Minutes later, he called back to announce that Manila had also been attacked. This particular report was erroneous; Manila and the Philippines were not attacked until several hours later. The fog of war had descended on the White House.

Despite such uncertainties and lapses of communication, President Roosevelt, for the next several days, would try to control the flow of information that was made public. FDR intended to shape the narrative that would give meaning to Japan's actions and America's reactions. At President Roosevelt's order, Early continued to update the media from the White House pressroom every few minutes throughout the day and early evening, giving further detail on the O'ahu attacks and adding news of each additional Japanese attack. To avoid public panic and to prevent the Japanese from knowing how vulnerable the Hawai'ian Islands were to a Japanese invasion, the White House deliberately shrouded the extent of the devastation at Pearl Harbor. Radio reports and newspaper coverage of the attacks were based almost completely on White House reports.

Well before President Roosevelt gave his "Day of Infamy" speech at 12:30 p.m., December 8, almost twenty-four hours after Japan began bombing and strafing O'ahu, news of the attacks had spread. People massed in front of the White House, waiting anxiously to hear more, hoping, perhaps, that the president would speak to them but also to draw near to Roosevelt, seeking comfort and offering support. They sang "God Bless America" and other patriotic songs. Hundreds stayed outside the gates all night.

The radio networks had been the first to break the news of Japan's attacks. Within minutes of the White House announcement, CBS was able to communicate with its affiliate station in Honolulu, which affirmed that the attacks were still ongoing. No radio networks were able to get news from the Philippines, and the White House's erroneous message about attacks on Manila continued to be disseminated—these false reports would not become true until ten hours after the attack began on O'ahu.

People were not sure, at first, what to make of the news or how significant it was. Three miles from the White House, the Washington Redskins were playing the Philadelphia Eagles in a late-season football game. The Redskins' management got word of the attacks soon after the game had begun but chose not to announce the news to the crowd. Instead, announcers made near-continuous calls over the public address system for various high-ranking military and civilian attendees at the game to report immediately to their respective offices.[4] Similar decisions were made across the nation at every sort of public assembly, from movie screenings to church services. While "the attack on Pearl Harbor" would soon be seen as the moment Americans' lives changed, the significance of the news was not fully apparent to everyone in those first moments and hours.

Similar mixed messages about the significance of the attacks came in the first address by someone of national political prominence. That person, oddly enough, was not the president. It was First Lady Eleanor Roosevelt. In her distinct upper-class warble, she spoke to the American people at 6:45 p.m. EST on her regularly scheduled NBC radio show, *Over Our Coffee Cups*. During this regular fifteen-minute program—which was somewhat incongruously sponsored by the Pan-American Coffee Bureau, a trade group representing seven Latin American nations that exported coffee to the United States—Mrs. Roosevelt commonly interviewed people about issues of national importance. The previous Sunday she had spoken with Nelson Rockefeller, the coordinator of inter-American affairs, about the impact the war in Europe was having on the nation's relationship with Latin America. On December 7, Roosevelt was scheduled to interview a young American soldier about war preparedness. She began, instead, with news of the Japanese attacks:

> Good evening, ladies and gentlemen, I am speaking to you tonight at a very serious moment in our history. . . . The State Department and Army and Navy officials have been with the President all afternoon. In fact, the Japanese ambassador was talking to the president at the very time that Japan's airships were bombing our citizens in Hawaii and the Philippines and sinking one of our transports loaded with lumber on its way to Hawaii [an inaccurate statement—the Japanese ambassador was meeting not with the president but with Secretary of State Cordell Hull]. . . . For months now the knowledge that something of this kind might happen has been hanging over our heads and yet it seemed impossible to believe, impossible to drop the everyday things of life and feel that there was only one thing which was important—preparation to meet an enemy no matter where he struck. That is all over now and there is no more uncertainty.[5]

Nonetheless, Eleanor Roosevelt's sober but ambiguous announcement that the "something of this kind [that] might happen" *had* happened was immediately followed with the previously scripted fifteen-minute interview, one that never referred to the shocking news of the day. On the day that soon would be remembered as one of "infamy," mainland Americans were not quite sure what to make of what was, in the minds of most, happening halfway around the world. And those in the most prominent positions, at least at first, offered little clear guidance.

It's worth noting that Mrs. Roosevelt, at least, portrayed Japan's aggression as attacks on "our citizens in Hawaii and the Philippines" (though she also suggested, oddly, that it did not really matter where the "enemy . . . struck."). In her politically progressive, humanitarian view, the people of the Philippines and Hawai'i—United States "citizens" all, according to her but not according to the US government (people of Hawai'i, yes; people of the Philippines, no)—were equally American and equally deserving of the support of their fellow citizens. Her egalitarian understanding and her rhetoric, as was true so often, were not to be echoed by her husband.

Almost immediately after the White House began issuing reports of the attacks, newspapers everywhere in the United States published a series of "extra" editions. Nearly every newspaper in the United States, in small towns and in big cities, headlined Japan's Pacific offensive, frequently putting out a special edition to do so. A great majority of those newspapers printed articles issued by the nation's major wire service, the Associated Press (AP). The AP stories, in turn, were based almost completely on the White House updates. This process suggests that Americans throughout the nation received a coherent—if sometimes incorrect or uncertain—message. But that was not the case. Because each paper's editors wrote their own headlines and chose from among several available illustrations (though not, that first day, from images of actual destruction wrought by the Japanese), readers found quite different versions of the attacks of December 7/8.[6] It was not yet "the attack on Pearl Harbor."

In fact, Pearl Harbor was not always accorded pride of place. It was frequently linked with—even subordinated to—Manila, as in "Japs Bomb Manila and Honolulu Base" (*Alexandria* [LA] *Daily Town Talk*); "Japs Bomb Manila, Hawaii" (*Las Cruces* [NM] *Sun-News*); and "Japs Bomb Hawaii, Manila" (*Reno* [NV] *Evening Gazette*). Even the *Honolulu Star-Bulletin*, after noting that "City Rocks to Blasts as Japanese Drop Bombs," ran a large, bold-faced, page-two heading: "President Roosevelt announced this morning that Japanese planes had attacked Manila and Pearl Harbor." A number of papers also headlined other American targets. "Japanese Planes Bomb Honolulu, Island of Guam," proclaimed the *Morning News* of eastern South Carolina. "Honolulu Bombarded: Hundreds Dead, Wake Island Reported Captured," reported the *Harrisburg* (PA) *Telegraph* "War Extra" (which also promised "Pennsylvania Ready For Any Call").

The story of a treacherous Japanese attack on American soil, likewise, had not yet consolidated. Many papers on December 7 portrayed a dawning war of empires. That's the logic that underlay headlines such as "JAPS ATTACK U.S. ISLANDS" (*Coshocton* [OH] *Tribune*) and "JAPAN ATTACKS U.S. IN PACIFIC" (*Galveston* [TX] *Daily*

This syndicated map, which ran in dozens of US newspapers on December 7, 1941, portrays a Pacific of imperial possession. Even though the map accompanied reports of the attacks, Pearl Harbor does not appear.

News). The *New York Times*, not yet read nationwide, offered a more internationalist version: "JAPAN WARS ON U.S. AND BRITAIN." In this version of the story, Japan had attacked US (and British) colonial possessions.

The war of empires was more clearly laid out in the syndicated map that many editors chose to illustrate their stories. The map shown on page 24, titled "War Starts in Pacific," ran in the *Hope Star*—the Arkansas hometown newspaper of Bill Clinton's family—and dozens of other papers. The map, clearly prepared before December 7, highlighted the various Pacific empires: those of the United States, Japan, Britain, the Netherlands, and France. It showed the sites of Japan's attacks and where various armies and navies were positioned. It displayed major hot spots: "British Rush Enforcements" in Burma; "Japs maneuvering" in Thailand and Borneo; "Dutch mobilize" in the "Netherlands Indies." "French Indochina" was coded black for Japanese control, as were parts of China. Guam was signified by an American flag. A US flag was also positioned on the "Philippine Islands," where, readers were informed, "U.S. Land, Sea Commanders Meet." Australia was pictured with the caption, "Australia proclaimed a station of war." Who proclaimed it such was not explained. Oddly, the Hawai'ian Islands are not pictured at all—the image undoubtedly had been drawn to explain the expected Japanese offensive in Southeast Asia and the Philippines. The map's caption, however, probably written by the *Hope Star* editor, does note that the "American air and naval base of Pearl Harbor lies beyond the right side of the map . . . 2,000 miles from California, with other war points in the Pacific ranging up to 8,000 and 9,000 miles distant."[7] The war, in this editor's version, was far away, staged on and over imperial lands and seas.

A second version of events, which assumes the existence of empires, portrays attacks on American force projection in the Pacific. The extra edition published by the *Sioux Falls* (SD) *Daily Argus-Leader* was headlined "350 Killed at Hawaiian Base"; it characterized Pearl Harbor as "the U.S. Navy's mighty fortress of the Pacific." That headline is in keeping with the AP story that ran in one of the *Brownsville* (TX) *Herald*'s extra editions: "Japanese airplanes Sunday attacked American defense bases at Hawaii and Manila. . . . The White House said that Japan had attacked America's vital outposts in the Pacific—Hawwai [*sic*] and Manila." Over in Paris, Texas, the language varied only slightly: "the Japanese attacked the two keystones of American defense in the Pacific." The second-level headline here? "U.S. Wins First Fight of New War."[8]

Again, a widely used illustration offers a more detailed version of the meaning of Japan's attacks. It portrays the same clash of empires but emphasizes that the United States, Great Britain, and Japan had turned the Pacific into a heavily militarized zone of conflict well before December 7. This map, titled "Broad Fighting Front for U.S., Japan," marked "outlying bases and stations" for the United States, the British, and the Japanese. The *Fresno Bee*'s editors, in captioning this syndi-

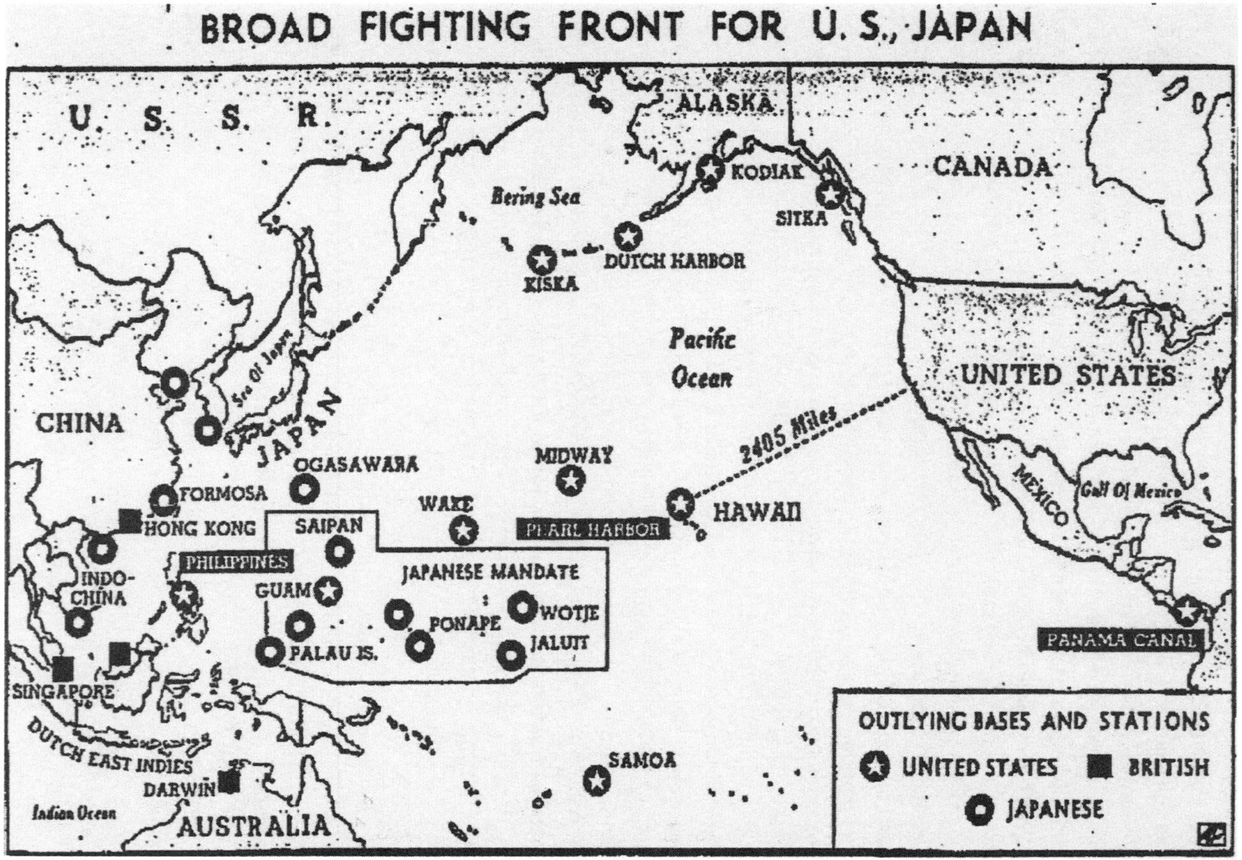

A second syndicated map offers a slightly different version of events. Presuming the existence of empire, it portrays a Pacific that was heavily militarized well before the attacks of December 7/8.

cated map, focused on military might and imperial interests: "The long string of American naval bases and air stations stretching from Panama to the Philippines all have been assigned roles in a master plan for Pacific defense. Britain's bases, centered on armed to the teeth Singapore, keep an eye on the East Indian corner. But Japan's roots stretch farther and farther from Tokio [*sic*]." This map and its caption make clear that even before the attacks, the United States and Japan had been vying for control of the Pacific world, fencing, as the caption's last line states, over "vital British-American trade lanes."[9]

A final version, which often coexisted with one or more of the above, portrayed the expansion of an existing war. Reflecting the United States' traditional focus on Europe, the *Alexandria* (LA) *Daily Town Talk* offered a lengthy subheading: "War Begun By Hitler Explodes Into World Conflict As Nippon's Bombers Strike in Pacific Isles." The *Odessa* (TX) *American* was more direct: "Japan's Bombs to Spread Nazi War to Entire World." Offering its readers a different historical trajectory, the *Kingsport* (TN) *Times*'s "First Extra" ran front-page photographs of the Japanese in Burma and China, where, the caption explained, "Japanese troops fight on, still far from victory after four years of war."[10]

In those first hours the narrative that would assume the power of myth—the story of a treacherous Japanese attack on Pearl Harbor, an attack on America itself—had not yet taken shape. Stories of empire and of imperial interests, of military installations and force projection, headlines that treated Wake Island, Manila, and Guam as equivalent to Pearl Harbor or Hawai'i—all framed the news of an attack that was not, in fact, universally understood as a moment that would change the future. But despite such lags in grasping the significance of the moment, and despite profound and fascinating differences in framing, the bottom line was the same throughout the mainland United States: "Japs Attack U.S."; "Japs Declare War on United States"; "Japan Launches Undeclared War on U.S." (Much more rare was the reverse headline: "U.S. At War With Japan.")[11]

World War II, from an American perspective, had begun. And President Franklin Roosevelt, after a near twenty-four-hour silence, would use his "bully pulpit" on December 8, 1941, to explain to the American people how to think about the advent of this new world war and America's place in it.

Even before Roosevelt knew the full extent of the Japanese attacks, the president knew what he wanted to say and where he wanted to say it. He would go to the Capitol and speak to Congress in an address that would be broadcast to the nation and read all over the world. At a meeting of his principal advisors that began a little more than an hour after Secretary of the Navy Knox had first reported the attack on O'ahu to the president, FDR announced that his speech would be brief and to the point. Secretary of State Hull argued for a different approach, insisting that the American people needed to understand how Japanese aggression in Asia and the Pacific and the United States' principled attempts to deter that aggression had led to Japan's deadly attacks. Hull urged the president to lay out a brief, of perhaps a half hour, that would detail Japan's deteriorating relationship with the United States and its subsequent acts of bellicosity. Roosevelt made clear that he would not write that kind of speech and, at about 4:15, he ended the meeting.[12]

With the room cleared, Roosevelt lit a cigarette and called in his secretary, Grace Tully. As she recalled, Roosevelt dragged on his cigarette and told her, "I'm going before Congress tomorrow. I'd like to dictate my message. It will be short." The dictated message, she later wrote, "ran under 500 words, a cold-blooded indictment of Japanese treachery and aggression, delivered to me without hesitation, interruption or second thoughts."[13] Tully typed up the speech and gave it to the president, who then made a few edits.

FDR met with his cabinet at 8:40 p.m. that night. "This [is] the most important cabinet meeting since 1861," he told them. After briefly describing the perilous situation in Hawai'i, Guam, Wake Island, and the Philippines, he read the latest draft of the speech he intended to give before Congress the next morning. Secretary of War Stimson joined with Secretary Hull in rejecting FDR's blunt declaration.[14] Stimson (who had been governor general of the Philippines, or, as he sometimes titled himself, "an Oriental Potentate," believed himself an expert on "the Oriental mind" and had little regard for the Japanese) thought that Roosevelt should emphasize "that Germany had inspired and planned this whole affair."[15] Hull (whose approach to Japanese aggressions had been, until the summer of 1941, one of extraordinary patience) argued that "the most important war in 500 years deserved more than a short statement."[16] Together, they argued forcefully that Roosevelt must detail for Congress and the American public Japan's aggressions in Asia and Pacific and trace the US attempts to curtail those aggressions through patient diplomacy. They wanted Roosevelt to deliver a speech about Japan's aggressive imperial ambitions in Asia and the Pacific.

Having conferred earlier in the day, the two men brought to the meeting a seventeen-page speech drafted by Assistant Secretary of State Sumner Welles, who had long clashed with those Roosevelt administration figures who had wanted to bring more pressure to bear on Japan.[17] Welles had vocally predicted that America's increasing economic pressures on Japan would lead to war.

The State Department–drafted speech differed almost completely from FDR's brief remarks. It began not with Japan's attacks but with a detailed history of the US role in Asia and the Pacific—though it was a history of a very specific sort. The United States, in this accounting, had long championed, in "our official relationships with the Pacific area . . . the sovereign rights of the countries of the

Far East" and "the principle of equal treatment." American imperialism is not mentioned. Nor is the US-Philippines War. Instead, a benign passivity explains America's burgeoning role in the Pacific: "A new phase opened at the end of the nineteenth century. Sovereignty of the Philippine Islands passed from Spain to this country; and this country pledged itself to equip the Philippines to become a free and independent nation." No mention is made of European control of large swaths of Asia and the Pacific islands. Japan's aggressions against China and the Dutch East Indies, in contrast, are narrated in detail, and condemned. In this narrative Japan's path of belligerency—fostered by German intrigue and support—led directly to the attacks on Hawai'i and the Philippines. "We are fighting," this speech contends, "in self defense; in defense of our freedom, of our liberties, and of our rights."[18] Exactly who the "our" is in this narrative is never made clear. But the message and purpose of this address was clear: the State Department believed that contrasting American beneficence in the Pacific with Japanese belligerence would best explain and legitimate the origins of the clash between the United States and Japan.

Harry Hopkins later aptly described the speech as a "long-winded dissertation on the history of Japanese relations leading up to this morning."[19] To quiet Stimson and Hull down, FDR took in hand a copy of the speech and promised to consider it. He did not. The twenty-five-sentence speech that FDR delivered the next morning, one that took just over seven minutes to present, did not discuss America's historical role in the Pacific or in Asia. It, like the State Department's version, ignored the many decades-long struggles among European nations, the United States, Japan, and the many diverse peoples of Asia and the Pacific over questions of sovereignty and power, and economic and cultural self-determination. In his address to the nation, Roosevelt focused exclusively on Japanese perfidy.[20]

Historians and columnists frequently point out the notable edit Roosevelt made on the first sentence of his first draft of this address. Originally, FDR had dictated the opening sentence as "Yesterday, December 7, 1941, a date which will live in world history . . ." FDR eventually crossed out "world history" and penciled in the far more potent and suggestive word, "infamy." With that one word change, FDR's argument was set: America was at peace with the world and was eagerly negotiating with the Japanese to solve their differences, when, without warning or cause, "the United States of America was suddenly and deliberately attacked by naval and air forces of the Empire of Japan."

The president made an additional significant edit to the early sentences of his speech, one that is rarely noted. Rather than naming Japanese bombing in "Hawaii and the Philippines," the new draft named only Hawai'i. There are good reasons for that revision. It had become clear by 6 p.m. that Manila had not (yet) been attacked, and FDR's point was that the Japanese had attacked even while still meeting with US officials in Washington, DC. But while FDR almost certainly removed the Philippines from this sentence for accuracy's sake, he also cut Manila and the Philippines from the other paired references with O'ahu/Hawai'i and—more significantly—did not restore them after Japan's attack on the Philippines was definitively reported. Thus FDR excised the Philippines from a sentence on "the distance ~~of Manila, and especially~~ of Hawaii, from Japan," and then from another on the results of "The attack~~s~~ of yesterday on ~~Manila and on the Island of O'ahu~~ the Hawaiian Islands."

Then the president offered, in cadenced tones, a listing of other places the Japanese had attacked.

> Yesterday, the Japanese Government also launched an attack against Malaya.
> Last night, Japanese forces attacked Hong Kong.
> Last night, Japanese forces attacked Guam.
> Last night, Japanese forces attacked the Philippine Islands.
> Last night, the Japanese attacked Wake Island.
> And this morning, the Japanese attacked Midway Island.

As the Philippines recedes into an incantation of distant shores and O'ahu becomes, in delivery, "an American island," FDR elides the American empire. In fact, as one would never know from Roosevelt's speech, Guam, the Philippines, and Wake and Midway Islands are all American possessions. Here they go unclaimed, jumbled with the British possessions of Hong Kong and Malaya and left with no mention of their national status or state of sovereignty. They are all simply places in "the Pacific area" attacked—seemingly inexplicably—by the Japanese. Roosevelt also makes no distinction between the colonial possessions of the United States and those of the British Empire. As Roosevelt portrays the attack on the "American island of Oahu" and a host of other places in the Pacific, he obscures the fact that the Anglo-American alliance of Pacific-Asian colonial possessions is now under attack by the Japanese empire.

Roosevelt, both in rejecting the State Department's lengthy exposition and in crafting his own narrative, chose not to complicate—or to clarify—Americans' understanding of whom exactly the Japanese had just attacked and for what reasons. In his powerful and effective speech, he simply notes: "The facts of yesterday and today speak for themselves." Congress agreed. Less than an hour after Roosevelt concluded his remarks, the Senate and the House declared war on Japan.

Across the Atlantic, Roosevelt's elision of empire and Japan's fateful decision to simultaneously attack both British and American possessions took a weight off the mind of Great Britain's prime minister, Winston Churchill. Just hours before the Pearl Harbor attack, Churchill had lunched with the US ambassador to Great Britain. Churchill was well aware that Japan was mobilizing its forces in Southeast Asia and the Pacific for some kind of offensive. Bluntly, he asked the American ambassador whether, if the Japanese attacked only British possessions, the United States would "declare war on them?" The ambassador had replied: "I can't answer that, Prime Minister. Only the Congress has the right to declare war under the United States constitution." The historian Steven Gillon, in describing this encounter, aptly concludes: "Churchill sat in silence. His empire stood on the brink of destruction, and the best his American counterpart could offer was a civics lesson."[21] Churchill's question, of course, became moot. The Japanese had attacked possessions of the British and the Americans, as well as those of the French and the Dutch. War had come for all.

Roosevelt likewise understood that this was now a global war, not simply a Japanese act of aggression against the United States. On December 9, the day following what would become known as his "day of infamy" speech, Roosevelt drew Americans around their radios for one of his signature "fireside chats."[22] At that point neither Germany nor Italy had declared war on the United States—though they would the following day. But Roosevelt by December 9 had already pivoted from his narrow focus on Japanese treachery to a broader, directly related theme: Japan, Germany, and Italy—"the Axis powers"—were not simply nations engaged in acts of international aggression but were "powerful and resourceful gangsters . . . banded together to make war upon the whole human race." His warning was crystal clear: the Japanese attacks were but one piece of a master plan. "All the continents of the world," he cautioned his anxious audience, "and all the oceans, are now considered by the Axis strategists as one gigantic battlefield." Thus Germany and Italy, Roosevelt declared, "consider themselves at war with the United States at this moment just as much as they consider themselves at war with Britain or Russia."

As President Roosevelt had framed Japan's attacks on the empires of Europe and the United States as a sudden act of deliberate deception in his previous speech, here he linked "the treachery committed by the military dictators of Japan" to the "course of Hitler and Mussolini in Europe and Africa." Roosevelt meant to shift America's focus and to prepare the nation for a global war. As he explained,

> We must realize for example that Japanese successes against the United States in the Pacific are helpful to German operations in Libya; that any German success against the Caucasus is inevitably an assistance to Japan in her operations against the Dutch East Indies; that a German attack against

> Algiers or Morocco opens the way to a German attack against South America and the Canal.
>
> On the other side of the picture, we must learn also to know that guerilla warfare against the Germans in, let us say Serbia or Norway, helps us; that a successful Russian offensive against the Germans helps us; and that British successes on land or sea in any part of the world strengthen our hands.

In this last address before war was formally declared between the United States and the Axis powers, Roosevelt wasted no words on the relationship among clashing empires in the Pacific and Asia. And Pearl Harbor, here, became not only shorthand for Japan's attacks on the United States but potentially only the first of many attacks by the Axis powers on the nation—and on the Western Hemisphere. "The attack at Pearl Harbor," he asserted, "can be repeated at any one of many points, points in both oceans and along both our coast lines and against all the rest of the Hemisphere." The United States, therefore, had to be prepared to defend its "hemisphere" from "crafty and powerful bandits" with "everything we've got." This is a striking pivot away from a Pacific war. Here President Roosevelt began the task of refocusing the anger of the American people away from Japan's Pacific attacks and toward the unified armed might of the entire Axis. He was laying the groundwork for the Europe-first strategy that would govern America's war plan.

Perhaps paradoxically, FDR's pivot from Japan's perfidy (in his "day of infamy" speech) to the threat posed by the Axis powers (in his fireside chat) also helped to solidify Pearl Harbor's position in the American narrative of war, for while the president never named Pearl Harbor in his address to Congress, he used "the attack on Pearl Harbor" as shorthand the following day. That shift, through no executive design, coincided with the first appearance of the rallying cry that would last the war's length: "Remember Pearl Harbor." The phrase first appeared in the Portland *Oregonian*'s afternoon edition on December 9, an echo, as historian Emily Rosenberg argues, of "Remember the Alamo" (and to a lesser extent, of "Remember the *Maine*"), and thus invested with the power of a familiar narrative, a "metaphor for a massacre by racialized primitives that rallied righteous revenge."[23]

The phrase caught on, whether picked up from the *Oregonian*'s headlines or coined independently by people for whom repurposing "Remember the Alamo" was an obvious move. Just over a week after the attacks, bandleader Sammy Kaye recorded "Remember Pearl Harbor," which would rise to number three on the charts in early 1942:

Let's REMEMBER PEARL HARBOR—
as we go to meet the foe—
Let's REMEMBER PEARL HARBOR
As we did the Alamo.[24]

"Remember Pearl Harbor" (and sometimes "Avenge Pearl Harbor") captioned official posters meant to strengthen public resolve for a long and costly war, urging Americans to enlist, to buy war bonds, and to "Work, Fight, Sacrifice." "Remember Pearl Harbor" was embroidered on pillows by mothers who'd sent their sons to war, cast on collectible silver coins, and laminated onto campaign-style lapel pins. It titled an eminently forgettable black-and-white movie released by Republic films in May 1942. And it provided a framework for events, defining the beginning of this war in a narrative that persisted long after hostilities ceased.

What did Americans remember when they "Remembered Pearl Harbor"? A version of events that shaped both the conduct of the war and the US role in the postwar Pacific world.

Japan had waged a devastating attack on US military installations on O'ahu, with damage centered on the Pacific Fleet anchored in Pearl Harbor. But it had also attacked and soon taken control of much of the Philippines, as well as Wake Island and Guam—all US possessions. "Remember Pearl Harbor" obscured that fact. President Roosevelt, in his recounting of Japanese treachery, never claimed those distant possessions, never vowed to free the people of those far lands who had lived their lives under the American flag. In one way, perhaps, that was partly to the good: as the Allies negotiated the shape of the postwar world, FDR looked to the end of colonial empires and supported self-determination. But more immediately, as Daniel Immerwahr argues in the chapter that follows, FDR wrote off the lives of hundreds of thousands of people by so defining them outside the boundaries of the United States.

The nation's focus on Pearl Harbor—while it worked to obscure the war of empires by portraying a sudden act of treachery and disavowing the nation's most distant colonial possessions—also solidified America's Pacific claim. As a shorthand version of the war's origins, "the attack on Pearl Harbor" rendered Guam and the Philippines and Wake Island inconsequential. But this shorthand positioned the islands of Hawai'i differently. "The attack on Pearl Harbor" was an attack on the United States. This association, in conjunction with the strategic role Hawai'i would play in the coming Pacific War, solidified connections with the islands and supported the long-standing efforts of Hawai'i's *haole* elite to gain statehood for the US Territory of Hawai'i.

In truth, there were differences between these possessions that helped to shape both the initial response and the eventual outcome. As much as anything, distance mattered. It's not that Hawai'i was close; Honolulu was almost 5,000 miles from the nation's capital and close to half that distance from San Francisco. The fastest ship from the West Coast took four days; fledgling commercial flights took close to twenty hours and cost as much as a luxury cruise. The other US possessions, however, lay even farther afield: Wake Island was roughly 6,700 miles from DC; Guam almost 8,000; Manila more than 8,500. All fell on the other side of the international date line.

More significantly, the Territory of Hawai'i had a different legal status from that of the Philippines, Guam, and Wake Island. It, unlike those possessions, was an incorporated territory, one legally considered an integral part of the United States. The Philippines, which the United States claimed in 1898 following the Spanish-American War, had—in the aftermath of the Philippine-American War—been allowed to move gradually toward independence. By 1935 the Philippines had been declared a commonwealth; it was scheduled to gain independence from the United States on July 4, 1945. Guam was (and remains) an unincorporated territory of the United States; Wake Island had no permanent indigenous population and was inhabited primarily by US military forces. This distinction between Hawai'i and the rest mattered, as incorporated territories traditionally gained statehood: the incorporated territories of New Mexico and Arizona had become states less than thirty years earlier, and most US states, after the original thirteen colonies, had been formed from incorporated territories. Hawai'i's legal status *did* distinguish it from these other US possessions in the Pacific.[25]

Most Americans, however, would not have been able to explain such distinctions. What distinguished Hawai'i from the other US possessions in the Pacific for most Americans was not its legal status or even its relative geographical proximity, but its familiarity. During the 1920s and 1930s, as radio and movies helped shape an increasingly national culture, Hawai'i had come to symbolize exotic romance. Americans bought sheet music for "Hawaiian" songs, from Al Jolson's "Along the Way to Waikiki" (1917) to Harry Owens's "Sweet Leilani" (which earned Bing Crosby his first gold record in 1938). From 1935 on, millions of Americans listened to performances from the luxury tourist hotels in Waikiki (and even to some music by Hawai'ian performers and composers) on the radio show "Hawaii Calls."[26]

It was film, however, that drew Hawai'i closest, offering a safely exotic paradise to American viewers in an age when the number of movie tickets sold weekly equaled about three-quarters of the US population. Hawai'i was such a frequent setting for movies—romances, in particular—that one *New York Times* film reviewer wrote sarcastically of "the well-known Hollywood suburb of Wackyki."[27] In these films Hawai'i usually served as a romantic backdrop for white Americans, its racial difference from the mainland majority offering those viewers a sense of the exotic but never threatening white supremacy.

The cultural familiarity of Hawai'i stemmed, in part, from economic and political ties. Leaders of a movement for statehood, dominated by the *haole* (white) elite and the "big five" corporations that had made fortunes from sugar production, were not blind to the importance of US public opinion. Hawai'i's familiarity was due, in large part, to their deliberate effort to integrate Hawai'i into the cultural imaginary of the nation, casting "the Paradise of the Pacific" as familiar, racially nonthreatening, and ready for statehood.

How this group had come to hold so much power in Hawai'i is a long and complex story, one central to the US presence in the Pacific.[28] In brief and without nuance, it is a tale of capitalist expansion and the conquest and subordination of the Hawai'ian people (even as members of Hawai'ian royalty played key roles in the transformation of the islands). By the late nineteenth century, descendants of US missionaries—who by that time exercised significant economic and political power—were seeking favorable terms for the export of sugar to the United States. At the same time, they were maneuvering to shift power from Hawai'i's ruler to the sugar oligarchy. In 1893, when Queen Lili'u'okalani pushed back against their power grab, a group of businessmen (most of them US citizens, but nonetheless raised in the islands) overthrew the Hawai'ian monarchy; this coup was supported by the US government minister and, at his behest, about 300 US Marines. While President Grover Cleveland disavowed the coup, his successor, President William McKinley, presided over the annexation of the Republic of Hawai'i in 1898. Hawai'i became a US territory in 1900, and its most visible leadership continued to be the *haole* elite—even as immigrants from the Philippines, Japan, China, and Portugal who came to work on sugar and pineapple plantations made the *haole* population an ever-smaller minority of the islands' people.[29]

While the US government in DC played no direct role in the overthrow of the monarchy, US military interests did shape that conflict and its aftermath. In 1873 the US military, concerned about Pacific defense, sought a Hawai'ian harbor. US military presence in the islands began in earnest when the United States traded the Kingdom of Hawai'i tax-free sugar imports for use of a small islet in the western O'ahu harbor Pu'uloa (which Americans called Pearl Harbor). Following Hawai'i's annexation, the US military expanded its reach, dredging Pearl Harbor, establishing army forts and airfields, and even purchasing the Diamond Head crater to place weapons for island defense. There were approximately 7,000 servicemen stationed in the islands in 1920, but as Japan more actively asserted its power in the Pacific, US forces increased. In May 1940 the US Battle Fleet was shifted from California to an advance position at Pearl Harbor; by September 1940, when the Axis powers signed their Tripartite Pact, there were 48,000 US troops stationed in Hawai'i. That growth would continue throughout the war, as Hawai'i's strategic importance became ever more obvious. In the US war that the attack on Pearl Harbor (and Guam, Wake Island, the Philippines, and a group of British colonies) precipitated, Hawai'i became the staging ground for the Pacific War. And fourteen years after the war's conclusion, Hawaii (lacking the *'okina* between the two "i"s) became the fiftieth US state.[30]

Perhaps Hawai'i would have become a state eventually, even if Japanese bombers hadn't unleashed such destruction early on the morning of December 7, 1941. There are a host of factors that make such an outcome plausible. But well before statehood, in the hours and days following the attacks of December 7/8, 1941, American portrayals of Hawai'i allowed it to claim a new, and more benign, kind of presence in the Pacific.

In the immediate aftermath of the attack, there was no clear, single narrative. Newspaper headlines offered a conflict of empires and imperial interests, attacks on US force projection in the Pacific, and Japanese assaults on an array of US possessions in which Hawai'i held no pride of place. Newspapers ran maps of the Pacific world that portrayed rival imperial claims and military installations—all prepared well before the "day of infamy," and at least one not even including the Territory of Hawai'i.

"Japs Attack U.S. Islands" and the assaults on "America's vital outposts in the Pacific" are both stories of American empire. "Remember Pearl Harbor" changed the frame. As the attacks on O'ahu, Guam, Wake Island, the Philippines, Thailand, Malaya, Singapore, and Hong Kong became the singular "attack on Pearl Harbor," the story of imperial rivalry disappeared, supplanted by an image of Japan's sudden sneak attack on the United States. In that shift—as when the United States claimed a fiftieth state whose population was comprised primarily of Asian and Pacific peoples—the United States positioned itself not as a Pacific empire but as a Pacific nation.

NOTES

1. This and the following account of Roosevelt's actions are drawn from Steven M. Gillon, *Pearl Harbor* (New York: Basic Books, 2011), especially 50–58. A great many reports of Roosevelt's responses to the attacks have been written, but Gillon provides a carefully researched narrative. Also useful is the account provided by Peter Grier, "Pearl Harbor Day," *Christian Science Monitor*, December 7, 2010, http://www.csmonitor.com/USA/2010/1207/Pearl-Harbor-day-How-FDR-reacted-on-December-7-1941.

2. Gillon, *Pearl Harbor*, 56.

3. Skipper Steely, *Pearl Harbor Countdown: Admiral James O. Richardson* (Gretna, LA: Pelican, 2008), 130–131.

4. Gillon, *Pearl Harbor*, 83.

5. "Over Our Coffee Cups," Eleanor Roosevelt papers project, https://www2.gwu.edu/~erpapers/teachinger/q-and-a/q21-pearl-harbor-address.cfm.

6. The sources of the headlines that follow are identified in the chapter text. All come from newspapers published December 7, 1941, as extra editions; they were accessed through newspapers.com. Quotes from articles or captions (as opposed to headlines) are cited in full.

7. "War Starts in Pacific," *Hope Star*, war edition, December 7, 1941, p. 1.

8. "Enemy Plans Blast Vital American Post; No Warning Is Given," *Brownsville Herald* extra edition, December 7, 1941, p. 1; "U.S. Wins First Fight of New War," Associated Press, December 7, 1941, as run in *Paris Texas News*, extra edition, December 7, 1941, p. 1.

9. "Broad Fighting Front for U.S., Japan," *Fresno Bee*, extra edition, December 7, 1941, p. 2A.

10. "U.S. at War with Japan," *Kingsport* (TN) *Times*, "First Extra" edition, December 7, 1941, p. 1, caption to photographs.

11. "Japs Attack U.S." appears in *Newport News* (VA) *Daily Press* and *Brownsville Herald*; "Japs Declare War on United States," *Santa Ana* (CA) *Register*; "Japan Launches Undeclared War on United States," *Daily Tar Heel* (Chapel Hill, NC); "U.S. At War With Japan," *Kingsport* (TN) *Times*; all headlines from extra editions, December 7, 1941.

12. Account is drawn from an article written by the director of the Franklin D. Roosevelt Presidential Library and Museum in association with an exhibit on Roosevelt and the first twenty-four hours after the Japanese attack on Pearl Harbor: Paul M. Sparrow, "How Roosevelt Crafted His 'Day of Infamy' Speech," *Poughkeepsie Journal*, December 7, 2016, http://www.poughkeepsiejournal.com/story/news/local/2016/12/06/how-roosevelt-crafted-his-day-infamy-speech/95039282/.

13. Ibid.

14. This account closely follows James C. Thompson Jr., "The Role of the Department of State," in *Pearl Harbor as History*, eds. Dorthy Borg and Shumpei Okamoto (New York: Columbia University Press, 1973), 85.

15. This material is taken from the December 7, 1941, diary entry of Secretary of Agriculture Claude R. Wickard, "FDR and Pearl Harbor," http://www.fdrlibrary.marist.edu/archives/pdfs/pearlharbor.pdf.

16. Ibid.

17. The entire draft speech, untitled and undated, along with supporting analysis, is available through the US National Archives collection, presented by the Franklin D. Roosevelt Library and Museum: "Day of Infamy: FDR's Response on December 7, 1941," https://www.google.com/culturalinstitute/beta/exhibit/QRXZUqsM.

18. Ibid.

19. Ibid.

20. Ibid.

21. All quotes are from Gillon, *Pearl Harbor*, 114.

22. "December 9, 1941: Fireside Chat 19: On the War with Japan," Miller Center, https://millercenter.org/the-presidency/presidential-speeches/december-9-1941-fireside-chat-19-war-japan. All quotes from the fireside chat come from this source.

23. Emily Rosenberg, *A Date Which Will Live* (Durham, NC: Duke University Press, 2003), 16, 14.

24. Recorded December 17, 1941; https://en.wikipedia.org/wiki/Sammy_Kaye_discography. Rosenberg, *A Date Which Will Live,* 16, also quotes these lyrics.

25. For an excellent pithy overview of these legal status issues, see Lanny Thompson, "The Imperial Republic: A Comparison of the Insular Territories under U.S. Dominion after 1898," *Pacific Historical Review* 71, 4 (November 2002), 535–574.

26. For a discussion of representations of Hawai'i, see Beth Bailey and David Farber, "The Fighting Man as Tourist: The Politics of Tourism and Culture in Hawai'i during World War II," *Pacific Historical Review* (November 1996), 641–660.

27. Frank S. Nugent, "The Screen" (Review of *Honolulu*), *New York Times*, February 23, 1939.

28. The literature on the annexation of Hawai'i by the United States is voluminous. For a good introduction, see Julia Flynn Siler, *Lost Kingdom: Hawaii's Last Queen, the Sugar Kings, and America's First Imperial Venture* (New York: Atlantic Monthly Press, 2012); and James A. Haley, *Captive Paradise: A History of Hawai'i* (New York: St. Martin's Press, 2014).

29. Individual works exist on the history of specific groups that originally came to the islands to work on plantations. Lawrence H. Fuchs, *Hawaii Pono: An Ethnic and Political History* (New York: Bess Press, 1997), offers an overview; this is an update of a 1961 social history of the islands.

30. On the US military in Hawai'i, see Stetson Conn, Rose C. Engelman, and Byron Fairchild, *Guarding the United States and Its Outposts* (Washington, DC: Center for Military History, 2000), especially chapter 6.

CHAPTER 2

"American Lives"

Pearl Harbor and War in the US Empire

Daniel Immerwahr

There are only three historical dates that most people in the United States know by heart. July 4, 1776, when the Declaration of Independence was signed, is one. September 11, 2001, the date of al-Qaeda's attacks on New York and Washington, is another. And then there is December 7, 1941, the "date which will live in infamy."

But Pearl Harbor is better known than it is understood. The event is usually remembered as an isolated strike by Japan on a US base in Hawai'i. What often slips from memory is the rest of Japan's blitzkrieg attack, which hit the US territories of Midway, Wake Island, Guam, and the Philippines all within a matter of hours (plus the British colonies of Malaya and Hong Kong and the independent nation of Thailand). Even Richard Nixon, who had served in the Pacific during the war, believed Hawai'i to be "the only piece of American territory that suffered directly from enemy attack in World War II."[1] Japan's other targets have been, as an army writer put it, "all but forgotten."[2]

Why? One might think it is because the Hawai'i attack dealt a more serious military blow than the others. But that isn't right. The army's official history judges the attack on the Philippines to be just as disastrous as the one at Pearl Harbor.[3] Indeed, one can argue, as the historian John Costello has, that the Philippines attack was the greater setback. At Pearl Harbor, the main Japanese achievement was the sinking of four World War I–era battleships (two of which were eventually returned to service). In the Philippines, the Japanese laid waste to the largest concentration of US warplanes outside North America—the foundation of the Allies' Pacific defense. And whereas the attack on Hawai'i was never repeated, the attack on the Philippines was followed by the Japanese conquest of the Philippines, which was the United States' largest colony.[4]

So why have the Japanese attacks of December 7/8 been metonymically reduced in public memory to a single event, "Pearl Harbor"? The answer has to do with the politics of empire, with the differential sense of which places and people "count" within the United States. Questions of inclusion arose at the very start, from the first attempts by Franklin Delano Roosevelt to narrate the Japanese attacks. And they shaped the war effort that followed. The sense among political and military leaders that certain US nationals were "Americans" and others were "foreign" had consequences that were wide-ranging and, I will argue, lethal.

Japan's lightning strike on the US Pacific empire was a crisis for Washington, but it was also an opportunity. By all accounts, Roosevelt was prepared to join the war and was concerned that peace-seeking sentiments among the public might prevent him. The Japanese attack offered a clear casus belli.

Yet, narratively, it was not clear *what* Japan had done. As Beth Bailey and David Farber showed in Chapter 1, newspapers in the twenty-four hours after the attack displayed a notable diversity in their descriptions of it. Was it primarily an attack on Hawai'i, the closest target to the US mainland and the first place the Japanese had struck? On the Philippines, the largest colony in the United States? On Guam, the colony most likely to fall under Japanese occupation? Or on Wake Island, where a sizeable contingent of mainland civilians and military personnel was stationed? (It is telling that the first US combat film about the war was *Wake Island,* released in 1942.[5])

"The facts of yesterday and today speak for themselves," Roosevelt insisted in his "infamy" speech. But we now know that Roosevelt wrestled in successive drafts to figure out what those ostensibly self-evident facts said. As Bailey and Farber discuss, Roosevelt had initially planned to present the event as a joint attack on Hawai'i and the Philippines. The first typed draft of the "infamy" speech, produced on December 7 in Washington, referred to a "bombing in Hawaii and the Philippines" and to attacks "on Manila and on the Island of O'ahu."[6] That formulation—Hawai'i and the Philippines—was also how Undersecretary of State Sumner Welles had put it in his draft of the speech (a draft that Roosevelt read but did not use) and how Eleanor Roosevelt had put it in her radio address on the night of December 7.[7]

But Roosevelt toyed with his draft throughout the day and into the night, making additions and deletions in pencil. At some point, he crossed out his references to the event as an attack on both territories and described it instead as a "bombing in O'ahu" or "on the Hawaiian Islands." The Philippines remained in the speech, but now only as an item on a terse list of Japan's other targets, a list that eventually included (once the fully tally was in) Malaya, Hong Kong, Guam, the Philippines, Wake Island, and Midway—presented in that order. That list blurred US and British colonies together, making them all seem vaguely foreign.

Why demote the Philippines? One reason might have been a genuine confusion in the White House as to what had happened. There was an early false report of an attack on Manila that was rescinded before the accurate report of the Philippines attack came in. The typed first draft captures the state of knowledge in the Oval Office in those early hours. Perhaps Roosevelt crossed out his prominent references to the Philippines once the initial report was corrected.

Yet that explanation just raises the question in a new way. By the evening, when Roosevelt had finished his day's editing of the draft, he *did* know, indubitably, that the Philippines had been struck. His final edits of the draft reflect this, since he penciled *in* references to the Philippines on the list of targets. Why didn't Roosevelt revert to the original Hawai'i-and-the-Philippines formulation, the one that his wife and his trusted undersecretary had chosen in their own descriptions of the event? Or, for that matter, why didn't he describe it as an attack on all of the inhabited colonies: Hawai'i, the Philippines, and Guam?

It's not hard to guess at Roosevelt's reasoning. He doubtless worried that the Philippines or Guam would seem too foreign to his audience. What if the public didn't *care* that Japan had attacked them? Opinion polls at the time suggested that few in the continental United States supported a military defense of those far western colonies.[8] Hawai'i, closer to the mainland, containing a large white settler population, and, for those reasons, potentially on the track to statehood, was a safer bet.

Roosevelt drove this point home with a further edit to his speech, made sometime between the third typed draft on the morning of December 8 and his delivery of the speech to Congress. Rather than having the Japanese squadrons bombing the "island of O'ahu," he had them bombing the "American island of O'ahu."[9] There, he continued, damage had been done to "American naval and military forces," and "very many American lives" had been lost.

American lives—those were the magic words. In his war message to Congress on the eve of the War of 1812, James Madison had accused the British of having "wantonly spilt American blood within the sanctuary of our territorial jurisdiction."[10] James Polk in his 1846 war message had charged Mexico with having "shed American blood on American soil."[11] Woodrow Wilson, in his war message in 1917, had told Congress that "American ships have been sunk, American lives taken."[12]

Roosevelt, in other words, was making a calculation. He was rounding the Philippines down to *foreign* and rounding Hawai'i up to *American*. That bit of political arithmetic in turn supported the narrative understanding of the Japanese attacks that Roosevelt advanced in his famous first sentence: "Yesterday, December 7, 1941—a date which will live in infamy—the United States of America was suddenly and deliberately attacked by naval and air forces of the Empire of Japan."

Two points are worth making about that sentence. First, in this rendition, the attack on Hawai'i is not an attack on the *empire of the United States* but on the *United States itself*, Hawai'i being (as Roosevelt had said in 1934) "an integral part of the nation."[13] Rhetorically encompassing Hawai'i within the "United States of America" allowed Roosevelt to insist that an attack on Pearl Harbor was an attack on US soil. It also allowed him to present the event as an attack by an empire upon a nation-state.

The second thing to notice is the date, December 7, 1941. That, too, supported Roosevelt's Hawai'i-centric presentation, because only at Hawai'i and Midway, out of all of Japan's targets, did the vagaries of the international date line put the event on December 7. In the rest of the theater, the event occurred on December 8 (which is the date that the Japanese ascribed to the attack, even to the part of it that occurred in Hawai'i). Though it's doubtful that Roosevelt so intended, his "date of infamy" conceit helped solidify his narrow construction of the event, writing the bulk of the US empire out of the narrative.

The reporter John Hersey was in Manila at the time. He recorded the scene as Filipinos tried to interpret the president's "infamy" speech as it came in over their radios. Roosevelt spoke, Hersey remembered, about Hawai'i and the "many American lives lost there," but he only mentioned the Philippines "very much in passing." The Filipinos around Hersey were confused. Roosevelt made the war "seem to be something close to Washington and far from Manila," Hersey wrote. But "to Manilans the war was here, now, happening to us, and we have no air-raid shelters."[14]

Roosevelt, in his "infamy" speech, offered an understanding of the United States, a way of mapping which parts of the polity were "American" and which weren't. But this wasn't his invention alone. In drawing that map, he responded to a larger cultural sense of the borders of "America."

The United States had, at the time of Japan's attacks, the fifth-largest empire on the planet. The nearly 19 million inhabitants of its colonies made up 12.6 percent of the US population. They numbered more than African Americans, remarkably. If you lived within the jurisdiction of the United States on the eve of World War II, you were more likely to be colonized than black by odds of roughly three to two.[15]

Yet, from the perspective of the US mainland, the millions of Filipinos, Puerto

Ricans, Hawai'ians, Alaskans, Zonians (from the Panama Canal Zone), Virgin Islanders, Guamanians, and American Samoans slipped easily from view. Consider the *New York Times* in a representative year, 1930. Its readers were nearly twice as likely to encounter articles about Poland or Brazil as they were about the Philippines. Hawai'i appeared in the *Times* seven times that year, Guam not once. In contrast, the paper ran more than six hundred articles about India, Britain's largest colony—nearly three times as many as it ran about all United States territories *combined*.[16]

World War II, which engulfed the United States' Pacific colonies, could have shone a light on the empire, forcing attention onto its possessions and their inhabitants. But for many mainlanders, the colonies remained an indistinct blur. Rand McNally, the major publisher of maps, produced a series of war atlases designed to help make sense of the geographically expansive war. Yet its wartime *Ready Reference Atlas of the World*—like many atlases at the time—listed Hawai'i, Alaska, Puerto Rico, and the Philippines as "foreign."

A class of seventh-grade girls at the Western Michigan College Training School in Kalamazoo found this puzzling. They wrote to Rand McNally to inquire. How could the attack on Pearl Harbor have been an attack on the United States if Hawai'i was foreign?[17]

"Although Hawaii belongs to the United States, it is not an integral part of this country," the publisher replied. "It is foreign to our continental shores, and therefore cannot logically be shown in the United States proper."[18]

The girls were not satisfied. *Hawai'i is not an integral part of this country?* "We believe this statement is not true," the girls wrote. It is "an alibi instead of an explanation." Further, they continued, "we feel that the Rand McNally atlas is misleading and a good cause for the people of outlying possessions to be embarrassed and disturbed." The girls forwarded the correspondence to the Department of the Interior, which oversaw most of the territories, and asked for adjudication.[19]

The girls were, of course, right. As an official clarified, Hawai'i was not foreign.[20]

Yet this wasn't the first time the Department of the Interior had handled a query of this nature. Its records are full of inquiries of this sort. Journalists, curious citizens, and government officials wrote in to ask very basic questions about what was part of the United States and what wasn't.

Those questions had consequences. War is a time of danger and sacrifice, a time when risks are apportioned. Who bore those risks had a lot to do with who got recognized as "American." It was a question of who was in and who was out—of whose lives mattered.

There are three ways in which colonized people's subordinate position within the United States shaped their fates during the war: in the preparations for war, the strategy adopted during the war, and the tactical decisions made during the fighting in the Pacific theater. In all three cases, the inhabitants of the territories were made to bear greater burdens and face greater dangers than their mainland compatriots.

The possibility of war with Japan had been on planners' minds since the start of the twentieth century, when Japan's anger over anti-Japanese discrimination in California led to a brief war scare. After World War I, Japan looked to be the most plausible potential enemy of the United States—Germany had been beaten down, France and Italy lacked navies, the Soviet Union was wracked with internal problems, and Britain seemed friendly.[21] Japan alone might plausibly attack. And if it did, it would surely attack the US Pacific territories first.

Despite watching this threat grow, mainland officials did very little to prepare the imperiled territories for a war. Just the opposite, in fact. In the Washington naval limitation treaty of 1921, the US government agreed to forgo strengthening its barely fortified western territories in exchange for securing an overall naval superiority to Japan. This decision left the Philippines and Guam "virtually defenseless," grumbled Captain Dudley Knox of the navy.[22] Yet even after Japan renounced the treaty in 1934, Congress hesitated to provide new Pacific defenses.[23]

"Plan Orange," the military's scenario for war with Japan, openly acknowledged that the United States would probably not be able to repel a Japanese invasion of the Philippines or Guam. Mounting sufficient coastal defenses would simply require more money than an indifferent federal government was willing to pay—it was "not within the wildest possibility," reported the commander of the army's Philippine Department.[24] Instead, the successive Plans Orange envisioned amassing a fleet in Hawai'i or on the West Coast and leaving only small forces in the westernmost territories. If Japan attacked, it would get the western Pacific colonies, but then (the thinking went) the United States could stage a counterattack and eventually win them back.

General Douglas MacArthur found this intolerable. Unlike most of his colleagues, MacArthur felt a deep attachment to the Philippines. His father had been the governor-general there, and MacArthur had spent much of his own career there as well. It was where he'd done his first tour of duty, where he first saw combat, where he first drew blood. Irate that the United States was *planning* to sacrifice the Philippines, MacArthur tried to revise Plan Orange. In his version, the United States would build up a large army in the Philippines, capable of holding the enemy off at the shoreline. But MacArthur was swimming against the tide, especially given that his attempted revision was advanced during the 1930s, a time marked by both hostility to military expansion and severe budgetary constraints.

The director of the War Plans Division regarded MacArthur's plan as "literally an act of madness."[25]

The most substantive step that the United States took to prepare for war with Japan was not to fortify the Philippines but to distance itself from it. In 1934 Congress passed the Tydings-McDuffie Act, making the Philippines a "commonwealth" and putting it on a countdown to independence. There were economic reasons for this: an independent Philippines could no longer send workers to the West Coast and could no longer ship its sugar tariff-free to mainland markets, where it might compete with domestic sugar producers. But there was a military logic, too. The Philippines was the "sore thumb" of US defense, which would cause "trouble if any unpleasantness comes in the Pacific," in one congressman's words.[26] Liberating it would also liberate the United States from the obligation to defend it.

As Theodore Roosevelt Jr. explained to the newly elected president of the commonwealth, Manuel Quezon, "The American people will not jeopardize their interests in the future for an independent Philippines any more than they will for any other nation, and most certainly will not engage in a war on their behalf unless the real interests of the United States were involved."[27]

So it fell to Quezon to build up the Philippines defenses himself, using the meager colonial treasury to do so. Douglas MacArthur took the extraordinary step of resigning his commission in the US Army in order to help. Yet the two found it difficult to get aid from Washington. A request for the US military to sell the Philippines some of its leftover World War I–era rifles met with hesitation and haggling. Unable to win sufficient help from the government, the Philippines was left facing an arms shortage, an ammunition shortage, and a shortage of funds. MacArthur asked Washington for a minor subsidy, $50 per trainee in the Philippine army (the US National Guard received a subsidy of $220 per trainee). This, too, was turned down.[28]

MacArthur believed the Philippines to be "an integral part of the United States," as deserving of defense as New York. But he had to admit by 1940 that the military forces there were "entirely inadequate for purposes of foreign defense" and were "little more than token symbols of the sovereignty of the United States."[29]

That was the story throughout the Pacific. The governor of Alaska begged Congress for defense aid. But Alaska, like the Philippines, was a territory, with no senators or representatives beholden to it. "We're not going to waste any money on Alaska" was the consensus, the governor recalled.[30]

It was only in mid-1941 that Congress got serious about Pacific defense. By then, however, it was too late. If you had made a flight around the Pacific in late 1941, this is what you would have seen: Hawai'i's defenses were substantial but incomplete, lacking especially long-range bombers. Guam had virtually nothing—its governor judged it to be "absolutely indefensible."[31] Alaska had a small collection of planes, but "by no stretch of the imagination," admitted its air force chief, could those planes "defend the territory against any attack in force."[32]

The Philippines, with its half-finished army, was also in a sorry state. Its soldiers had canvas shoes, coconut-bark helmets, outmoded rifles, artillery that dated from 1898, and very little by way of ammunition.[33] The air force collected in the Philippines—including thirty-five B-17 "Flying Fortresses"—was the mainstay of the entire Pacific defense and a relative bright spot. But a confidential report from the high commissioner to Roosevelt warned of "glaring deficiencies" that remained in Philippine defenses.[34]

That report was sent on November 30, 1941. A week later, it would be proved entirely correct.

The war began, for the United States, with the December 7/8 attacks. Despite nine hours' warning, MacArthur—for reasons that remain elusive—failed to get his planes off the ground. Japanese pilots found them an easy target, and within a short span of time they laid waste to the air force in the Philippines (MacArthur's air commander deemed it "one of the blackest days in U.S. military history").[35] The collapse of the flimsy Pacific defenses and the onset of war turned abstract questions about the United States' defense priorities into immediate ones. Guam was conquered within hours. Wake Island was under siege. The Philippines was in a bad spot. What would Roosevelt *do*?

The president answered clearly enough. "I give to the people of the Philippines my solemn pledge that their freedom will be redeemed and their independence established and protected," he said in a message to the colony. "The entire resources, in men and material, of the United States stand behind that pledge."[36]

Those were strong words. Yet they were also, when one looked closely, evasive ones. Philippine freedom would be "redeemed," yes, but didn't that imply that it would first be lost? Also, the president had said nothing about *when* all this would happen. Immediately after making the statement, Roosevelt sent his press secretary, Steve Early, to clarify its timeline. Early scolded journalists for reading "too much of the immediate rather than the ultimate" into the president's pledge. "You must consider distances," he pleaded.[37]

But Filipinos took the promise seriously. Rumors circulated of a massive convoy, miles in length, brimming with food and equipment, on its way. "In our mind's eyes we saw the vast fleet of steel gray ships steaming toward us, their bows cutting the waves sending up a multi-colored spray," a Filipino officer recalled.[38] Even MacArthur believed that Washington was preparing a relief effort.

Yet only a trickle arrived. Worse, Filipinos could hear *all* of Roosevelt's speeches, not just the ones aimed at him. They heard him stress the German enemy over the Japanese one. They heard his firm resolve to defend England.

Barely a week after pledging the entire resources to Philippine defense, Roosevelt delivered his State of the Union address. "It was bitter for us not to be able to land a million men in a thousand ships in the Philippine Islands," he said. But, he explained, "we have been faced with hard choices." An attack on Japan would come "in proper time."[39]

Manuel Quezon vibrated with anger. "I cannot stand this constant reference to England, to Europe. I am here and my people are here under the heels of a conqueror," he exclaimed. "How typically American to writhe in anguish at the fate of a distant cousin while a daughter is being raped in the back room."[40]

Quezon petitioned Roosevelt. "This war is not of our making," he pointed out.[41] What right did the United States have to drag the Philippines into a war and then abandon it? Why was Washington defending the imperialist powers of Europe while letting its own people perish? "While enjoying security itself," Quezon told Roosevelt, "the United States has in effect condemned the sixteen millions of Filipinos to practical destruction."[42]

Quezon demanded immediate independence. That way, he reasoned, he could declare neutrality and negotiate to have both Japan and the United States withdraw their forces.[43] MacArthur endorsed the plan, warning Roosevelt that "the temper of the Filipinos is one of almost violent resentment against the United States."[44]

Now it was Roosevelt's turn to be irate. "You have no authority to communicate with the Japanese government," he scolded Quezon.[45] "So long as the flag of the United States flies on Filipino soil," he promised, "it will be defended by our own men to the death."[46]

"To the death" was not just stirring rhetoric; it was the likely outcome. The Roosevelt administration had already agreed with Britain on a "Germany first" strategy for the war, which meant prioritizing Europe. Germany first was, the historian Louis Morton has rightly written, "the most important single strategic concept of the war."[47] It dictated how the United States fought at every level: where it sent its ships, how and when it negotiated, which technologies it prioritized. And that stance held firm during the war.

Germany first, however, meant Japan second. In particular, it meant that the United States would offer only relatively light resistance as Japan extended its Greater East Asia Co-Prosperity Sphere over Southeast Asia, the Pacific, and much of China, at least until Hitler was under control. It meant looking the other way as US colonies fell. Was the United States truly willing to see that happen, Britain's prime minister, Winston Churchill, asked. The US secretary of war,

Henry Stimson, a former governor of the Philippines, reassured him: "There are times when men have to die."[48]

In March 1942 Roosevelt ordered MacArthur, Quezon, and other top-ranking officials out of the Philippines. The colony could not be defended. The Japanese took Guam, Wake, and the Philippines. And in June, Japan bombed Dutch Harbor in Alaska and conquered the islands of Agattu, Attu, and Kiska, part of Alaska's Aleutian island chain.

"Somebody ought to be impeached," grumbled Manuel Quezon when he heard the Alaska news.[49]

The Japanese occupation of the Philippines, Guam, and part of Alaska was brutal. The Aleuts were rounded up and sent to Japan as prisoners of war, where half of them died.[50] The men on Wake Island were largely sent to a POW camp in China. The Philippines and Guam were run with harsh discipline. Unprovoked beatings and barely provoked executions were common, as was the confiscation of food and anything else that might serve the war. By 1944, starved Manilans were dropping dead in the streets.[51]

As usual, it was MacArthur among top officials who evinced the most concern on behalf of his beloved Philippines. It was "American territory," he loudly reminded his colleagues, where 17 million people were "undergoing the greatest privations and sufferings because we have not been able to support or succor them."[52] The United States, he insisted, had an obligation to oust Japan as soon as possible.

MacArthur's sense was not widely shared, though. Although Hollywood and the press paid careful attention to the mainlanders who had been trapped on Wake Island and the Philippines, concern for the other US nationals—the Filipinos, Aleuts, and Guamanians—was much harder to find. In fact, the remaining Aleuts were rounded up by the United States itself and interned, for their own "protection," in filthy camps where more than 10 percent died.[53]

The Filipino journalist (and future president of the United Nations General Assembly) Carlos Romulo made a frantic tour of 466 mainland towns and cities in two and a half years in an attempt to raise awareness.[54] But he struggled to get his message through. In a despondent moment, Romulo confessed to being "shocked and horrified" by mainlanders' indifference.[55] Washington seemed to him to be "crowded with little Neros, each fiddling away blithely" while the empire burned.[56]

The reconquest of the Japanese-held parts of the United States began with the Aleutians in 1943. The battle over the island of Attu cost hundreds of US soldiers their lives. The 2,000 Japanese entrenched on the island had fought to the death.

Guam was harder. The United States began its assault with air raids, which struck Guamanians and Japanese alike. Again, the Japanese dug in, trading fire with their assailants for *months*. The United States finally launched a round-the-clock attack using planes and ships that lasted for thirteen days straight. This was bombardment on "a scale and length of time never before seen in World War II," the US Marine Corps' official history concluded.[57]

Worried that that Guamanians might aid the US invasion, and fearing that they were at the end of their lives, anyway, the Japanese troops turned on the populace. Beheadings, rapes, and indiscriminate shooting were common. Japan's soldiers marched the entire native population of some 18,000 to the south of the island, massacring many there. In the aftermath, a US soldier recalled encountering a pile of decapitated corpses: "The heads lay like bowling balls all over the place."[58]

Around 15,000 Japanese soldiers died on Guam, and hundreds of Guamanians. In retaking Guam, the US military laid waste to Guam's capital, bombing and shelling every major structure in the town: the museum, the hospital, the governor's residence, the courthouse. Over the course of the war, about four-fifths of the homes in Guam had been destroyed.[59]

The United States then interned thousands of "liberated" Guamanians, over their objections, in camps while the navy tore down the rest of the capital to build it up as a forward base from which to fight the war.[60]

The Philippines came last. Yet again, Japanese forces were entrenched. MacArthur worried the most about Manila, which was the first (and as it turned out, only) major city in which the United States would fight Japan on the ground. As they had at Guam, the Japanese turned on the city. They took out the power and water systems. They dynamited factories and warehouses, and the flames predictably spread toward residential areas. As civilians fled into the street (or as the soldiers no doubt thought of it, the "battlefield"), they were shot down.[61] The diaries kept during the battle of Manila are replete with other stomach-churning atrocities: pregnant women disemboweled, babies bayoneted, whole families slaughtered. Prepared to die, the Japanese troops felt few moral constraints.

MacArthur's men entered this bloodbath with caution. Dislodging the Japanese while protecting Filipino lives was a delicate operation. When MacArthur's air commander suggested simply napalming a part of the city, Intramuros, from the skies, MacArthur dismissed the suggestion out of hand. Intramuros was inhabited by a "friendly" population, he reminded. Aerial bombing was "unthinkable."[62]

But as the battle for Manila wore on, MacArthur's army grew less and less patient. The Japanese were holed up throughout the city; storming their emplacements one by one with small arms was a dangerous proposition. Six days into the battle, the lead division, the Thirty-Seventh Infantry, saw nineteen of its men killed in a single day. That was, of course, nothing compared to the daily deaths

A US tank drives through the wall that had formerly demarcated Intramuros, 1945. (American Historical Collection, Ateneo de Manila University)

of Manilans. But to the division's commander, General Robert S. Beightler, it was "alarming."[63]

Beightler switched tactics. Rather than engage the Japanese in direct combat, clearing Japanese emplacements using small arms, he would simply destroy any building in which they might be hiding. "Putting it crudely, we really went to town," Beightler reported. "To me, the loss of a single American life to save a building was unthinkable."[64]

That's a sentence worth reading twice. In Beightler's mind, the trade-off he was facing was between "American lives" and architecture. But, as Beightler well knew, many of those buildings were inhabited—by enemy soldiers and, in many cases, by Filipinos as well. It's just that, by his fateful logic, Filipinos were not "Americans."

Not only the Thirty-Seventh, but the other divisions attacking Manila turned up the heat. Though Intramuros was spared napalm bombs from planes, it was nevertheless, with MacArthur's approval, comprehensively destroyed. During one manic hour on February 23, the closely packed (and still inhabited) section of the city had three tons of explosives hurled at it *per minute*. Shells struck, more than one per second, "hurtling like lightning bolts from the hands of an angry god," as one observer wrote.[65] "We made a churned-up pile of dust and scrap out of the imposing, classic government buildings," Beightler boasted.[66]

Within a week of the fighting, US shelling of the whole area in front of advancing troops became, as one report put it, "the rule rather than the exception."[67] Any structure containing Japanese soldiers, or suspected to contain them, was a target. "Block after bloody block was slowly mashed into an unrecognizable pulp," recorded the Thirty-Seventh's official history.[68]

That included refugee centers, such as the Philippine General Hospital, which the Thirty-Seventh fired at for two days and nights even though it contained more than 7,000 civilians—and very few Japanese soldiers.[69] These were "days of terror," remembered a Filipino trapped inside the hospital. "I can still hear the screams of the wounded clearly to this day."[70] Other refugee shelters—the Remedios Hospital, the Concordia Convent—met similar fates.

The sixth-largest city in the United States—larger than Boston or Washington, DC—had for a month of fighting been converted into an abattoir. Bodies decomposed everywhere, many bearing the marks of torture or mass execution. The stench was unbearable.

"The largest buildings had been transformed into mere piles of rubble and debris. Over areas, miles square, hardly one stone was left on top of another. It was as if all the forces of destruction had operated together, and that even this had been exceeded," wrote a local journalist. "This seemed demonic work."[71]

Demonic, maybe, but not indiscriminate. The "better to lose a building than an American life" logic succeeded in protecting mainland soldiers. In the month of fighting, 1,010 of them died. Compare that to the 16,665 Japanese troops who perished.[72] And compare *that* to the 100,000 Manilans killed. For every "American life" lost, a hundred Manilans died.

Or so we think. Mainland lives lost were counted with to-the-last-digit precision, but Filipino lives lost were at best informed guesses. The 100,000 figure, accepted by the US Army, was based on extrapolations from figures submitted by undertakers after the war.[73]

A soldier carries a stunned young woman through the wreckage of Manila. (American Historical Collection, Ateneo de Manila University)

At any rate, Manila wasn't the only place hit. Smaller towns and cities were bombarded as well. "We levelled entire cities with our bombs and shell fire," admitted the high commissioner. "We destroyed roads, public buildings, and bridges. We razed sugar mills and factories." In the end, he concluded, "there was nothing left."[74]

Senator Millard Tydings led a survey of the colony after the war. He estimated that 10 to 15 percent of its buildings had been destroyed, and another 10 percent damaged.[75] After the war, Filipinos submitted claims on behalf of 1,111,938 war deaths, which is the number the government accepted.[76] Add Japanese (518,000) and mainland fatalities (the army counted slightly more than 10,000) and the total climbs to more than 1.6 million.[77] Such numbers are regrettably imprecise, especially on the Filipino and Japanese side, but their scale is correct.

World War II in the Philippines rarely appears in US history textbooks. But it should. It was by far the most destructive event ever to take place on US soil.

Oscar Villadolid, a boy at the time, remembers a scene from the aftermath of Manila's "liberation." A GI came down his street handing out cigarettes and Hershey bars. Speaking slowly, he asked Villadolid's name. When Villadolid replied easily in English, the soldier was startled. "How'd ya learn American?" he asked.[78]

The soldier wasn't the only GI to receive this surprise. The Thirty-Seventh Infantry Division's official history contains multiple stories of soldiers baffled upon encountering English-speaking Filipinos.[79] In Villadolid's case, however, we have a record of the encounter from the Filipino side. Villadolid patiently explained that when the United States conquered the Philippines, it had instituted English in the schools. This only compounded the GI's confusion. "He did not even know that America had a colony here in the Philippines!" Villadolid marveled.[80]

Take a moment to let that sink in. This was a soldier who had taken a long journey across the Pacific. He had been briefed on his mission, shown maps, told where to go and whom to shoot. He had very likely put his life on the line, perhaps seen his comrades die. Yet at no point had it dawned on him that he was there to reclaim a US colony and that the people he was "liberating" were, just like him, US nationals.

He thought he was invading a foreign country.

NOTES

Excerpts from this chapter appeared originally in *How to Hide an Empire: A History of the Greater United States,* by Daniel Immerwahr. Copyright © 2019 by Daniel Immerwahr. Reprinted by permission of Farrar, Straus and Giroux.

1. Press Conference of Vice President Nixon, International Airport, Seattle, August 5, 1960, *The American Presidency Project*, ed. Gerhard Peters and John T. Woolley, www.presidency.ucsb.edu (hereafter *APP*).

2. Elizabeth M. Collins, "After Pearl Harbor, Soldiers Held out for Months against Japanese Invasion of the Philippines," December 8, 2016, www.army.mil/article/179370.

3. Louis Morton, *The Fall of the Philippines* (Washington, DC: Office of the Chief of Military History, Department of the Army, 1953), 88.

4. John Costello, *Days of Infamy: MacArthur, Roosevelt, Churchill—The Shocking Truth Revealed* (New York: Pocket Books, 1994), 4.

5. An excellent account of Wake Island and its place in the public imagination is Gregory J. W. Urwin, "The Defenders of Wake Island: Their Two Wars, 1941–1945," in Gunter Bischof and Robert L. Dupont, eds., *The Pacific War Revisited* (Baton Rouge: Louisiana State University Press, 1997), 111–137.

6. Draft 1, Significant Documents Collection, Franklin D. Roosevelt Presidential Library and Museum (hereafter FDR Library).

7. Speech, December 7, 1941, Eleanor Roosevelt Papers, Speech and Article File, December 1941–January 1942, FDR Library.

8. Earl S. Pomeroy, *Pacific Outpost: American Strategy in Guam and Micronesia* (Stanford, CA: Stanford University Press, 1951), 140.

9. For the final available draft of the speech, the third, see Franklin D. Roosevelt, Master Speech File, 1898–1945, FDR Library. We do not have a copy of the final version, the speech that FDR read from.

10. James Madison, Special Message, June 1, 1812, *APP.*

11. James K. Polk, Special Message to Congress, May 11, 1846, *APP.*

12. Woodrow Wilson, Address to a Joint Session of Congress Requesting a Declaration of War Against Germany, April 2, 1917, *APP.*

13. Franklin Delano Roosevelt, Remarks in Hawai'i, July 28, 1934, *APP.*

14. John Hersey, *Men on Bataan* (New York: Alfred A. Knopf, 1942), 365.

15. Daniel Immerwahr, "The Greater United States: Territory and Empire in U.S. History," *Diplomatic History* 40 (2016), 376n. The 12.6 percent figure includes military personnel stationed in the territories, and the comparison includes African Americans in the territories.

16. *New York Times Index: Annual Cumulative Volume Year 1930* (New York: New York Times Company, 1931).

17. Letters collected in 9-0-1, Administrative, World's Colonies; Box 67, Folder: "World's Colonies—General"; Office of Territories Classified Files, 1907–1951; Record Group 126, Records of the Office of Territories, NARA, College Park, MD (this record group hereafter ROT).

18. Helen Johnson of Rand McNally to Donna Kowalski, circa 1942, in ibid.

19. Barbara Frederick to Harold Ickes, January 14, 1943, in ibid.

20. Ruth Hampton to Barbara Frederick, January 30, 1943, in ibid.

21. Louis Morton, "Germany First: The Basic Concept of Allied Strategy in World War II," in Kent Roberts Greenfield, ed., *Command Decisions* (Washington, DC: Office of the Chief of Military History, Department of the Army, 1960), 11–47.

22. Dudley W. Knox, *The Eclipse of American Sea Power* (New York: American and Navy Journal, 1922), 53.

23. Issue discussed in Julius W. Pratt, *America's Colonial Experiment: How the United States Gained, Governed, and in Part Gave Away a Colonial Empire* (New York: Prentice-Hall, 1951), 338.

24. Johnson Hagood to Herbert Hoover, 1929, quoted in Richard H. Rovere and Arthur Schlesinger Jr., *The MacArthur Controversy and American Foreign Policy* (New York: Farrar, Straus and Giroux, 1965), 44. On Plan Orange in general, see Edward S. Miller, *War Plan Orange: The U.S. Strategy to Defeat Japan, 1897–1945* (Annapolis, MD: Naval Institute Press, 1991).

25. Louis Morton, *The War in the Pacific: Strategy and Command: The First Two Years* (Washington, DC: Center of Military History, 1962), 34.

26. Rep. James G. Strong in *Independence for the Philippine Islands: Hearings Before the Committee On Insular Affairs, House of Representatives*, 72d Congress, 1st sess., 340.

27. Roosevelt to Quezon, quoted in Theodore Roosevelt Jr., *Colonial Policies of the United States* (Garden City, NJ: Doubleday, Doran, 1937), 187.

28. D. Clayton James, *The Years of MacArthur*, vol. 1 (Boston: Houghton Mifflin, 1970), 608.

29. MacArthur to Quezon, October 1940, reprinted in ibid., 541–542.

30. Ernest Gruening, *Many Battles: The Autobiography of Ernest Gruening* (New York: Liveright, 1973), 295.

31. Lewis H. Brereton, *The Brereton Diaries: The War in the Air in the Pacific, Middle East, and Europe, 3 October 1941–8 May 1945* (New York: William Morrow, 1946), 17.

32. Galen Roger Perras, *Stepping Stones to Nowhere: The Aleutian Islands, Alaska, and American Military Strategy, 1867–1945* (Vancouver: UBC Press, 2003), 53.

33. Shoes: Glen M. Williford, *Racing the Sunrise: Reinforcing America's Pacific Outposts, 1941–1942* (Annapolis, MD: Naval Institute Press, 2010), 102; helmets: Daniel D. Holt and James W. Leyerzapf, eds., *Eisenhower: The Prewar Diaries and Selected Papers, 1905–1941* (Baltimore: Johns Hopkins University Press, 1998), 405; artillery: Richard Connaughton, *MacArthur and Defeat in the Philippines* (Woodstock, NY: Overlook Press, 2001), 155.

34. High Commissioner's Office to FDR, November 30, 1941; "Civilian Defense" folder, box 1; High Commissioner–Pol/Econ; ROT.

35. Brereton, *Brereton Diaries*, 44.

36. Roosevelt, Message of Support to the Philippines, December 28, 1941, *APP*.

37. Quoted in Hersey, *Men on Bataan*, 257.

38. Rigoberto J. Atienza, *A Time for War: 105 Days in Bataan* (Philippines: Eugenia S. vda. de Atienza, 1985), 119.

39. Roosevelt, State of the Union address, January 6, 1942, *APP*.

40. Charles A. Willoughby and John Chamberlain, *MacArthur: 1941–1951* (New York: McGraw-Hill, 1954), 56.

41. Douglas MacArthur to Emory S. Adams, January 28, 1942, *Foreign Relations of the United States: 1942*, vol. 1 (Washington, DC: United States Government Printing Office, 1960), 889 (hereafter *FRUS*). Manuel Quezon describes the interchange in *The Good Fight* (New York: D. Appleton-Century, 1946), 259–274.

42. Douglas MacArthur to George Marshall, February 8, 1942, *FRUS 1942*, 894.

43. Ibid.

44. Ibid., 896.

45. L. T. Gerow to Douglas MacArthur, February 11, 1942, *FRUS 1942*, 900.

46. George Marshall to Douglas MacArthur, February 9, 1942, *FRUS 1942*, 898.

47. Morton, "Germany First," 11.

48. William Manchester, *American Caesar: Douglas MacArthur, 1880–1964* (Boston: Little, Brown, 1978), 241.

49. Michael P. Onorato, ed., *Origins of the Philippine Republic: Extracts from the Diaries and Records of Francis Burton Harrison* (Ithaca, NY: Cornell University Southeast Asia Program, 1974), 154.

50. The ordeal is detailed in Nick Golodoff, *Attu Boy*, ed. Rachel Mason (Anchorage: National Park Service, Alaska Regional Office, 2012).

51. Daniel F. Doeppers, *Feeding Manila in Peace and War, 1850–1945* (Madison: University of Wisconsin Press, 2016), 324–325.

52. Willoughby and Chamberlain, *MacArthur*, 235–236.

53. Dean Kohlhoff, *When the Wind Was a River: Aleut Evacuation in World War II* (Seattle: University of Washington Press, 1995).

54. Carlos P. Romulo, *My Brother Americans* (Garden City, NY: Doubleday, Doran, 1945), 21.

55. Frank S. Adams, "Visitor from Bataan," *New York Times*, June 24, 1945.

56. Romulo, *My Brother Americans*, 8.

57. Henry I. Shaw, Bernard C. Nalty, and Edwin T. Turnbladh, *History of U.S. Marine Corps Operations in World War II*, vol. 3 (Washington, DC: Government Printing Office, 1966), 448.

58. Quoted in Robert F. Rogers, *Destiny's Landfall: A History of Guam* (Honolulu: University of Hawaii Press, 1995), 192.

59. Ibid., 201.

60. On this sort of "friendly" internment, which occurred on many Pacific islands, see Lamont Lindstrom and Geoffrey M. White, *Island Encounters: Black and White Memories of the Pacific War* (Washington, DC: Smithsonian Institution Press, 1990), 61.

61. Three overviews are indispensable to understand the Battle of Manila: Robert Ross Smith, *Triumph in the Philippines* (Washington, DC: Office of the Chief of Military History, 1963); Alfonso J. Aluit, *By Sword and Fire: The Destruction of Manila in World War II, 3 February–3 March 1945* (Manila: National Commission for Culture and the Arts, 1994); and Richard Connaughton, John Pimlott, and Duncan Anderson, *The Battle for Manila* (London: Bloomsbury, 1995).

62. Quoted in Smith, *Triumph*, 294.

63. Robert S. Beightler, *Report after Action: Operations of the 37th Infantry Division, Luzon P.I., 1 November 1944 to 30 June 1945 (M-1 Operation)*, September 1945, 51, New York Public Library.

64. Beightler, *Report on Activities*, quoted in Connaughton et al., *Battle for Manila*, 175–176.

65. William A. Owens, *Eye-Deep in Hell: A Memoir of the Liberation of the Philippines, 1944–45* (Dallas: Southern Methodist University Press, 1989), 122; Aluit, *Sword and Fire*, 355.

66. Beightler, *Report*, quoted in Connaughton et al., *Battle for Manila*, 176.

67. XIV Corps, *Japanese Defense of Cities as Exemplified by the Battle for Manila* (Army Chief of Staff, G-2, Headquarters, Sixth Army, July 1, 1945), 20.

68. Stanley A. Frankel, *The 37th Infantry Division in World War II* (Washington, DC: Infantry Journal Press, 1948), 283.

69. Aluit, *Sword and Fire*, 389; Frankel, *37th Infantry*, 281–283.

70. Miguel P. Avanceña, quoted in Aluit, *Sword and Fire*, 391.

71. A. V. H. Hartendorp, *The Japanese Occupation of the Philippines*, vol. 2 (Manila: Bookmark, 1967), 604–605.

72. Connaughton et al, *Battle for Manila*, 174.

73. On the 100,000 figure, see Aluit, *Sword and Fire*, 398–399.

74. Paul V. McNutt, address at Beta Theta Pi Fraternity, November 27, 1946; "McNutt, P.V., Correspondence and Speeches, 1945–46" folder, box 7; Office of the High Commissioner of the Philippine Islands, Records of the Washington, DC, Office, 1942–46; ROT.

75. Millard Tydings, "Report on the Philippine Islands," June 7, 1945, 22, in "Philippine Rehabilitation Commission" folder, series 4, box 2, Papers of Millard E. Tydings, Special Collections, Hornbake Library, University of Maryland.

76. Numbers reported in Quirino, "Our Bid for Survival," 1947, in Juan Collas, ed., *The Quirino Way: Collection of Speeches and Addresses of Elpidio Quirino* (n.p., 1955), 51; and also in Joaquin M. Elizalde, Secretary of Foreign Affairs, "The Case for the Prompt Ratification of the Japanese Peace Treaty," 1952, 5, both in American Historical Collection, Rizal Library, Ateneo de Manila University.

77. Japanese figures: Miki Ishikida, *Toward Peace: War Responsibility, Postwar Compensation, and Peace Movements and Education in Japan* (New York: Center for US-Japan Comparative Social Studies, 2005), 12; mainland: 10,640 dead (not counting the Leyte and Samar campaigns) according to Smith, *Triumph in the Philippines*, 652.

78. Oscar S. Villadolid, *Born in Freedom: My Life and Times* (Quezon City: Colet-Villadolid Publications, 2004), 191.

79. Frankel, *37th Infantry*, 227–229.

80. Villadolid, *Born in Freedom*, 191. A similar story appears in Frank Mathias, *G.I. Jive: An Army Bandsman in World War II* (Lexington: University Press of Kentucky, 1982), 133. The army's guide given to soldiers en route to the Philippines, *We Return to the Philippines* (Brisbane: Information and Education Section, HQ, USAFFE, c. 1944), praises Filipinos for their friendship and notes that they speak English, but it never clearly explains why.

CHAPTER 3

Japan and the "Spirit of December 8"

Jeremy A. Yellen

December 8, 1941, was a strange day in Japan. As poet and novelist Itō Sei passed by his neighbor's house in Tokyo at around 1 p.m., he overheard the radio broadcast of the attack on Pearl Harbor, the invasion of Malaya, and the declaration of war against the United States and Britain. Exhilarated by the news, he decided to see what things were like in town. But whatever he saw felt subdued and not out of the ordinary. This was mystifying, Itō felt, for a country that had just declared war.[1] He took a bus to Shinjuku, which was too quiet for his liking. No other passenger even mentioned the war in passing. Itō itched to scream out, "At last, war has finally begun!" But he kept quiet, convinced that he was the only person excited by the news. From Shinjuku he made his way toward Ginza, where his strange day continued. He passed through Yotsuya, Hanzōmon, and Hibiya before noticing anything resembling excitement. Things finally changed when he reached the National Theater (Nihon Gekijo) in Yūryakuchō. He saw university students who seemed "a little worked up, speaking with frowns on their faces. But passersby were all sullenly reading the newspaper." Itō finally went home and was restless that evening. Thrilled by what Japan had accomplished, he noted in his diary, "This is splendid. Japan's attack is every bit as magnificent as that of the Russo-Japanese War."[2]

What a difference a day made. In his diary on the following day, Itō reflected on the excitement boiling over in Tokyo. "Today everyone is beaming with joy [*kishoku arite akarui*]. This is entirely different from yesterday."[3] He surmised that nobody spoke of the war the previous day owing to the initial shock of the news. But given time to digest the gravity of Japan's success, shock turned to joy. Not two months later, he came to view the war in even more vivid and upbeat terms. On February 15, 1942, the day that Singapore fell, Itō could not contain his pleasure. "This war is bright," he wrote. "It certainly has brightened Japan even more than it has been since before the China Incident. And the gloominess [that had pervaded] just before the Greater East Asia War is also gone. This war is good. Bright."[4]

As Samuel Yamashita's chapter in this volume shows, Japanese subjects met the decision to wage war against the "Anglo-Saxon powers" with a mixture of emotions, from concern and dismay to exhilaration.[5] Nonetheless, the pure excitement displayed by people like Itō Sei must be seen as the dominant narrative. The attacks of December 8 mobilized support from the broader populace, many of whom, like Itō Sei, now saw the war as "good" and "bright." This support was understandable. Government propaganda and media reports since the 1930s had emphasized that Japan was a long-term victim of Anglo-American arrogance and belligerence. Many Japanese thus rejoiced at the decision to strike back against their persecutors. Moreover, the stunning success of that strike, in the space of little more than a day, swept away the weariness and distress from four years of a drawn-out and demoralizing war in China. For those who had misgivings about the "China Incident," the undeclared total war raging in China, the war against the "Anglo-Saxon powers" placed the conflict in China in a new context. They now believed in good faith that Japan was fighting a "holy war," not to exploit its neighbors but to liberate Asia from the West.

The dizzying success of the attacks of December 8 generated a festive atmosphere and a sense of popular excitement for Japan's expanded war. In this sense, the outbreak of war brought about perhaps the most powerful moment of what Louise Young has called "imperial jingoism."[6] The outbreak of war against the United States and Great Britain ensured popular commitment to Japan's effort to build a new empire that reached across Greater East Asia, from the cold woods of Sakhalin to the jungles of Indonesia, and from the Philippine tropics to the jungles and deltas of Burma.

MOBILIZED BEHIND JAPAN'S "BRIGHT" WAR

Itō Sei was by no means the only person who thought of Japan's war against Britain and America as both "good" and "bright." The broader public, too, was ecstatic. Many across Japan remembered the excitement as immediate and overpowering. Ikezaki Tadataka, a politician who earlier in his career wrote as a critic under the nom de plume of Akagi Kōhei, learned of the attack after taking a train to Ōsaka. He made his way to his office, only to find it buzzing with delight. "One and all," he wrote on December 14, 1941, "not even one person was unexcited.

Even [Nozaki's] timid wife had a smile on her face and tears in her eyes. Looking upon this, I suddenly felt my own eyes water. In that moment," he continued, "there were no words to express my state of mind. *At last we have done it!*" Ikezaki could not stop thinking about the momentous, history-changing decision to open hostilities against the Anglo-American powers. "This," he wrote, "is the most epoch-making event in the six-thousand years of world history."[7]

Of course, not everyone celebrated. Some who had substantial knowledge of the limits of Japanese power viewed the expanded war with dread. Ozaki Yukio, a maverick independent politician who had been critical of the growing influence of the military in public life, noted his concerns about the outbreak of war against the Allied powers. What worried him most was "the ecstatic response" of the people to Japan's military achievements. He thus responded by expressing his views on the war, in private, through two poems:

桶狭間の奇勝におごり本能寺の
奇禍を招ける人な忘れん

Okehazama no	Forget not he, whose
Kishō ni ogori	Arrogance in triumph at
Honnōji no	Okehazama
Kika o manekeru	Invited calamity
Hito na wasuren	On the grounds of Honnōji

詰手なき将棋をさしつつ勝ち抜くと
嘯く人のめでたからずや

Tsumete naki	A fool's errand
Shōgi o sashi tsutsu	To press on playing shogi
Kachi nuku to	Deceiving oneself
Usobuku hito no	That victory lies ahead
Medetakarazu ya	Despite no hope of checkmate[8]

Both poems served as private, diary-bound warnings. The "arrogance in triumph" of Ozaki's first poem referred to Oda Nobunaga, one of the three unifiers in Japan's warring states period. Although Nobunaga had achieved a great victory in the Battle of Okehazama in 1560, he would later be forced by one of his retainers to commit suicide. Pride, Ozaki hints, was Nobunaga's undoing. The second poem is an even harsher indictment of the decision to wage war against the Allied powers despite having no real way to win. Wishful thinking alone never won wars. Both poems thus point to the misplaced jingoism in the wake of the attacks of December 8 and suggest that the seeds had already been sown for Japan's future defeat. Far from feeling jubilant, Ozaki felt that the public should instead be worried.

Others responded in a similar way. Prince Higashikuni—Hirohito's uncle—lamented in his diary on December 8, "With this, I knew that Japan had taken its first step to ruin, and I was disheartened."[9] Former prime minister Konoe Fumimaro and former foreign minister Matsuoka Yōsuke were similarly despondent.[10] Konoe spent a dejected day on December 8 at the Peers Club in Tokyo. His downcast mood provided a stark contrast to the popular excitement among Japan's nobility. He later told his aide and son-in-law, Hosokawa Morisada, "Our luck will not last more than two or three months at best."[11] Matsuoka, too, reportedly wept in dismay. He told his private secretary, Saitō Yoshie, "I am now painfully aware that the signing of the Tripartite Pact was the biggest mistake of my lifetime. . . . When I think of this, it will bother me even after I die."[12] Finally, political scientist Nanbara Shigeru bemoaned the war through the following *tanka* poems that convey his distress.

人間の常識を超え学識を超えておこれり日本世界と戦う

Ningen no	Beyond common sense
Jōshiki o koe	Beyond any learning
Gakushiki o	It has happened—
Koete okoreri	Japan,
Nihon sekai to tatakau	At war against the world

日米英に開戦すとのみ八日朝の電車のなかの沈痛感よ

Nichi Bei-Ei ni	Only the attack
Kaisen su to nomi	On America and England
Yōka asa no	Explains the sorrow
Densha no naka no	Permeating the train car
Chintsūkan yo	On the morning of the eighth[13]

Those who had profound doubts about Japan's war, however, largely kept those thoughts private. It would have taken great personal courage, conviction, and sacrifice to speak out in opposition. Openly opposing the war, after all, would have invited both legal punishment and social ostracism, and perhaps even attempts at assassination. From the early 1930s, political assassinations had become so widespread that they were an essential aspect of Japanese political life. Moreover, no powerful organization existed that could shield or support those who would speak publicly in resistance. The state, in fact, had used the Peace Preservation Law in the years since 1925 to control "thought crimes" and to suppress dissident organizations or heterodox ideologies. With no support for public action and fears of social ostracism or even personal harm, those who opposed the war kept their sentiments private. This is one reason why the Home Ministry could boast on December 9, 1941, that "there is a deep sense that the system of national unity [*kyokoku itchi taisei*] is strengthening more and more," and that "where public peace is concerned there is no unrest."[14]

The Home Ministry was correct—most Japanese citizens were electrified by the news. Lt. General Satō Kenryō, who from 1942 to 1944 served as the director of the Army Ministry's Bureau of Military Affairs, noted that whereas some may have been angry that Japan "did something stupid" and others lamented Japan's "certain defeat," many more met the war with high morale.[15] Yatsugi Kazuo, the founder of the National Policy Research Association (Kokusaku Kenkyūkai), remembered the news of Japan's war as generating an "uninterrupted tumult of excited phone calls from friends, shouting 'At last, we've done it!'"[16] This high morale was evident among writers in particular. Writers were quick to express their excitement at the imperial rescript declaring war through liberal use of such terms as "deep emotion" [*kangeki*] and "tears of gratitude" [*kanrui*]. Echoing this sentiment, novelist and playwright Nagayo Yoshirō wrote, "I never thought I would live to see such a happy, enjoyable [*tsūkai*], and auspicious [*medetai*] day. The oppressive gloom that covered us like dark clouds over our heads for the past several months, or past twelve years, has vanished with the brilliant imperial edict [declaring war]."[17]

Second-year middle school student from Sendai Itabashi Kōshū recalled his own excitement at the news. "I felt as if my blood boiled and my flesh quivered," he recalled. "The whole nation bubbled over, excited and inspired. 'We really did it! Incredible! Wonderful!' That's the way it felt then." Itabashi noted that cost-benefit analyses never entered the equation. "We simply hit out," he noted. "Our blood was hot! We fought. Until the very end, no one considered the possibility that Japan could lose."[18]

Itabashi's sense of the nation's "blood boiling over" was reinforced by popular magazines and mass media institutions. Often calling for the "annihilation" [*gekimetsu*], the "obliteration" [*zenmetsu*], the "destruction" [*hōkai*], or the "defeat" or "overthrow" [*datō*] of the Anglo-Saxon enemy, mass media institutions helped create a mood of jingoistic hysteria. Japan would fight its war of "self-preservation and self-defense" with little regard for consequences, and with little thought to costs. This sense of lashing out in self-defense is wonderfully illustrated in a political cartoon for popular entertainment magazine *Kingu* [King]. Drawn shortly after the Pearl Harbor attacks, the illustration shows a diminutive Japanese man knocking the breath out of his larger, more imposing Anglo-Saxon foe, leaving the impression that this first punch is only the beginning of a thorough thrashing.

A *Japan Times & Advertiser* political cartoon, drafted in English but intended both for domestic and foreign consumption, makes an even stronger point about

"Taking It the Hard Way," *Japan Times & Advertiser*, December 10, 1941. (Courtesy of *The Japan Times.*)

the obliteration of the Anglo-Saxon powers. It highlights a sense of shock, dismay, and fear among the ABC powers (America, Britain, and China) as they confronted the realities of Japanese power. Uncle Sam, John Bull, and Marshall Chiang are all left reeling, at the point of toppling over from Japan's heavy punch. And like the political cartoon that appeared in *Kingu*, this creates a sense that Japan's first punch is only the beginning.

Other students viewed Pearl Harbor and the attacks of December 8 in a similar light. Yamaguchi Masahiko, a fifth-year student at Waseda Gakuin Middle School, noted in his diary on December 8, 1941, that "Britain and America should be afraid" and recorded the special day as inspiration to renew his desire to pass the higher-school exams.[19] And Kuroda Saburō, who was then a student at Tokyo Imperial University, wrote in his own diary, "Such a delightful day like today won't come again [*kyō mitai ni ureshii hi wa matatonai*]." The delight of December 8, he noted, left a "refreshing feeling" in his heart. The following day, Kuroda took to

The Japanese Empire lashes out in the name of "self-preservation and self-defense." Taken from "Ei-Bei gekimetsu! Kagayaku daisenkuwa to tsugi no senkyoku o kataru," *Kingu,* February 1942, 43. (Courtesy of the National Diet Library, Tokyo, Japan)

his diary again, hinting at his desire to learn more about Japan's victories. "For some reason I felt restless all day. I tried to read books, but after a while I'd fidget and rise to my feet. Ah, when will the evening newspaper arrive!"[20]

Kyoto Imperial University professor Komaki Saneshige listened with students to the 11:30 a.m. radio news that reported Japan's military successes as well as the declaration of war. He wrote on December 31, reflecting at length on the meaning of Japan's attack on Pearl Harbor three weeks earlier, "University students swarming around the radio gave three cheers of 'banzai.' But long before that I had been privately weeping. Then, without thinking, I joined with a young member of my classroom and cried on the main street." He later went to lunch with the same person, and neither could hold back their tears. "Choked by tears [*kyoki aetsu*], I prostrated myself toward His Majesty from afar, and cried out in my heart 'thank you very much,' 'thank you very much.'" With the emperor's declaration, he believed that a war had begun to bring the Imperial Way to the forefront of global politics.[21]

Renowned political scientist and Tokyo Imperial University professor Yabe Teiji met the news with a mix of excitement and concern. In his diary on December 8, 1941, Yabe wrote, "Today is the first day of a historic age." At 12:30 p.m., after grading examination papers and inputting the results into his student's records, Yabe turned on the radio and heard the imperial rescript declaring war. "The brilliant sun was shining down as if this was a warm and peaceful spring day," he penned, "and as I listened [to the radio] I watched the refined crimson of the camellias. The radio invited the sense that this was somebody else's business, and I thought the fight for our country's very existence had more than ever plunged into a decisive battle. Upon thinking that sometime enemy planes might attempt an air raid here, I shuddered."[22] Over the following days, he noted with glee about the successes of the Imperial Japanese Navy. On December 9 Yabe wrote, "The navy's Hawaiian operation is one of the greatest triumphs in the history of war." The following day, he "shuddered" again when learning of the sinking of the British Royal Navy battleship HMS *Prince of Wales* and the battlecruiser HMS *Repulse.* "Navy *banzai!*," he rejoiced.[23] This excitement translated into political involvement in Japan's new order. Beginning in January 1942, Yabe would play a pivotal role in both the Navy Ministry's brain trust, the Naval Intelligence Division, and the National Policy Research Association, helping craft new visions and principles for the Greater East Asia Co-Prosperity Sphere.

Five days after the outbreak of war, on December 13, 1941, throngs of supporters rushed to Hibiya Park to celebrate the war against the Anglo-Saxon enemy. Tens of thousands of people crowded together in this central Tokyo park to express their enthusiasm and joy at Japan's great military successes. Prime Minister Tōjō Hideki addressed the rally, feeding into the frenzy by drawing attention to Japanese dreams for centrality in global affairs. "The victory of Japan," he thundered, "will be the victory of the East Asia Co-Prosperity Sphere, as well as the victory of the creation of the new world order." The crowd responded with a "rousing and thunderous banzai for the humiliation of the haughty Anglo-Saxons."[24]

What makes this flood of support truly striking was the fact that Japan struck from a position of great weakness. Those knowledgeable of the sources of Western power keenly understood Japan's vulnerability. A prime example is Iwakuro Hideo, a section chief in the Army Ministry's Bureau of Military Affairs. Iwakuro was a firebrand mid-echelon officer who advocated strongly for the Axis alliance, but who also took part in the first round of exploratory conversations in Washington, DC, to avoid war with the United States. In August 1941, while traveling back to Japan aboard the *Ryūta Maru,* Iwakuro drew up a graph that highlights the depth of Japan's materiel deficiencies.

Iwakuro's Assessment of Japan's Vulnerability

Area	*US Production*	*Ratio: Japan/United States*
Steel manufacturing	95 million tons	1/20
Oil production	110 million tons	1/100
Coal production	500 million tons	1/10
Electric power	1,800 kW	1/6
Aluminium	600 thousand tons	1/6
Aircraft production	120 thousand	1/5
Automobile production	6.2 million	1/50
Ships	10 million tons	1/2
Industrial workers	34 million people	1/5

Note: Taken from Iwakuro Hideo, *Sensō rikugun bōryaku hishi* (Tokyo: Nihon Keizai Shinbun Shuppansha, 2015), 329.

In all, Iwakuro argued that Japan maintained only one-tenth the productive capacity of the United States.[25] Moreover, this knowledge was not limited to Iwakuro and others in the know. Elites and mass media outlets never hid Japan's materiel deficiency and technological limitations. To the contrary, they readily admitted Japan's relative weaknesses, but they emphasized that any deficiencies could be counterbalanced by *Yamato damashi*, or Japanese spirit. It was spirit, not materiel or technology, that led to triumph in war. This emphasis on the primacy of spirit, in fact, had been argued since the Russo-Japanese War, and would be argued again in 1941. According to Iwakuro, this belief that spirit trumps technology led decision-makers into a "war that Japan had no prospects of winning."[26]

The attacks of December 8 energized the public for a variety of reasons. First, they provided a sense of excitement that Japan would finally take retribution for a long history of victimization in international affairs. By 1941 many Japanese had come to believe that their nation was dragged into a world of power politics in which the cards were unfairly stacked against them. The rejection of the Japanese delegation's proposed racial equality clause at Versailles in 1919 and the so-called Japanese Exclusion Act of 1924 served as constant reminders of the low regard for which Japan was held. Government propaganda in the wake of the Manchurian Incident in 1931 reinforced a narrative of Japan as isolated in a hostile world. Japan's war in China, the decision to join the Tripartite Pact, and the occupation of French Indochina only increased this sense of victimization. The United States responded by imposing "moral embargoes," followed by a broader array of economic sanctions. By late July 1941, after Japan occupied southern French Indochina, the United States froze all Japanese assets. Great Britain and the Dutch East Indies soon followed suit. The freezing of assets, which soon turned into a full embargo, represented a major challenge to Japan. Not only did Japan lose access to 88 percent of its oil needs but it also lost three-quarters of its foreign trade.

By August 1941 the Japanese mass media had reached a "war-fevered" pitch. Media outlets complained of an "ABCD encirclement": that they were fenced in by America, Britain, China, and the Dutch.[27] Those countries, which had a long history of racism toward Japan, now threatened Japan with economic ruin. In a diary entry in November, US ambassador to Japan Joseph Grew noted the prevailing mood: "It is always we who threaten; it is always we who are the potential aggressor, never Japan. Thus does the United States wholly 'misunderstand' Japan's peaceful intentions . . . and thus do we render an adjustment of relations impossibly by 'encircling' (a word so loved by the Nazis) innocent and unoffending Nippon."[28] Moreover, the Japanese media presented the Hull Note of November 26, which called on Japan to return to the status quo ante of the 1920s, as an "ultimatum."[29] Although the Hull Note was never intended as an ultimatum, its presentation as such confirmed the sense that Japan was once again being bullied and humiliated, and asked to return to a third-power status.[30] Given this context, it is not surprising that many Japanese reacted to the attacks of December 8 with glee, relishing the fact that "war has finally arrived."[31] Pearl Harbor broke the impasse in international politics, provided a sense of retribution for a longer history of victimization, and gave the nation a new goal around which the people could mobilize.

Strikingly, the December 8, 1941, imperial rescript declaring war on America and Britain reinforced this victim narrative. Japan, the rescript stated, had only the purest of motives. It only sought stability, peace, friendship, and "prosperity in common with all nations." But Japan's enemies failed to understand its true intentions. Instead, they presented new challenges at every turn. They threatened Japan with military preparations, obstructed Japan's "peaceful commerce," and even severed economic ties, "menacing gravely the existence of our Empire." Japan had patiently endured this foreign menace, but the time for waiting had passed. The imperial rescript concluded, "Our Empire for its existence and self-defense has no other recourse but to appeal to arms and to crush every obstacle in its path." Japan, in short, was victimized into taking up arms.[32]

This sense of victimization, and the glory of retribution, is perhaps best summed in "December 8," a long-form poem by famous poet Takamura Kōtarō.

Kioku seyo, jūnigatsu yōka	Remember December 8,
Kono hi sekai no rekishi aratamaru.	the day world history changed.
Anguro Sakuson no shuken,	The day Anglo-Saxon power
kono hi tōa no riku to umi to ni hitei saru.	was denied across the land and sea of East Asia.
Hitei suru mono wa warera Japan,	It was our Japan that denied them,

byōtaru tōkai no kuni ni shite,	the small country in the Eastern sea,
mata kami no kuni taru Nippon nari.	the Land of the Gods, Nippon.
So o ji shimetamau Akitsu Mikami nari.	Ruled over by a living God.
Sekai no tomi o sōdan suru mono,	The powerful clan of Anglo-America,
kyōgō Bei-Ei ichizoku no chikara,	monopolists of global wealth,
warera no kuni ni oite hitei saru.	was denied in our own country.
Warera no hitei wa gi ni yoru.	Our denial was our justice.
Tōa o Tōa ni kaese to iu nomi.	We only demand the return of East Asia to East Asia.
Karera no sakushu ni rinpō kotogotoku yasetari.	Our neighbors grow thin from their exploitation.
Warera masani sono sōga o kudakan to su.	It is we who will break those claws and fangs.
Warera mizukara chikara o yashinaite hitotabi tatsu.	We who build our strength and rise up.
Rōjaku danjo mina tsuwamono nari.	Young and old, men and women: soldiers all.
Taiteki hi o satoru ni itaru made warera wa tatakau.	We fight until our great enemies see the error of their ways.
Sekai no rekishi o ryōdan suru.	World history has been severed in two.
Jūnigatsu yōka o kioku seyo.	Remember December 8.[33]

Second, the Pearl Harbor success gave an emotional boost and positive news for a people who had made great sacrifices for the war in China. Although the China Incident was met in 1937 with a surge of popular enthusiasm, four years of inconclusive fighting had dampened popular zeal. Japanese subjects were told that they were fighting a "holy war." But this was a war with no clear purpose, with no foreseeable end, and for which significant sacrifices were demanded. Clothing was in short supply. The government placed raw cotton on a rationing system in February 1938 and encouraged the use of the factory-produced "staple fiber" made from wood pulp. But staple fiber was weak and tended to fall apart when exposed to water.[34] There was a shortage of food as well. Beginning in April 1941 Japan introduced a rice rationing system in its six biggest metropolitan areas. This system limited rice purchases to 330 grams per day for people between the ages of eleven and sixty, and rationed rice even more for young children and the elderly. By that December, the system was in use throughout most of Japan. Rationing hit city dwellers hard. Most were no longer able to eat three square meals of white rice and miso soup. Instead, they often supplemented their rice intake by mixing in barley, millet, potatoes, and kabocha squash.[35] Moreover, queues for sugar, vegetables, and other foods were a common sight in major metropolitan areas. The government even encouraged austerity. Starting in July 1940 the slogan "Luxury is the Enemy" [*zeitaku wa teki da*] appeared throughout the nation. Moreover, in March 1941 the Army Ministry News Department began publicizing the motto "minimum livelihood, maximum honor" [*saitei no seikatsu, saikō no meiyo*].[36] Both slogans encouraged sacrifice and even deprivation for the greater good of Japan's war in China. The success at Pearl Harbor gave greater meaning to those sacrifices and helped restore pride and motivation in Japan's imperial adventure abroad.

Third, the attacks of December 8 helped intellectuals and pundits make sense of the China Incident. Perhaps the most forceful and passionate argument was made by Takeuchi Yoshimi, a scholar of Chinese literature. Takeuchi penned a declaration entitled "The Greater East Asia War and Our Resolve" for the January 1942 edition of *Chūgoku bungaku* [Chinese Literature]. "History has been made," he wrote. "The world has transformed in one night. We saw this with our own eyes." The expanded war gave a sense of mission and resolve where one was lacking. "December 8, the day we received the imperial rescript that declared war, the Japanese people's resolve burned as one. It was a refreshing feeling."[37] Before December 8, Takeuchi had believed that war was something that should be averted. War, after all, was miserable and wretched. But Pearl Harbor made him realize that such thoughts were misguided. Like Itō Sei, Takeuchi now recognized that the war was "bright." Why was he hit by this sudden realization? Because the attacks of December 8 gave true meaning to Japan's "holy war" in China.

For Takeuchi, the "holy war" had made little sense owing to Japan's historical love for its elder Asian brother. In fact, it engendered a sense of shame and self-doubt. Takeuchi had worried that Japan was fighting to little purpose. He wrote, "Shamed by our unworthiness, we have disregarded the significance of the so-called holy war. We Japanese until just now have been suspicious that, under the pretext of constructing East Asia, we have in fact been bullying the weak." But the events of December 8 changed things. "Frankly speaking," Takeuchi continued, "suddenly we had a different feeling [*niwaka ni onajigatai kanjō*] about the China Incident." December 8 wiped clean any sense of dislocation and gave the war a clear purpose and historical importance. The China Incident was the first step toward a grander project—the liberation of Asia from the yoke of Western imperialism. "The new significance," Takeuchi wrote, "of spreading the new order in East Asia and liberating its peoples is our resolution to which we can devote painstaking efforts. This is a resolution that nobody can distort."[38] Pearl Harbor thus convinced Takeuchi that the true conflict was not with China but with the powerful adherents of the old order—the United States and Great Britain.[39]

Others felt the same way. In the January 1942 edition of *Bungei shunjū*, the fascist Japanese Century Group penned an article that noted the existence of "some dissatisfaction" with the description of the China Incident a "holy war."[40]

But those dissatisfactions, the article claimed, resulted from an incomplete understanding of history. Although the China Incident was the first to be called a "holy war," the group insisted that all of Japan's modern wars from 1894 were part of one larger "holy war based on the noble cause of ridding [Asia] of imperialist aggression." In this sense, the Greater East Asia War represented the culmination of Japan's long-term fight with Western imperialism and colonial control.[41] Kyoto School philosopher Kōsaka Masa'aki confidently argued the same. "The 'truth' of the Japan-China Incident," he maintained, "lies in the liberation of East Asia from the old British and American world."[42] Even popular magazines like *Kingu* now could speak of the true "historical significance" of the Greater East Asia War, a "continuation of the *Bakumatsu* era [cry of] 'Revere the Emperor, Expel the Barbarians!'"[43] Pearl Harbor thus gave new meaning to the China Incident. No longer a fight between Asian brothers—now the Incident was recast as an integral part of a broader crusade against Western imperialism. It became the first step in the effort to create an "Asia for the Asians."

This meaningful crusade even baptized doubters into new believers. Aono Suekichi, a left-wing literary critic who had been briefly imprisoned in 1938 for suspected thought crimes, now found himself remade anew a servant of Japan, willing to die for the emperor. This conversion is striking. Aono had been a member of the first Japanese Communist Party, which was founded in 1922, and had briefly worked to rebuild the party after its dissolution in 1924 before becoming a critic at the proletarian journal *Bungei sensen* [Literary Battlefield]. But Pearl Harbor changed his outlook. On January 1, 1942, he wrote in his diary, "It's a truly clear day today, one that makes me want to say that the world is at peace. It is as if heaven and earth too are cheering this victorious new year. I feel strongly that Japan is the land of the gods."[44] Literary critic Honda Akira found himself similarly moved. "The declaration of war against Britain and the United States cleared up my mind." He continued, "With this, the meaning of our holy war has become apparent, and our war aims have also become simple and clear. I have a renewed sense of courage, and all has become easier to accomplish."[45]

The jingoistic mood inspired by the outbreak of war was best captured by novelist Dazai Osamu. In February 1942, Dazai published in *Fujin Kōron* [Women's Review] a comic piece about how one "impoverished" housewife spent the momentous day of the Pearl Harbor attack. The piece, "December 8," is at once humorous and slightly subversive, blending the personal and the political to parody how families reacted to the news. The story begins with the clear-headed housewife hearing a radio announcement about the outbreak of war against American and British forces. She immediately recognizes that everything has changed. "As I listened, I felt I had become a different person. . . . Japan, too, from this morning has become a different Japan."[46] From there, Dazai's piece caricatures a populace that is nervous but united in cause, willing to forego even their most basic needs to help their country "smash" the enemy.

> At breakfast, without thinking, I asked my husband, "Will Japan really be alright?"
>
> "If not, we wouldn't have gone to war. We'll definitely win," he replied, sounding very stiff. My husband always tells lies, so his opinions are never reliable. At the same time, I decided that I would try hard to believe this particular statement.
>
> While I was cleaning up the kitchen, I contemplated many different things. Is it simply their different eye color and hair color that gives me such feelings of animosity toward them? I'd like to beat the living daylights out of them. This is a completely different feeling from when we were fighting in China. I can't stand even the thought of those callous brutes of American soldiers hulking about on our dear and beautiful Japanese soil. If you take but one step on our sacred soil, your feet will rot away. You aren't worthy. Pure soldiers of Japan, please go ahead and smash them! From now, we at home may suffer from shortages of many kinds, but you need not worry about us. We don't mind.[47]

Dazai did not shy away from making implicit mockery of the popular mood. At the end of the story, the housewife leaves the public bathhouse, carrying her baby on her back, to a pitch-black night. A blackout, she realizes. As she takes careful step after careful step, feeling her way back home, she begins to panic. At that point, the housewife gets a lesson in faith:

> From behind, I heard a man walking toward me in rough, awkward gait while singing "Summoned by the Emperor" completely out of tune. *Gohon gohon*, he coughed twice in his peculiar way, and I knew who it was.
>
> "This is hard on Sonoko," I said.
>
> "What's the matter with you," he responded in a loud voice. "You people have no faith—that's why this dark road is hard on you. Me? I have faith, so this dark road feels like broad daylight. Follow me," he said and briskly walked ahead.
>
> My amazing husband. Who knows how sane he really is?[48]

The husband's stress on faith is telling. Faith, after all, was what the popular mood called for. Faith that Japanese spirit and gumption would prevail over enemy technology and materiel. Faith that Japan's war aims were achievable. Faith that Japan's leaders knew where they were going—that they were not simply, to paraphrase Prime Minister Tōjō Hideki, "taking the plunge" off Kiyomizu Temple with little possibility of great gain.[49] Was this sane? In poking fun at the popular mood, Dazai walked a thin line between comedy and subversion. In the process, he wrote a story that highlights, in an indirect yet powerful way, the extent to which Pearl Harbor and the attacks of December 8 united Japanese subjects in the service of empire. In Pearl Harbor's wake, groups in control of state policy could be assured of broad public backing for the war effort.

IMPERIAL JINGOISM AND THE SPIRIT OF DECEMBER 8

As Donald Keene has noted, the Pearl Harbor attack created a "festive mood" or "carnivalesque atmosphere" [*omatsuri kibun*] that continued throughout much of 1942.[50] This carnivalesque atmosphere was evident in both the popular mood and the policymaking mindset. Japan's rapid advance in Asia generated unbridled optimism. The broader public looked with awe and pride upon Japan's successive victories in Hong Kong, Malaya, Singapore, the Dutch Indies, Burma, and the Philippines. This sense of pride, self-confidence, and faith in Japan's mission was epitomized by what writer Kamiya Shigeru referred to as "the spirit of December 8." Kamiya wrote, "Today even small children stand before a world map, dreaming dreams of advance after advance, thinking *'here too, here too*!'"[51]

This "spirit of December 8" took shape as enthusiasm for Japan's expanded war for mastery over Asia, and a willingness to sacrifice at home for the sake of victory abroad. Many subjects became proactive participants in efforts to boost morale. On November 15, 1942, in the lead-up to the first anniversary of the Greater East Asia War, Japan's mass party, the Imperial Rule Assistance Association, in cooperation with the leading newspapers of the day (the *Asahi shinbun*, *Yomiuri shinbun*, and *Tokyo nichi-nichi shinbun*), invited the public to craft slogans that best captured the resolve to win the war.[52] In the following ten days, the newspapers received more than 320,000 responses. On November 27, 1942, the newspapers announced the ten winning slogans.[53] "We shall not want until victory!" [*hoshigarimasen, katsu made wa*] and "lacking, lacking, [we are] lacking in ideas" [*taranu taranu, kufū ga taranu*] constituted the best known of the winners. The second slogan referred to the deprivations and sacrifices made in daily life, as even daily necessities were requisitioned for the war effort. But far from being negative and backward-looking, this slogan spun deprivation in a positive light. It hinted that Japanese subjects could make up for any shortages though good ideas and a penchant for ingenuity. These slogans, too, became emblematic of the "spirit of December 8." They highlighted the continued enthusiasm and willingness to mobilize for wartime Japan's imperial project, whatever the cost to their daily lives.

The "spirit of December 8" thus manifested as a moment of imperial jingoism, perhaps even surpassing the jingoism that appeared in the wake of the Manchurian Incident of 1931. In this sense, the decision to wage war against America and Britain initiated what might be thought of as an imperial moment. From the cloudless wintry morning of December 8, as Japanese leaders began to contemplate the possibilities of a new type of empire reaching across Asia, they could be assured of broad public support for Japan's wartime goals. But this was an ephemeral moment in time. Japan's imperial moment lasted but a year; it would fizzle out when it became apparent that Japan did not have the material wherewithal to match its imperial dreams.

NOTES

1. Itō Sei was not the only one who noticed the strangeness of December 8. His feelings were echoed by famous *benshi*, actor, and narrative artist Tokugawa Musei. Tokugawa wrote in his own diary on December 8 that he emerged into a changed world. "I go out front. The city feels completely different from the Kobe of yesterday. Even the greenhouse cyclamen and Western-style houses [*seiyōkan*] that can be seen from the street look different." See Tokugawa Musei, *Musei sensō nikki*, vol. 1 (Tokyo: Chūō Kōronsha, 1977), 11.

2. Itō Sei, *Taiheiyō sensō nikki*, vol. 1 (Tokyo: Shinchōsha, 1983), 9–11.

3. Ibid., 12.

4. Just before this statement, he noted how happy he was that East Asia would have more than enough sugar. See ibid., 59.

5. See Chapter 4 in this volume.

6. Louise Young uses this term to describe the popular reaction to the Manchurian Incident of 1931, but it is also an apt description for the situation in 1941. See Louise Young, *Japan's Total Empire: Manchuria and the Culture of Wartime Imperialism* (Berkeley: University of California Press, 1998).

7. Ikezaki Tadataka, "Sono hi no kangeki: Namida urumu," *Shin joen* (February 1942), 60–61. He wrote this on December 14, 1941, less than one week after Pearl Harbor.

8. The originals can be found in Ozaki Yukio, *Minken tōsō shichijūnen* (Tokyo: Yomiuri Shinbunsha, 1952), 183; these translations are taken from Jeremy A. Yellen and Andrew Campana, "Japan, Pearl Harbor, and the Poetry of December 8th," *Asia-Pacific Journal: Japan Focus* 14, 24/3 (December 2016), https://apjjf.org/2016/24/Yellen.html.

9. Higashikuni Naruhiko, *Higashikuni nikki: Nihon gekidōki no hiroku* (Tokyo: Tokuma Shoten, 1968), 103.

10. There is more than a hint of irony to this. Konoe and Matsuoka, after all, were in many ways responsible for Japan's drift toward Pearl Harbor and the opening of hostilities against Great Britain and the United States.

11. For Konoe's views, see Yabe Teiji, *Konoe Fumimaro*, vol. 2 (Tokyo: Kōbundō, 1952), 467; and Oka Yoshitake, *Konoe Fumimaro: A Political Biography* (Tokyo: University of Tokyo Press, 1983), 161.

12. Quoted in Jeremy A. Yellen, "Into the Tiger's Den: Japan and the Tripartite Pact, 1940," *Journal of Contemporary History* 51, 3 (July 2016), 576.

13. Nanbara Shigeru, *Keisō: kashū* (Tokyo: Sōgensha, 1948), 173. The translation is taken from Yellen and Campana, "Japan, Pearl Harbor, and the Poetry of December 8th."

14. Quoted in Yoshimi Yoshiaki, *Grassroots Fascism: The War Experience of the Japanese People*, trans. Ethan Mark (New York: Columbia University Press, 2015), 96.

15. Satō Kenryō, *Dai tōa sensō kaikoroku* (Tokyo: Tokuma Shoten, 1966), 220–221.

16. Yatsugi Kazuo, *Tōjō Hideki to sono jidai* (Tokyo: Santen Shobō, 1980), 115–116.

17. Quoted in Yasuda Takeshi, "Jūnigatsu yōka no shisō," Hashikawa Bunsō, Kano Masanao, and Hiraoka Toshio, eds., *Kindai Nihon shisōshi no kiso chishiki: Isshin zenya kara haisen made* (Tokyo: Yūhikaku, 1971), 441.

18. Haruko Taya Cook and Theodore F. Cook, *Japan at War: An Oral History* (New York: New Press, 1992), 77–78.

19. Aoki Masami, *Senjika no shomin nikki* (Tokyo, 1987), 153. In an interesting metaphor for Japan's fate, he later failed his entrance exams.

20. Sugimura Masaru, *Nikki ni miru taiheiyō sensō* (Tokyo: Bungeisha, 1999), 20–21.

21. Komaki Saneshige, "1941-nen no omoide," *Bungei shunjū* (February 1942), 10–13.

22. December 8 entry, Yabe Teiji, *Yabe Teiji nikki: ichō no maki* (Tokyo: Yomiuri Shinbunsha, 1974), 481.

23. December 9 and 10 entries, in ibid., 481.

24. *Japan Times & Advertiser*, December 14, 1941, p. 1.

25. Iwakuro Hideo, *Sensō rikugun bōryaku hishi* (Tokyo: Nihon Keizai Shinbun Shuppansha, 2015), 329. Iwakuro was remarkably accurate. The most careful recent scholarship in Japanese has shown that Japan overall had one-twelfth the productive capacity of the United States. See Yamada Akira, *Gunbi kakuchō no kindaishi: Nihongun no bōchō to hōkai* (Tokyo: Yoshikawa Kōbunkan, 1997).

26. Iwakuro, *Sensō rikugun*, 327.

27. Ibid., 327. The notion of an "ABCD encirclement" was widely publicized throughout the Japanese mass media by August 1941.

28. Joseph C. Grew, *Ten Years in Japan* (New York: Simon and Schuster, 1944), 481.

29. See, for instance, "Sanagara saigo tsūchō no atsukai," *Yomiuri shinbun*, November 28, 1941, p. 1.

30. The Hull Note was not, in fact, a cause for war. The decision for war had, for all practical purposes, already been made. And the naval strike force had left port for Pearl Harbor on November 26, the day before the Hull Note arrived in Japan.

31. See Ikezaki, "Sono hi no kangeki: Namida urumu," 60.

32. The English translation of the imperial rescript is taken from *Japan Times & Advertiser*, evening edition, December 8, 1941, p. 1. For the original Japanese-language document, see Japan Center for Asian Historical Records (JACAR), reference code A03022539800.

33. Takamura Kōtarō, "Jūnigatsu yōka," *Takamura Kōtarō zenshū*, vol. 5 (Tokyo: Chikuma Shobō, 1994) 50–51.

34. Simon Partner, *Toshie: A Story of Village Life in Twentieth-Century Japan* (Berkeley: University of California Press, 2004), 84–85.

35. Taiheiyō Sensō Kenkyūkai, ed., *Taiheiyō sensō ga yoku wakaru: "shinjuwan" kara hajimatta Nichi-Bei no shitō no subete* (Tokyo: Nihon Bungeisha, 2009), 98–100.

36. Ibid., 100.

37. Takeuchi Yoshimi, "Dai tōa sensō to warera no ketsui," *Chūgoku bungaku*, no. 80 (January 1942), 481.

38. Ibid., 482–483.

39. Japanese historians have made this point as well. See, for instance, Katō Yōko, *Sore demo, Nihonjin wa "sensō" o eranda* (Tokyo: Asahi shuppan, 2009), 335.

40. The Japanese Century Group was, according to *Chūō Kōron* editorial chief Hatanaka Shigeo, a "fascist critic group." Its most active members were Daitō Bunka Gakuin professor Saitō Shō, Nishitani Yahē, *Yomiuri shinbun* reporter Hanami Tatsuji, and Izawa Hiroshi. See Kakeno Takeshi, "Senjika media no hensei to tenkai: Bungei shunjūsha hakkō 'genchi hōkoku' sōmokuji (ka)," *Saitama gakuen daigaku kiyō*, No. 11 (December 2011), 366.

41. Nihon Seikisha Dōjin, "Seisen no hongi," *Bungei shunjū* (January 1942), 88–101. Hayashi Fusao popularized this very argument in the 1960s. See Hayashi Fusao, *Dai tōa sensō kōteiron* (Tokyo: Banchō Shobō, 1964).

42. Kōsaka Masa'aki, "Dai tōa kyōeiken e no michi," *Kaizō* 24, 1 (January 1942), 34.

43. "Ei-Bei gekimetsu! Kagayaku daisenkuwa to tsugi no senkyoku o kataru," *Kingu* (February 1942), 41.

44. Donald Keene, *Nihonjin no sensō: Sakka no nikki o yomu* (Tokyo: Bungei Shunjū, 2009), 18.

45. Quoted in Yasuda Takeshi, "Jūnigatsu yōka no shisō," 441.

46. Dazai Osamu, "Jūnigatsu yōka," *Dazai Osamu zenshū*, vol. 5 (Tokyo: Chikuma Shobō, 1990), 16.

47. Ibid., 19.

48. Ibid., 25.

49. In justifying the decision to go to war, Tōjō stated in October 1941, "There may be times in the life of a man when he has to close his eyes and jump from the veranda of the Kiyomizu Temple." See Ben-Ami Shillony, *Politics and Culture in Wartime Japan* (New York: Oxford University Press, 1981), 44.

50. See Donald Keene, *Sakka no nikki o yomu Nihonjin no sensō* (Tokyo: Bungei Shunjū, 2009), 40.

51. Kamiya Shigeru, "Jūnigatsu yōka no kokoro," *Bungei shunjū* (February 1942), 119. Cited in Yellen and Campana, "Japan, Pearl Harbor, and the Poetry of December 8th."

52. "Kokumin ketsui no hyōgo boshū," *Tōkyō Asahi shinbun*, November 15, 1942; see also *Yomiuri shinbun*, November 15, 1942.

53. "Kokumin ketsui no hyōgo," *Tōkyō Asahi shinbun*, November 27, 1942; see also *Yomiuri shinbun*, November 27, 1942.

CHAPTER 4

Popular Japanese Responses to the Pearl Harbor Attack

December 8, 1941, to January 8, 1942

Samuel Hideo Yamashita

At seven in the morning on December 8, 1941, Japanese sitting down to breakfast heard the following radio broadcast: "An Imperial Army and Navy Headquarters announcement: At six in the morning on December 8, our imperial country's army and navy forces initiated hostilities with American and British forces in the Western Pacific." Needless to say, the news came as a surprise, but it also had another, unexpected, effect.

After four and a half years of a seemingly unending war in China and months of frustrating negotiations with the United States—which had produced what one prefectural official described as an unmistakable "stifling tension"—the news of the attack offered a sense of relief.[1] Forty-one-year-old Sakamoto Tane, who lived in Kōchi, a port city on the island of Shikoku, expressed those feelings in her diary when she wrote, "At long last the war has started."[2]

At 11:00 a.m. an imperial rescript formally declaring war on the United States, Britain, and their allies was issued, followed by a huge, spontaneous response. In many cities, people made their way to local shrines to pray for victory, and this went on for several days.[3] The *Asahi* newspaper (*Asahi shinbun*) described what happened in Hiroshima City on December 9: "Yesterday's excitement turned today to a determination to serve in ways that could lead to certain victory, and in the cold rain that had been falling from early morning, crowds of ordinary people went to pray for certain victory at the *gokoku* [protect-the-nation] shrine and other shrines and shrine precincts everywhere."[4] Unsolicited contributions for national defense and donations of metal goods also came streaming into government offices and police stations.[5] Excitement and enthusiasm were everywhere.

People were suddenly interested in the news again, as shown in what happened in Yokohama, a major port city on the eastern seaboard: Five hundred people applied to register their new radios, and seventy brought in radios needing repair, their dials broken from continuous twisting and turning for better reception.[6] Many Yokohama-ites also felt sure the enemy would start bombing Japanese cities. The Yūrindō Bookstore reported that "a lot of books on air defense were sold," and a department store "did a brisk business in air defense goods, metal helmets, and the like." In addition, on the afternoon of December 8 and all the next day, the Odeonza Movie Theater in Yokohama noticed a drop in the number of moviegoers.[7]

These spontaneous reactions to the news of the attacks were part of a larger popular response that occurred throughout Japan.[8] The surviving documentary record reveals two types of popular responses. One was a dramatic public response orchestrated by the central, prefectural, municipal, and village governments and overseen by scores of officials, and the other was a genuinely private response, recorded in personal journals and recounted in postwar memoirs.

Both types of responses are significant. The public responses show us what specific institutions, tactics, and practices the central, prefectural, and municipal governments used to mobilize the general population for war and how they deployed the official discourse devised after Japan invaded China in July 1937. In contrast, the private responses tell us much about how ordinary people felt about the December 8 attacks and the idea of war with the United States and Britain and how they responded, if at all, to the government's staged public events. Most telling here is the variety of responses: on the one side, hundreds of thousands of Japanese, caught up in the war fever that swept across the nation, turned out to participate in the public events that took place in the days and weeks after December 8; and even those who did not turn out for these events were enthusiastic, even ecstatic. On the other side, many individuals expressed reservations about the attacks and prospect of war with two great powers, and some were genuinely unhappy, or even depressed.

PUBLIC RESPONSES

The central government had been preparing the population of the home islands and colonies for war for nearly four and a half years, using huge public rallies, mass rituals, and even countrywide moments of reverential silence. The first mass ritual occurred in 1937. On November 3, the anniversary of Emperor Meiji's birthday, all imperial subjects were asked to face the imperial palace in Tokyo and to bow at precisely 9:00 a.m. In 1938, the same ritual was performed on

New Year's Day (January 1), National Foundation Day (February 11), and the emperor's birthday (April 29). To recognize the achievements and sacrifices of the country's military forces, the government also orchestrated a minute of silence on designated days—Army Day (March 10), Navy Day (May 27), and a "Moment to Express Gratitude to Soldiers and Sailors" (October 7). The first anniversary of the Marco Polo Bridge Incident,[9] on July 7, 1938, found 10,000 people in Tokyo marching from Yasukuni Shrine, the shrine for soldiers and sailors, to the imperial palace, and everyone else in Japan and the colonies observing a minute of silence at noon.[10] According to historian Kenneth Ruoff, these "public celebrations . . . provided imperial subjects with a sense of participating in affairs of the nation" and "no single event came as close to achieving, at least for a minute or so, nearly total simultaneous and uniform and national participation as did the precisely timed mass rituals."[11] These carefully planned public events that took place after the December 8 attacks had the population of the home islands and colonies expressing together their loyalty and devotion to the government, their commitment to the war effort, and their fervent desire for "certain victory."

Exactly how did the central and prefectural governments respond to the attack on Pearl Harbor? Surviving records suggest that the first official responses, coming just hours after the early morning broadcast on December 8, were the work of prefectural governors eager to generate support for the war among their constituencies.[12] The governor of Fukui Prefecture attempted to persuade his constituents to support the war effort by describing how Japan's efforts to maintain the peace in East Asia had been thwarted at every turn by the United States and Britain:

> Today the [emperor] graciously issued a declaration of war against both America and England. This is truly [a moment of] unendurable gratitude and excitement. It has been four and a half years since the China incident, and our country has steadfastly maintained the stability of East Asia. The imperial country—the immovable country that has worked to contribute to the peace of the world and the welfare of humanity—has come to this impasse. Not only have both America and England not revised their rigid view that eternally subordinates East Asia. They also have blocked in various ways the resolution of the China incident and have conspired and acted, in concert with other enemy states, to disrupt the economic relations of our country, enticed other countries to increase their military power all around our country, and amplified the threat to the existence of our imperial country.
>
> The government of our imperial country maintained peace in the Pacific to the bitter end and was anxious to stop the spread of war and calamity throughout the whole world and humanity. Patiently and prudently [we] have negotiated time and again with America for eight long months, and with the

> spirit of compromise that the existence and authority of our imperial country permitted, we have worked for a peaceful solution, exhausting what should be exhausted and doing what should be done. But America vainly deployed fanciful rules, failed to recognize the crystal-clear realities [existing] in East Asia, perverted its material power, and failed to grasp the true power of our imperial country. Together with other countries, America has increased the military threat to our imperial country and has gone to extremes to achieve its subordination, and in this way, the methods and hopes for maintaining peace in the Pacific by nonthreatening means were completely lost, which has jeopardized the stability of East Asia and the existence of our imperial country. In the end, the imperial rescript declaring war on both America and England was issued.[13]

This narrative offers an official explanation of the December 8 attacks, one in which the United States and Britain are the aggressors and Japan is the innocent victim. In other places, the tense standoff between the United States and Japan was described as a "national crisis" and the attacks as a "breakthrough."

The governor of Hiroshima Prefecture, for example, issued the following public statement:

> Today, His Highness graciously issued a rescript declaring war against both America and England. It is a truly terrifying and emotional situation, one that finds the people of our prefecture silently rectifying their hearts, humbly embracing the sacred will, and looking forward to putting the imperial consciousness at ease. . . . The gentlemen in the prefecture already believe, without a doubt, in the resolve they have shown today, and they will never stop praying that they will be able to rise up in our tradition of certain victory and no defeat and, with all the people of the prefecture, to become a single unit, advancing on the single path that will resolve all difficulties.[14]

Obama Hachiyo, the governor of Shizuoka Prefecture, advised his constituents:

> The two million people of our prefecture would do well to focus on making explicit their resolute organizations, believing in certain victory; along with the entire prefecture, they should observe the sacred will; they should not err in their deportment; and they should complete the preparations long awaited. Recognizing that the conflict will be long, each of us should pledge to complete his or her main tasks, overcome the ten thousand difficulties, overthrow the enemy countries, and move toward their annihilation.[15]

A day later, on December 9, Yamagata Saburō, the governor of Ibaraki Prefecture, urged his constituents to support the war effort:

> Embracing the belief in certain victory in sacred wars that our ancestors passed on to us, we will offer ourselves and become a foundation for the rise of Asia. Exercising self-discipline and self-awareness, with neither arrogance nor sloth, giving our all and enduring, armed, and strong sturdy organizations . . . we should expect to advance to overcome this unprecedented situation.[16]

Although different, these official statements shared a vocabulary well known to most Japanese since the start of the Sino-Japanese War in July 1937, one that stressed the importance of each citizen joining all the others in doing everything possible to bring about "certain victory." In August 1937 the cabinet of Prime Minister Konoe Fumimaro had taken the first steps to mobilize the nation, issuing the "Guidelines for the Execution of the National Spiritual Mobilization" and encouraging local communities and schools to join together in sending off conscripts, supplying people for labor brigades, and contributing to savings-bond campaigns. As the war in China continued, the government took other steps, such as dissolving labor unions; reorganizing political parties into a single party, the Imperial Rule Assistance Association; and creating national organizations for journalists, workers, women, and youth.[17]

In September 1940 the government designated the first day of every month as "Raising Asia Public Service Day" and enjoined its citizens "to remember [on that day] the hardships of the battlefield and to exercise self-discipline and self-reflection in their daily lives." Beginning with "the nation as one, exhausting loyalty and serving the country with dogged perseverance," the government also circulated slogans such as "extravagance is the enemy," "hoarding is the enemy," and "think of the troops at the front," plastering them on walls in cities and towns throughout the country.[18] By December 8, 1941, the words "sacred will," "sacred wars," "certain victory," "self-rectification," "endurance," "self-discipline," and "sacrifice" were regarded as code in an official discourse well known to Japanese.

These words appear in the resolutions that city councils passed in response to the news of the attacks. The city council of Niigata City in northwestern Japan convened an emergency meeting at 2:30 p.m. on December 8, which eighteen council members attended. The head of the council proposed that they send, on behalf of Niigata's citizens, a telegram reading, "We, the one hundred and sixty thousand citizens [of Niigata], pledge to serve to the death" to the prime minister, the war minister, the navy minister, and the commander in chief of the combined fleet. The council agreed and reaffirmed as well their commitment to complete unfinished projects.[19] Many other town councils adopted proclamations and res-

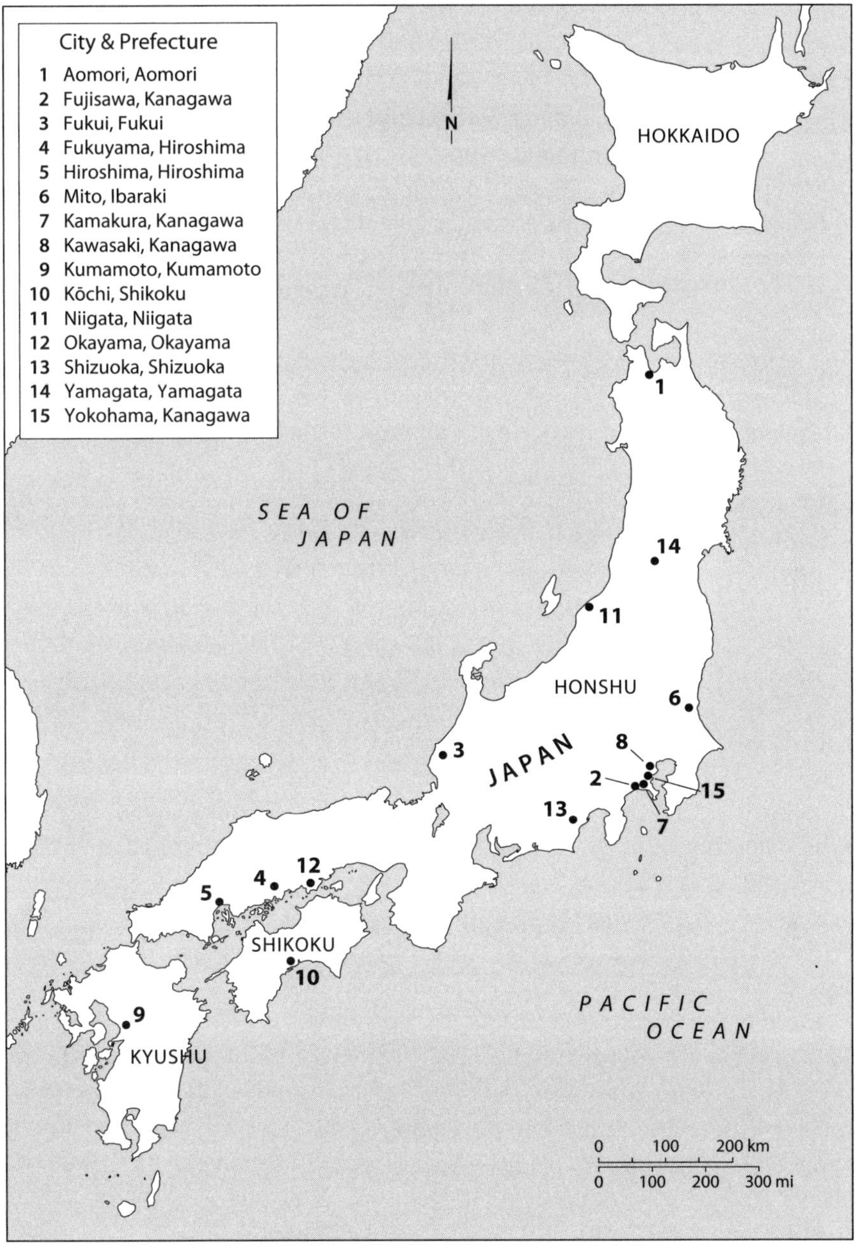

Public Responses to the Pearl Harbor Attack

olutions calling for the attainment of the goals of the "sacred war." The Nagano city council also met in special session on December 8 and passed two resolutions. The first one read: "With the enthusiasm of this city's population, we convey our determination to break through the national crisis," and the second one: "We pledge to struggle forward to offer up our determination to die and to complete the enterprise of the sacred war."[20] The same was done, within days, in four cities in Kanagawa Prefecture: Yokohama, Fujisawa, Kawasaki, and Kamakura.[21] On December 10 the council of Fukuyama City, a small town just east of Hiroshima City, adopted the following resolution, which was addressed to the emperor:

> The imperial rescript declaring war was proclaimed here and given to 100 million countrymen. The retainers cannot contain their fear and excitement, and our Fukuyama City earnestly embraces the sacred will and pledges to give its all for the enterprise of Eight Corners Under One Roof and the immovable policies of the imperial country. By doing this we will advance to a breakthrough of the nation's problems, exhaust loyalty and service to the country, and expect to do our best to put the imperial mind at ease.
>
> Now our country has risen up against two of the world's strongest countries as our enemy, along with unprecedented national problems. We have hardened our resolve for certain victory and no defeat, and we expect to advance the entire city along the single path to the attainment of the goals of the sacred war.[22]

Inspired by Fukuyama's example, many villages nearby adopted resolutions that "made the world an enemy."[23] Prefectural, municipal, and village officials were using the language of the official discourse to encourage their constituencies to work toward achieving the "goals of the sacred war."

Within days of the attacks, the Home Ministry sent out instructions to provincial officials. Huge pro-war rallies, some organized solely by prefectural authorities and held in major cities and prefectural capitals, were one result. On December 10, Hiroshima Prefecture convened the "Great Assembly of the Prefectural Population for Certain Victory Against America and England" in the large open space in front of the *gokoku* shrine. Seventy thousand people turned out for the meeting and were addressed by the prefectural governor.[24] In these events, the "annihilation of the Americans and British" became part of the official wartime discourse.

Other rallies were organized by alliances of prefectural and municipal authorities, local branches of the newly formed Imperial Rule Assistance Association, veterans' organizations, local newspapers, and other bodies. The "Festival to Pray for Military Victory," held on the morning of December 10 in Kumamoto City in Kyushu, had multiple sponsors: the Municipal Association of the Kumamoto

Jingikai, the Kumamoto City Home Front Service Association, and the Kumamoto branch of the Imperial Rule Assistance Association. Because the Kumamoto municipal public hall could not accommodate the 30,000 people who came to the rally, they spilled out into the space in front of the hall and along the Tsubogawa River all the way to the Gōkyō Bridge. That afternoon, a "Grand Assembly of Kumamoto Prefectural People for the Annihilation of the Americans and British" was convened in the same public hall, sponsored by the prefecture, the city, local branches of the Imperial Rule Assistance Association, the reservists' association, and local newspapers. Attending were 3,000 individuals—mostly officials and veterans—who adopted various declarations and resolutions.[25] On the same day, a "Great Assembly for the Annihilation of American and England" was held at the *gokoku* shrine in Kanazawa City, with 20,000 people attending.[26]

On December 11 in northern Japan, the Niigata branch of the Imperial Rule Assistance Association and the *Niigata Daily News* (*Niigata nichi-nichi shinbun*) sponsored a "Great Citizens Assembly to Pray for Victory in War" held at the Hakusan Shrine, and the 20,000 attendees heard their mayor call for "giving one's all and one's self to the country" and "pledging to hold firmly to the ideals of certain victory and to perform sincerely cooperative service."[27]

On December 14, Okayama City, in central Japan, staged a rally that began at 8:00 a.m. and was attended by representatives chosen from different groups in the city. The speakers ranged from the governor of the prefecture and the mayor to members of the municipal assembly and heads of the community councils.[28] Those attending the rally adopted the following resolution:

> The gracious proclamation of the imperial rescript pertaining to both America and England has been issued, and our feelings of awe and excitement are overflowing. Standing now at the crossroads of the emperor's rise or fall, we and all of our city's citizens will do our very best to carry out the sacred will. We will hold tightly to our steadfast unity and our belief in certain victory, contemplate our manly spirit, and staunchly embrace our defense of the home front. And at the source of the Grand Ruler's authority, we expect to realize the goals of the sacred war and put the sacred consciousness at ease.[29]

The rally finally ended at 8:00 p.m.

On December 15 the Mito City branch of the Imperial Rule Assistance Association held a "Great Prefectural Assembly for the Destruction of America and England and Certain Victory" in the plaza in front of the prefectural office, and even though it was snowing, 10,000 people showed up, representing organizations from throughout the prefecture.[30] A similar "Certain Victory General Assembly of the Prefectural Population" rally was held in Yamagata City in northern Japan on December 16, with 2,000 people attending. The rally began with a procession through the city, led by the prefectural governor and representatives from various cities and districts in the prefecture, who carried a banner that read, "Punish America and England."[31] The broad representation at the Yamagata event was typical of these regional events.

"General Citizens Assemblies for Certain Victory" were held across the country in small towns and villages.[32] City, town, and village councils also passed resolutions pledging their communities' total support and sacrifice, which were sent on to Tokyo. In addition, the Shinto establishment helped bring the war to rural communities, with the main shrine in each prefecture sending emissaries to shrines in every town and village. A special New Year's issue of the *Eastern Daily News* (*Tōō nippō*) recounted what happened in Aomori in northern Japan:

> The gracious proclamation of the imperial rescript pertaining to both America and England has been issued, and our feelings of awe and excitement are overflowing. Standing now at the crossroads of the emperor's rise or fall, we and all of our city's citizens will do our very best to carry out the sacred will. We will hold tightly to our steadfast unity and our belief in certain victory, contemplate our manly spirit, and staunchly embrace our defense of the home front. And at the source of the Grand Ruler's authority, we expect to realize the goals of the sacred war and put the sacred consciousness at ease.[33]

The Aomori officials were following instructions sent out by the Home Ministry, a reminder that the public responses to the news of the December 8 attacks were orchestrated by the central and provincial governments to create the impression that all Japanese were fully behind their government and willing to do everything possible to ensure that Japan win this "sacred war." Of course, we cannot know whether there was complete unanimity.

PRIVATE RESPONSES

The private responses to the news of the attacks on Allied installations in Southeast Asia and the Pacific were another popular reaction to the news of the December 8 attacks. These private responses both resembled and differed from the broader public responses and also varied among themselves. Since most Japanese had not expected the attacks, the news was as exciting as it was dramatic. In fact, many people were too excited to do more than simply record the early morning

Individual Responses to the Pearl Harbor Attack

announcement in their diaries as if they were reliving the moment when they first heard the news and the excitement they felt. Takeya Nobuyo, a forty-two-year-old housewife living in Pyongyang in Korea, a Japanese colony, wrote in her diary simply: "December 8 War started with England and America."[34] Others rehearsed the main facts—"America and Britain," "The two strongest powers in the world," "strongest Pacific Fleet in the world," or "several warships sunk"—as if to confirm what they had heard.

Nearly everyone reacted enthusiastically to the victories of December 8. Although they had no understanding of how those attacks fit into a larger strategy, most recognized that going to war with the "two greatest powers in the world" would not be the same as fighting the Chinese and would demand more of them. Young men, predictably, were the most excited about the expansion of the war. A twenty-two-year-old railway switchman in Yokohama wrote in his diary: "The thing that should have come finally has come. The 'It's coming!' thing that I expected came before I knew it, and my youthful blood was simply bubbling forth. All individualistic feelings have completely flown away, and we are in the thrall of huge patriotic and nationalistic feelings."[35] A nineteen-year-old farmer in Nakayama Village in Nagano Prefecture, had an almost identical reaction: "My gut feeling was that 'At last, they finally did it!' and my heart jumped for joy!"[36] Their excitement and enthusiasm are understandable, and of course, most of these young men would be drafted and sent off to the war.

Teenagers, as well, were enthusiastic but also guarded. Tsushima Tsukasa, a fifteen-year-old farm boy in northern Japan, later remembered where he was when he first heard about the attacks and what he felt.

> I was on my way to school, when a classmate shouted excitedly, "Hey, I couldn't hear it clearly on the radio at home, but early in the morning Japan's naval aircraft made a surprise attack on Pearl Harbor and sank American warships. No, or was it yesterday morning?" For an instant, I couldn't believe my ears. "Impossible," I thought. Attacking an American naval base smack dab in the middle of the great expanse of the Pacific, was that true? In my heart, in the midst of joy, unease crept in.

At school, Tsushima and his classmates lined up for the morning assembly and were told by their principal,

> A notice has come, right at this moment, from the Prefectural Education Office. According to an Imperial Headquarters announcement, yesterday at dawn, our navy launched a surprise attack on Pearl Harbor and, with waves of attacks on American ships, sank them and produced huge battle

> results. With this, war has broken out between our country and America and England. Recognize the gravity of the situation; brace yourselves; and devote yourselves to the way of learning.

In his diary, he recalled, too, that "everyone was agitated when they heard these words" and remembered his own feelings: "But from now on, what in the world would my country do to manage the conflict with the Chiang Kai-shek government, and had it also started a war with America and England that could be won? My unease intensified."

Tsushima tried to calm his anxieties by calling on his knowledge of Japanese history:

> Moreover, my inner self was really agitated. How should we younger ones take over the war? We must defend Japan, a sacred country with a 2,600-year history.
>
> For example, even if there were no prospect of victory, if we somehow faced this challenge, I was sure that the divine gods [*kamikaze*] would rise up and help us.
>
> This was clear from the actual history of the battles of Bunei [1264–1275] and Kōan [1278–1288]. This is what I was told, and my youthful heart trembled mightily.

Still, he knew that his life would soon be quite different.

> From this point on, I would happily graduate from middle school, but would I be able to enter [one of] my choices—Ichikō or Nikō [the top high schools in the country]? But if the war situation gets worse while I am a student, I would be drafted and probably would have to go to the battlefield with a weapon.
>
> It was a single day in which it was as though a wedge had been driven into my heart.[37]

In the end, Tsushima ended up not at Ichikō or Nikō, but at Morioka Agricultural Technical School. We will never know if the outbreak of war on December 8 affected this outcome.

Itabashi Kōshū, a thirteen-year-old student in Sendai, in northeastern Japan, felt the same as Tsushima did. Looking back years later, he remembered that his "blood boiled" when he got the news of the attacks.

> I was in the second year of middle school that day, Pearl Harbor Day. "Well, we really did it!" I thought. The sound of the announcement on the radio

still reverberates in my ears. (He hums a few bars from "The Battleship March," the unofficial navy anthem played on the radio to set the tone for the victory announcements.) "News Special, News special," high pitched and rapid. "Beginning this morning before dawn, war has been declared on the Americans and British." I felt as if my blood were boiling, and my flesh shook. The whole nation bubbled over, excited and inspired. "We really did it! Incredible! Wonderful!" That's the way it felt then.

Itabashi explained:

I was brought up in a time when nobody criticized Japan. The war started for me, in the brain of this middle-school student, as something that should happen, something that was natural. Every day, we sent warriors off with cheers of "*Banzai! Banzai!*" War was being waged in China. "Withdraw your forces," America ordered Japan. If a prime minister with foresight had ordered a withdrawal, he probably would have been assassinated. Even I knew that withdrawal was impossible! There was the ABCD encirclement—the Americans, British, Chinese, and Dutch. They wouldn't give us a drop of oil.[38]

Itabashi entered the naval academy in late 1944 but did not see action.[39]

Mishima Yūichi, an eighth grader in Osaka, was another teenaged boy who responded enthusiastically to the news of the December 8 attacks. He was on a school excursion on December 8, which he described that night in his diary:

December 8 (Monday)

Japan declared war on America and England.

Today was a clear and bracing early winter day.

I got off [the train] at Sakurai Station and walked about seven hundred meters along fields while staring at the running peaks of Mounts Tennōzan and Otokoyama beyond them. I offered General Nogi's "Lord Kusunoki's Parting Message to His Son" and "General Tōgō's Inscription of Emperor Meiji's Poem." Minase Shrine was a truly quiet and divine site, and I prayed while thinking of the three emperors from long ago [Emperor Go-Toba, Emperor Tsuchimikado, and Emperor Juntoku].

Then I walked for about an hour toward Mount Tennōzan, through a forest of bamboo, pine, and walnut trees, stepping carefully on the fallen leaves, and was relieved when I got to the summit. I ate my box lunch and listened to Terano-sensei's stories.

The return trip was from Yamazaki, and I finally got to read about our going to war with America and England in the newspaper and was surprised and tense.

On the day that war was declared, a school excursion. To a most exalted site where many historical events came together. This was completely by accident, but it became a truly unforgettable day.

Mishima's entry continues with references to two leading icons of loyalty, the warriors Kusunoki Masashige (?–1336) and Toyotomi Hideyoshi (1536–1598).

I went to school and, for the first time, realized that war had broken out with America and England. Because I wrote that I got up at seven o'clock, I did not hear the six o'clock news. I probably never turned on the radio.

That morning was cold. I blew into my palms and rubbed them, and because my feet were cold, I stamped the ground in the schoolyard to pass the time. Perhaps because there was a small meeting, the teachers did not come out for some time. Because of that I felt the cold more than usual.

Our departure was later than scheduled.

"Lord Kusunoki's Parting Message to His Son" hit home. Until now, we had been standing on this side of the wall of adult war. That wall has [now] been destroyed, and war is blowing toward us. I thought that Kusunoki Masayuki's resolve—which left the present up to his father, Masanari—to repair to the battlefield had become our lot.

The big camphor trees at the Minase Shrine towered peacefully up into the sky. Up there, later, the new aircraft called the Zero, large numbers of them, flew over at high speed. When the cold sound of metal disappeared, quiet returned to the precincts.

On the summit of Mount Tennōzan, when I heard that these were the remains of the ancient battlefield where Toyotomi Hideyoshi attacked and punished Akechi Mitsuhide, I thought the roar of the flames of war will come from the skies in the south and the east, becoming a soundless sound.

Mishima's identifying with well-known icons of loyalty is not surprising, as these historical figures were featured as models in prewar ethics and history textbooks.[40] He closed his December 8 entry with an ominous "In the evening, I had the feeling that darkness and an oppressive air were closing in on and pressuring me."[41] Mishima, like Tsushima and Itabashi, reacted patriotically to the news that war had broken out but was anxious as well. All three boys had the good fortune to be too young to be conscripted and so survived the war.

The reactions of teenaged girls were similar to those of the boys, with one fundamental difference: they knew that they would not be conscripted for military service. Kondo Toshi, a student at a girls' high school in Okazaki in central Japan, wrote in her diary that day:

> "Today, the eighth, before dawn, our imperial army and navy forces in the western Pacific commenced hostilities with the Americans and British." I wanted to keep listening to the succession of battle reports that followed this announcement, but time was short, and I went to school. After the review of the class at the morning assembly ended, the principal spoke. Everyone tensed up but did not move and listened with eyes wide open. When the teachers came to our classrooms, they had us listen to more news broadcasts. In fourth period we learned that our country had declared war with the issuance of an imperial rescript. After lunch, all the students at the school were asked to assemble in the schoolyard, and we listened to the principal speak again. We then went to the Kōyama Hachiman Shrine to offer our prayers for military success. Even after I got home, between the continuing news broadcasts and the excitement [about the outbreak of war], I was not able to study for my examinations. When there was a naval victory, the "Battleship March" was played before the news broadcast, and when there was an army victory, "Though the Enemy Was Many Tens of Thousands Strong" was played—this to arouse the feelings of our countrymen. This continued until one in the morning.[42]

Kondo was torn: she wanted to study for her examinations, but the "continuing news broadcasts and the excitement [about the outbreak of war]" made it impossible. Like hundreds of thousands of Japanese citizens around the country, she and her classmates were led to the local Hachiman shrine to pray for the country's success in the "sacred war."

Kimura Toneko, a thirteen-year-old schoolgirl at the Keimei Academy, a special elite private school in Tokyo for children who had been educated abroad, had mixed feelings about the December 8 attacks because she had lived in the United States and still had friends there and because her banker father was still working in the United States. Not surprisingly, her response is a mixture of excitement and uncertainty:

> Today is a very exciting day.
>
> At one o'clock the emperor of Japan declared war against England and America.
>
> It was so sudden that I could not believe my ears.
>
> To fight against the places and friends I love is very hard, because my father is still there. I especially disliked and feared this news.

> Almost once every hour, the school bell rang for us to meet downstairs, where we listened to the speeches about this war.
>
> It seems that as soon as the war was declared, the Japanese warships bombed some parts of Hawaii and sank some American ships.
>
> But what surprises me most is the way in which our people take it. They are as calm as ever, never leaving their jobs or anything. We will live like we always have and not be afraid of anything.[43]

Like Kondo, Kimura did not welcome the prospect of fighting the American and British enemy, as the boys did.[44]

In their diaries, two Kyoto girls simply recorded what they heard at school on the morning of December 8. Twelve-year-old Kawabata Fumiko's entry for that day begins, "At long last war with America and England broke out."[45] Nine-year-old Nishikawa Hisako wrote down verbatim what she had heard that morning: "The principal's speech. At long last a big war with America and England has started. This war is different from the Incident [the Sino-Japanese War], and we will have to do it in the open, and in the end, we must win. All of you, too, will have to do your very best."[46] After the speech, Nishikawa reported that she and her classmates went to a local shrine, presumably to pray for Japan's victory.[47] Even though both girls' diary entries for December 8 begin with the same "At long last war . . . ," and one of them states that these were her principal's words, the sense of relief conveyed in these words was not what the girls felt. Rather, these were the feelings of their principals, teachers, and perhaps most Japanese.

As the government hoped, many people were ecstatic when they heard the news. Cartoonist Yokoyama Ryūchi was still asleep when the news of the attack was first broadcast. "My wife woke me with the words 'War's broken out!' I was thrilled. Happy, all the indecisive gloom cleared off just like that."[48] Morishita Jirō, a teacher in Tokyo, wrote in his diary on December 8, "Because our armed forces have scored what were called huge victories, Japanese are pleased and in high spirits."[49] Tezuka Nuizō, a Christian in his sixties, could hardly contain his excitement, writing in his diary: "Praise! Thanks! Prayers! To be loved, one should love. Isn't this extraordinary? Isn't this wise? To declare war against America and England. At eleven o'clock. The emperor who defends the grace of God. He who is above the gods and spirits. Amen. Amen."[50] Tezuka's fusion of patriotism and Christianity is one of the most bizarre reactions to the news of the attack.

Forty-one-year-old Sakamoto Tane, who was married to a judge and lived in Kōchi, a port city on the island of Shikoku, wrote the following at the end of what proved to be a long day:

> Six o'clock in the morning a special news broadcast [reported] that imperial navy forces entered a state of war with England and the United States in the western Pacific, and at long last the war has started. At eleven o'clock in the morning, an imperial rescript declaring war was issued. There were news reports on the radio from time to time, and until the end of the day, things did not calm down.
>
> According to a report at one o'clock, before dawn this morning, imperial naval forces carried out a death-defying attack on the American fleet and air power in the vicinity of Hawaii, and bombed Singapore, achieving great military results.
>
> According to the 8:40 report in the evening, [our forces] sank two battleships and smashed four heavy cruisers, with no losses on our side—things were moving ahead at great speed. We listened intently to the radio and went to bed at midnight.[51]

Sakamoto's private account, filled with both excitement and amazement, is typical of how many Japanese felt in the immediate aftermath of the news of the nation's victories.

Some Japanese, however, were disappointed that the negotiations in Washington, DC, had not led to a peaceful settlement. Kamiyama Mitsuo, a twenty-four-year-old man from Osaka who fancied himself a poet, was one of them. He had hoped "for a solution that did not involve fighting," and his December 8 diary entry reads:

> This morning at eleven o'clock, the declaration of the Japanese-American War and an imperial rescript were given to us. By that time, Japan had attacked and sunk American warships. With the China incident still unresolved, Japan now must do battle with a strong enemy. The world at this moment is at the height of disorder. In the end, where will the first glimmer of hope for a world at peace come from?—we can't know. It was my thought that we would avoid coming to blows with America to the extent possible, and in principle, this was the case. I had hoped for a solution that did not involve fighting. This was the case even with the China incident.[52]

Resigned, Kamiyama continued, "But now that matters have come to this, there is nothing one can say. My heart is calm. There is still something I believe in. In regard to the goals of the state, I [still] have my principles."[53] Something of a Marxist, he saw himself as "a person of moral conscience" and had railed so fiercely against those of his friends who found "personal meaning" (*ikigai*) in the Sino-Japanese War that he feared being arrested and punished for being "antipatriotic" and a "traitor." After the war, he wrote that he had predicted Japan's defeat and destruction and blamed "not America and England but the confused, blind and ignorant."[54]

Other Japanese were truly sorry that war had broken out. No one was sorrier than Takahashi Aiko, a Tokyo housewife but hardly a typical one. Although she had been born and raised in Japan, she had spent her twenties and early thirties in Los Angeles, where she met and married her doctor husband. Both her children were born there, and the family returned to Japan in 1932, just months after Japanese troops streamed into, and took over, Manchuria. Never in her wildest dreams had Takahashi imagined that Japan and the United States would go to war.

> We firmly believed that no matter how bad our relationship with America got, it would never come to war. For example, it was as regrettable as it could be for Japan. Why, because the political problem of which position was correct was a separate issue. In fighting, one expects that the absolute and final goal is winning. . . . No matter what sort of diplomatic negotiations took place, we never imagined that the solution would be waging war. This was because I thought it was like a child challenging an adult [to a fight].[55]

As the last sentence of her comment on the outbreak of war reveals, Takahashi believed that Japan was so obviously inferior to the United States that it would never go to war. This is how she put it in her long diary entry for December 8:

> If we said, "Look at the everyday lives [of people] in Japan and America, there is no comparison," the response was, "Because America is an extravagant country, peaceful science there has developed; but when it comes to military science, Japan has complete confidence vis-à-vis America. There is no need to worry." The person who said this was an admiral in our family, which gave his comments a certain weight. Because it was someone of that sort saying this, when this was said, we might have thought, well, splendid preparations [for war] have been made, but we could not feel assured and believe this. Even if we looked at the washboard I was using in the kitchen, even though the Japanese and the Americans used the same materials, the American washboard was rationally made. The Japanese washboard seemed to be imitating the shape of the American one, but it was made without paying attention to rationality or physics. With just one or two differences in the carved shape of the washboard, the soap slipped, the water spilled on my chest, and the way water was stopped at the bottom was bad, and the stability of the board was not a given. When one uses a Japanese Western-style toilet,

> the placement of the handle was not thought out scientifically, and one can't flush the toilet with one hand and has to use two hands. When the steam from a covered pot condenses, it does not fall into the pot but forms droplets on the outside of the pot and spills on the floor. Even in matters as insignificant as these, Japanese forget the utility of science, and in a society that feels no inconvenience or lack of freedom, I wondered whether our science was really superior to that of other countries and felt unsure.[56]

Like Kamiyama, Takahashi recognized that her absolute certainty that Japan could not win the war could be seen as "pro-American and unpatriotic," so she kept those feelings to herself. Even the radio her family had brought back from Los Angeles seemed to betray them: it caught fire on December 9 and charred the ceiling, leading the family to conclude that "the American radio found broadcasting Japan's war news distasteful."[57]

Forty-eight-year-old Tomizuka Kiyoshi agreed with Takahashi. Like her, he believed that Japan could not defeat the Western powers. His reasoning, while different, was not unrelated. He was a leading aeronautical engineer who had graduated from Tokyo Imperial University and had studied in England, France, and Germany and was currently teaching at his alma mater. He also had published a specialized work in his field—*Aeronautical Engines* (*Kōkū gendōki*; 1937)—and a more popular work—*The Construction of a Scientific Japan* (*Kagaku nihon no kensetsu*; 1940). As a specialist, Tomizuka was convinced that Japan could not win a modern war, and he never missed a chance to say so publicly. By coincidence, he was presenting his views on the morning of the Pearl Harbor attack:

> On the morning of December 8, 1941, I was scheduled to deliver a lecture at the Tokyo Municipal Officials Institute and then, in the afternoon, to attend a meeting of the Central Cooperation Assembly of the Imperial Rule Assistance Association. I left my house hurriedly and went to the assembly hall in Sendagaya, where I lectured until noon, forcefully presenting my pet theory, namely, that "because Japan was poor in resources and scientific technique was lacking, no matter how much we persevered, there would be no victory in a modern war." No one opposed me. My hosts at the lecture did not tell me that the Tōjō cabinet had declared war on America and Britain that morning. . . . I intended to give a good lecture, and then went to Tokyo Hall for an Imperial Rule Assistance Association meeting. I expected the hall to be open, but not a soul was there. The hall was empty. I thought it was strange and asked someone in the vicinity, who said the meeting today had been called off. When I asked, "Really? Why?" he responded, "We started a war with America and England. There was a radio broadcast this morning.

> Didn't you hear it?" I was dumbstruck. If that's the case, "my lecture this morning was inappropriate," I thought.[58]

Apparently Tomizuka's colleagues at the Aero Research Center at Tokyo Imperial University felt as he did.

> My friends at Aero Research said privately that victories of Japan's air units would last for half a year at most. After that, they would probably decline. If they can last until this point, that would be good, but if they can't, Japan will find itself in a bad way—this is our view. In Germany for some time, the established view was that "if the war extends into winter, Germany will lose": this was because the oil researchers assumed that without winterized oil, both military vehicles and artillery would come to a halt in the dead of winter. Now it had become winter. Already the fate of Germany was fixed! This was the view of my colleagues and me.[59]

Tomizuka reported that even Admiral Yamamoto Isoroku, who as commander in chief of the combined fleet had overseen the planning and execution of the Pearl Harbor attack, felt the same as he and his colleagues did.[60] Inexplicably, Tomizuka continued to be in demand as a lecturer, even after he was branded as a "defeatist."[61]

Recognizing that Japan simply was not up to the task of defeating the United States, some Japanese were shocked that their forces had attacked American and British installations. Usui Hajime, who lived just beyond the western edge of Tokyo, thought the attacks defied common sense. "After all, the war in China was not going well, and declaring war on the world's greatest countries, America and England . . . was simply inconceivable."[62] Despite the government's efforts to treat the attacks of December 8 as monumental victories that portended continuing success, some Japanese did not agree with that rhetoric.

Indeed, some Japanese were furious with their leaders. Saitō Mutsuo was studying for his college entrance examinations at the time of the attacks. Having been educated in the 1930s as Japanese nationalism began to strengthen, he was shocked by his father's response to the Pearl Harbor attack. Even though the son was excited and pleased about the attack, the father, an insurance salesman, was not.

> When everyone was talking about victory, my father was pessimistic. You see, he knew about the outside world. He knew what sort of a country America was. He said: "What do they think they are doing, going to war with America? Don't they know how rich and powerful it is and how strong American industry is? Japan can't hope to defeat a country like that."

> Naturally, I argued with him. "Didn't you hear what they said on the radio? We've wiped out the American fleet," I said. "The whole Pacific is open to us now. Of course we're going to win."
>
> But it was a matter of education, really. Father had been educated in the Taishō age. He'd been brought up with liberal ideas. We'd been taught to believe that Japan was invincible, the Land of the Gods, and so on. But Father, I think, believed that something terrible had started.[63]

Like many of his countrymen, young Saitō "thought after we heard the news that the Americans might start to bomb us right away. So what I did was—I didn't go to cram [school] that day—I went down to the nearest store and bought some strong rice-straw paper and a pot of glue. It probably sounds rather silly now, but I spent the whole morning of the day that war broke out going around the house and covering the windows with sheets of paper to protect us from flying glass."[64] Saitō was not alone. As noted earlier, many Japanese immediately bought books on civil defense or helmets in preparation for these attacks.

In the days and weeks after the Pearl Harbor attack, however, all the news was good, and the "war fever" that had gripped Japan when its forces invaded China in the summer of 1937 intensified.[65] Indeed, the news was so good that by the start of the new year, even the skeptics and doubters had become believers. Tokugawa Musei (1894–1971), a well-known actor, wrote in his diary on December 8, "Iwai-kun let me know, through the half-open curtain of my room, about the news of the declaration of war against England and America. Hey, it's come. Finally come. Kokkuri's prediction was two days off. Listened to Prime Minister Tōjō's announcement to the entire nation in the curtains. His words were pretty difficult, so I wondered how this would play but, in any event, a historic broadcast."[66] A day later, he questioned what he had heard: "Got up unusually early and read the newspaper from one side. Two American battleships sunk and four heavily damaged; four cruisers heavily damaged and one aircraft carrier sunk. Because these results were a little too amazing, they didn't register. I could only imagine that the Japanese navy used magic, and no matter how much one shouted 'banzai,' I wasn't persuaded."[67]

Tokugawa even wondered what the start of war with America and Britain had to do with him. "I thought about how I as an individual was linked to the Japan-America War. What sort of function was I as an individual to fulfill? Or perhaps I wouldn't be fulfilling any function at all."[68]

For several weeks, he wrote little or nothing about the war in his diary even as Japanese forces scored victory after victory, advancing into Manila and taking Hong Kong. What finally prompted him to mention the war was his four-year-old son, who surprised him on the morning of December 27 by pretending to be a railway station conductor and announcing, "The enemy is coming, the enemy is coming. On Track 2 the enemy is coming. On track 3 the enemy is coming!"[69]

Four days later, on New Year's Day, Tokugawa dutifully reported in his diary that he and his family had drunk the "first water," offered it to their ancestors, and dined on New Year's fare and spiced saké. But his long New Year's Day entry also clearly reveals a dramatic change in his view of the war:

> It was an unprecedented New Year's. Reading just the headlines [in the newspapers], my chest swelled with pride:
>
> "Advancing into the Southwest Pacific—The Rising Sun Flag"
>
> "All of Malaya, Controlling the Skies"
>
> "Imperial Forces' Fierce Pursuit in the Philippines"
>
> "The General Attack Situation in Manila, Contact with the Crack Encircling Force from the North and South"
>
> "Wild Eagles Suppress Xiangang, Five Evening Bombing Raids"
>
> "Xiangang Now Streets of Death, Warning to Entire City"
>
> "Fierce Attacks on Guangdong"
>
> "On Shidi River Encircling Australian Forces, Penetrating Attacks on Both West and East Banks"
>
> "Fierce Fighting, Australian Forces Defeated"
>
> "American-English Anguished Discussion Not Effective in Averting Defeat"
>
> "When Singapore Falls, India, the Heart of England, Will Quake"
>
> "The Cutoff of the Burma Road, Dutch Assistance Facilities Destroyed in Fierce Bombing"
>
> "The Hudu Tragedy of American Defeat Reports"
>
> "The Beginning of a Decisive Battle with American-Philippine Forces, the Pan Pan District in North Manila"
>
> "Overcoming the Enemy in a Fierce Thirty-Six-Hour Battle"
>
> These are the headlines I gathered when I glanced at the four newspapers our house receives—*Miyako*, *Yomiuri*, *Nichi-nichi*, *Asahi*.
>
> Have we had newspapers with fabulous headlines like these up to now?[70]

Even the skeptic Tokugawa Musei had come around.

CONCLUSION

Most Japanese were thrilled by the success of the December 8 attacks. Hundreds of thousands of people attended the prefectural and municipal events held across the country. Even small town councils passed resolutions supporting the "sacred war" that promised that their communities would make sacrifices to ensure a "certain victory." Local shrines hosted the visits of emissaries from the Shinto establishment, who joined villagers in praying for Japan's victory. Those who could not turn out for the rallies and assemblies and had radios listened faithfully to the daily broadcasts of the latest war news, eager to hear if Japanese forces were "annihilating and destroying" the American and British enemies.

The same excitement and enthusiasm exhibited at public events is found in the personal journals and diaries of many Japanese. Children and teenagers were the most enthusiastic about the December 8 attacks, reflecting the nationalism they had learned in school and the influence of their teachers. Most adults were excited by the news of Japan's victories, and many simply felt a sense of relief. But others were disappointed by the outbreak of war with the United States and Britain—usually those who had some knowledge of Japan's capacity for war or some familiarity with the United States or Britain. In their eyes, the December 8 attacks were a terrible mistake and Japan was destined to lose.

With the string of military victories that ensued—on the Malay Peninsula, Singapore, Hong Kong, and Manila—the "concerns and unease" of many of the skeptics were swept away.[71] During the New Year's holiday (December 31 to January 4), there was so much interest in the latest newsreels that the crowds queuing up at movie theaters in Yokohama were large enough that the police had to be called to manage them.[72] Then on January 8, the government renamed "Raising Asia Public Service Day" as "Imperial Rescript Observance Day." From that day on until the end of the war, on the eighth day of each month, Japanese observed a moment of reverential silence at precisely 11:59 a.m.; every house flew the Japanese flag; and restaurants and cafés closed.[73] "Imperial Rescript Observance Day" became another of the mass rituals performed across the nation that reminded Japanese, as one account put it, that "every day is a battle."[74] Of course, the war with the Western powers had only just begun.

NOTES

1. Fukui-ken, comp., *Fukui ken-shi* (Fukui: Fukui-ken, 1996), tsūshi-hen 6, kingendai 2, 287; and Nagano-ken, *Nagano ken-shi* (Nagano: Nagano ken-shi kankōkai, 1989), 521.

2. Kodera Yukio, comp., *Senji no nichijō: aru saibankan fujin no nikki* (Tokyo: Hakubunkan, 2005), 115.

3. Okayama-ken hensan iinkai, comp., *Okayama ken-shi* (Okayama: Okayama-ken, 1989), kindai 3, 17.

4. *Asahi shinbun*, December 10, 1941. The several "nation-protecting" shrines (*gokoku jinja*) across Japan were provincial branches of the Yasukuni Shrine in Tokyo, which was founded in 1869 to honor those who fought and died in the war to restore imperial rule.

5. Ibaraki-ken, comp., *Ibaraki ken-shi* (Ibaraki: Ibaraki-ken, 1984), 891; and *Nagano ken-shi*, 519.

6. Radio ownership was still surprisingly limited: 40 percent of urban homes and only 10 percent of rural households had a radio.

7. Ishino Akira, *Kanagawa ken-shi gaisetsu* (Tokyo: Rekishi toshosha, 1980), 472.

8. Besides Pearl Harbor, the Japanese also attacked the Philippines, Hong Kong, Malaya, Guam, and Wake Island, as well as Makin and Tarawa in the Gilbert Islands.

9. The Marco Polo Bridge Incident was the skirmish between Japanese and Nationalist Chinese troops that took place on the outskirts of Beijing and became the pretext for the Japanese invasion of China.

10. Thomas Havens, *Valley of Darkness: The Japanese People and World War Two* (New York: Norton, 1978), 17; and Kenneth James Ruoff, *Imperial Japan at Its Zenith: The Wartime Celebration of the Empire's 2,600th Anniversary* (Ithaca, NY: Cornell University Press, 2010), 56–58.

11. Ruoff, *Imperial Japan at Its Zenith*, 56–58.

12. Toyama-ken, *Toyama ken-shi* (Toyama: Toyama-ken, 1984), tsūshi-hen 6, kindai-ge, 1063.

13. Fukui-ken, *Fukui ken-shi*, 287–288.

14. *Asahi shinbun*, December 9, 1941.

15. Shizuoka-ken, comp., *Shizuoka ken-shi* (Shizuoka: Shizuoka-ken, 1997), 226.

16. *Ibaraki ken-shi*, 891.

17. Havens, *Valley of Darkness*, 55–60.

18. Kanazawa shi-shi hensan iinkai, comp., *Kanazawa shi-shi* (Kanazawa: Kanazawa-shi, 2006), tsūshi-hen 3 (kindai), 453–456; Toyama-ken, *Toyama ken-shi*, 1060.

19. Niigata shi-shi hensan kindaishi bukai, comp., *Niigata shi-shi* (Niigata: Niigata-shi, 1996), 337–338.

20. *Nagano ken-shi*, 517.

21. *Kanagawa ken-shi*, 471.

22. Fukuyama shi-shi hensan iinkai, comp., *Fukuyama shi-shi* (Fukuyama: Fukuyama shi-shi hensan iinkai, 1978), 893.

23. Ibid.

24. Hiroshima-ken, comp., *Hiroshima ken-shi* (Hiroshima: Hiroshima-ken, 1981), kindai 2, tsūshi 6, 743.

25. Shin kumamoto shi-shi hensan iinkai, comp., *Shin Kumamoto shi-shi* (Kumamoto: Kumamoto-shi, 2003), tsūshi-hen 7, kindai 3, 959.

26. *Kanazawa shi-shi*, 456.

27. Niigata shi-shi hensan kindaishi bukai, comp., *Niigata shi-shi* (Niigata: Niigata-shi, 1996), tsūshi-hen 4, kindai (ge), 338.

28. The Home Ministry created the community councils in 1940, each consisting of several hundred households, in the cities and entire villages in the countryside. By the end of 1940, 180,000 had been created.

29. Okayama shi-shi henshū iinkai, comp., *Okayama shi-shi: sensai fukkō-hen* (Okayama: Okayama-shi, 1960), 18.

30. *Ibaraki ken-shi*, 892–893.

31. Yamagata-ken, comp., *Yamagata ken-shi* (Yamagata: Yamagata-ken, 1986), kingendai-hen (ge), 837–838.

32. For information on what was done in Ibaraki and Hiroshima Prefectures, see *Ibaraki ken-shi*, 338, and *Hiroshima ken-shi*, 743–744.

33. Hachinohe shi-shi hensan iinkai, comp., *Hachinohe shi-shi* (Hachinohe: Hachinohe-shi, 2014), 398.

34. Takeya Nobuyo, *Kibō no hana o mune ni: ichi shufu no senjika nikki* (Tokyo: Chūō kōrōn jigyō shuppan, 2006), 383.

35. *Kanagawa ken-shi*, 471.

36. Komatsu Shigeyoshi, *Tsuisō shōwa nijūyonsai*, cited in Nagano-ken, *Nagano ken-shi* (Nagano: Nagano ken-shi kankōkai, 1989), 519.

37. Tsushima Tsukasa, *Kokki: nikki ga kataru senji no chūgakusei* (Tokyo: Bungeisha bijuaru āto, 2008), 79–81.

38. Haruka Taya Cook and Theodore F. Cook, *Japan at War: An Oral History* (New York: New Press, 1992), 77.

39. Ibid.

40. See Samuel H. Yamashita, "Confucianism and the Japanese State, 1904–1945," in *Confucian Traditions in East Asian Modernity: Moral Education and Economic Culture in Japan and the Four Mini-Dragons*, ed. Tu Wei-ming (Cambridge, MA: Harvard University Press, 1996).

41. Mishima Yūichi, *Shōwa no sensō to shōnen to shōjo no nikki* (Osaka: Tōhō shuppan, 1995), 67–68. Kusunoki Masashige (1294–1336) was remembered as a warrior who gave his life for the Emperor Go-Daigo in 1336, and his "Parting Message to His Son" was taught to Japanese students in modern times.

42. Shinpen okazaki shi-shi henshū iinkai, comp., *Shinpen okazaki shi-shi* (Okazaki: Shinpen okazaki shi-shi hensan iinkai, 1991), 1231–1232.

43. Toneko Kimura Hirai and Taro Kimura, *Dear Gloria: Homesick for America in Wartime Japan*, ed. Gregg Ramshaw (Pittsburgh: Carnegie Mellon University Press, 2011), 73.

44. Of course, Kimura got the sequence of events wrong: she has Japan declaring war first and then attacking Pearl Harbor. We later discovered that this indeed was how things were supposed to have unfolded had there not been problems with the teletype machine at the Japanese embassy in Washington, DC. See Gordon W. Prange, *At Dawn We Slept: The Untold Story of Pearl Harbor* (New York: McGraw-Hill, 1989), 466–467, 489–490, 502, 554.

45. Kawabata Fumiko, *Shōjo no mita taiheiyō sensō* (Tokyo: Shinpūsha, 2005), 60.

46. Nishikawa Hisako, *Enikki shōjo no nichibei kaisen* (Tokyo: Sōshisha, 1992), 11.

47. Ibid.

48. Cook and Cook, *Japan at War*, 96.

49. *Nagano ken-shi*, 520.

50. Ibid.

51. Kodera, comp., *Senji no nichijō*, 115.

52. Kamiyama Mitsuo, *Taiheiyō sensō senji nikki-sho* (Tokyo: Kindai bungeisha, 1995), 11–12.

53. Ibid.

54. Ibid., 1.

55. Takahashi Aiko, *Kaisen kara no nikki* (Tokyo: Takahashi Aiko, 1955), 5.
56. Ibid., 5–6.
57. Ibid., 7.
58. Tomizuka Kiyoshi, *Aru kagakusha no senchū nikki* (Tokyo: Chūō kōrōnsha, 1976), 4.
59. Ibid.
60. Ibid., 5–6.
61. Ibid., 6.
62. Usui Hajime, *Senji shōmin nikki* (Tokyo: Kaiensha, 1976), 26.
63. Tessa Morris-Suzuki, *Showa: An Inside History of Hirohito's Japan* (London: Athlone, 1984), 98. During the Taishō period (1912–1925), Japan instituted its first party governments.
64. Morris-Suzuki, *Showa*, 97–98.
65. Louise Young, *Japan's Total Empire: Manchuria and the Culture of Wartime Imperialism* (Berkeley: University of California Press, 1998), 58–68.
66. Tokugawa Musei, *Musei sensō nikki* (Tokyo: Chūō kōrōnsha, 1977), i, 11.
67. Ibid., 12.
68. Ibid.
69. Ibid.
70. Ibid., 25–26.
71. Oita-ken sōmu-bu sōmu-ka, comp., *Oita ken-shi* (Oita: Oita-ken, 1988), 319. See Donald Keene's study of intellectuals' responses to the outbreak of war: *So Lovely a Country Will Never Perish: Wartime Diaries of Japanese Writers* (New York: Columbia University Press, 2010).
72. *Kanagawa ken-shi*, 472.
73. See Ruoff, *Imperial Japan at Its Zenith*, 58.
74. Fukuyama shi-shi hensan iinkai, *Fukuyama shi-shi*, 894.

CHAPTER 5

Identities and Alliances

China's Place in the World after Pearl Harbor, 1941–1945

Rana Mitter

The news of Pearl Harbor, and the attacks associated with it, was received rather differently by two of China's leaders. In China's temporary wartime capital at Chongqing, Chiang Kai-shek, the leader of China's National government (Guomin zhengfu), realized that the entry of the United States into the war in Asia would change China's fortunes completely. He wrote immediately to President Franklin Roosevelt, pledging a new "common battle." A thousand miles away in Nanjing, Zhou Fohai, a senior minister in the collaborationist government of Wang Jingwei, working with the Japanese occupiers, noted mournfully: "Now the Pacific becomes a killing ground."[1]

The two men had very different views of the best outcome of the war. But both shared one understanding: that Pearl Harbor turned what had been a Sino-Japanese War into one that would be part of something truly global. Having attacked both the United States and British Empire, Japan had gambled that it could finally subdue China and hold off two major Western powers simultaneously. Yet Japan had not fully grasped that the widening of the war fundamentally changed China's position too.

When war had broken out between China and Japan in July 1937, China was swiftly forced into a struggle to plan and sustain resistance. The Sino-Japanese War did not, as Japan's commanders had hoped, lead to the sudden collapse of China's government or morale. But it also did nothing to strengthen China's position in the global order. There were numerous expressions of sympathy for China from around the world, but there was little concrete sense that the invasion of

China and the retreat of the Nationalists (Guomindang or Kuomintang) to the interior was a matter of great concern to the wider world, other than that it damaged the possibility of commerce and trade in Asia.

The attacks of December 7/8 would have different results. The entry of the United States and Great Britain into the war in Asia was an important moment, but it did not *immediately* change conditions within China. However, the attacks and their aftermath did launch a major shift within China that would have enormous implications for the postwar Pacific and, indeed, the entire globe. The attack on Pearl Harbor prompted politicians, intellectuals, and key members of the military to begin thinking differently about Chinese identity. Those changes heralded the initial moves that would propel China into a new position in the postwar world.

In 1942, when FDR first put forward the idea of China as one of "four policemen" who would oversee the postwar order, the skepticism of many westerners, from Winston Churchill on, was not hard to see. Churchill described China contemptuously as little more than a "faggot vote" for the United States in the postwar era.[2] This reluctance to take the new Chinese role seriously was perhaps unsurprising, considering how weak and limited in its capacity China was in comparison with the other Allies, and most historians have concentrated on China's weakness in the war years.

Yet this version of the narrative has focused so much on the inadequacies of China's status as a wartime ally that it has obscured the suddenness and immensity of China's change of fortunes in comparison to where it had stood in 1937. The post–Pearl Harbor wartime period raised China to a position in global order that would have been hard to imagine had it not become part of a wider alliance. It also enabled Chinese at all levels during the war to expand their horizons and think of China's role being recast as a sovereign actor in a more globalized world.

Following Pearl Harbor, China was able to think of its role in a range of new contexts. In the prewar era, its involvement with internationalism had been ambivalent because of the nature of China's membership in organizations such as the League of Nations; China had had partial sovereignty but still did not have full autonomy on areas such as the right to set its own tariffs. After Pearl Harbor, it was clear that China would become a genuinely sovereign actor; the key moment was the signing of the treaties ending extraterritoriality in 1943, which meant that the privileges granting some foreigners immunity to Chinese law were ended. China would also become a mentor to the colonial world, able to flaunt its status as a rare independent non-Western state; here, Chiang's February 1942 visit to the Indian independence leaders Jawaharlal Nehru and Mahatma Gandhi in India was an important event. The international alliance also enabled policy debates in China to move beyond policies of survival and to consider what a postwar China might look like; thus, the wartime consideration of Western and indigenous ideas of social welfare became part of this discussion.[3] Wartime China was a place of lively and often fierce political debate in which Communists, Nationalists, and a variety of other political parties and intellectuals were all involved.

After Pearl Harbor, China's relationship with the Western powers changed considerably. It fought in cooperation, although hardly smooth cooperation, with its American and British counterparts in 1941–1942. By the start of 1943 the old "unequal treaties," which forced China to cede territory and trading rights against its will, had finally been abandoned, and the old system of "extraterritoriality," which gave special privileges to foreigners in China, was ended. By the end of that year, China had taken part in the Cairo Conference—the only occasion when a non-Western leader (Chiang Kai-shek) sat with the two major Western Allied leaders (FDR and Churchill) in equal status. During this whole period, various actors tried to project their own visions of what postwar China might look like. However, the pivotal nature of Pearl Harbor for China was clear; it was the moment when it took the first steps toward the standing as a major international power that it enjoys today.

CHINA'S PARTIES: THE RESISTANCE

How was the aftermath of Pearl Harbor seen by the major political actors in China who had been fighting Japan for four years since 1937, and how did they exploit the opportunities that it presented? China's ruling Nationalists, under the leadership of Chiang Kai-shek, had spent much of the period from 1927 to 1937 in open conflict with the Chinese Communists, with each side determined to eliminate the other. During this period, Mao Zedong had become one of the most prominent leaders of the Chinese Communist Party (CCP). When war broke out between China and Japan in 1937, the two warring Chinese sides formed an uneasy alliance against the invaders. The alliance had begun to break down by 1940, yet it still held, at least in name, by the summer of 1941.

The Chinese Communist Party knew that China had just experienced a major turning point. Operation Barbarossa, the German invasion of the USSR six months earlier, had already meant that the CCP had been able to declare its hand as part of a wider "antifascist" alliance on June 23, 1941, the day after the assault had begun. A statement attributed to Mao Zedong declared that the "Soviet Union's sacred war of resistance against fascist aggression is being waged not only in its own defense but in defense of all the countries and all the nations struggling to liberate themselves from fascist enslavement."[4] Yet this was, in the end, a statement more symbolic than substantial. The outbreak of war between the USSR and Germany did not lead to significant changes in China's military situation. There was no prospect of immediate Soviet involvement in the war in China (and indeed, it would not come about until August 1945), making the CCP's expression of solidarity with the USSR principally about positioning rather than strategy.[5]

Pearl Harbor, in contrast, was a concrete change in China's circumstances. "On the part of the United States, Britain, and other countries who have risen to resist this aggression," declared the CCP Central Committee on December 9, 1941, "it is a just war of liberation in defense of independence, freedom and democracy." Furthermore, "China must establish a military alliance with Britain, the United States, and other friendly countries fighting Japan."[6] The CCP's commitment was to an international war, even if its contributions were confined to its own base areas in China.

Behind the rhetoric, there was some cynicism on the part of the top CCP leaders. Mao Zedong wrote a private letter to Zhou Enlai just a couple of days later, in which he was more critical of the proposed new allies, asking, "Do those indolent British and American military and political personnel have the necessary stamina?" He also noted that, usefully for the party, "the possibility of the Guomindang's attacking the border regions will be reduced" as a result of Pearl Harbor.[7] Nonetheless, he saw the importance of the expansion of the war, predicting (correctly) that Hong Kong, Malaysia, Burma, and the Dutch East Indies might be vulnerable, and (less accurately) that Australia and New Zealand might become so as well. As the fighting continued, Mao hoped that "strongholds such as Singapore, Manila and Darwin" might be held to allow a counterattack against an exhausted Japan after around six months or so. He also believed that the outbreak of a Pacific War would allow for the swift defeat of Germany. Mao's wide-ranging assessment made clear that he considered China's struggle, and the CCP's, to be part of a global matrix of interactions: World War II, rather than a war between two East Asian countries.

However, the CCP's actions and decisions about engagement with the war against Japan would not directly change as an immediate result of Pearl Harbor. In contrast, the attack led to a swift and thorough rethinking of Chiang Kai-shek's national government's plans not just for a Chinese victory but also for a new formation of postwar regional order in Asia. On December 20, 1941, just days after Pearl Harbor, Chiang detailed in his diary what he wanted as part of the postwar settlement: Tibet and Kowloon from Britain, Outer Mongolia and Xinjiang to return or be secured for China, Manchuria and Dalian to be seized back from Japan, and the end of extraterritoriality, concession areas, and manifestations of imperialism in general. A year later, on November 9, 1942, Chiang had drawn up a ten-point plan to work with America, with the following key points:

(A) Long term alliance
(B) Return Manchuria/Luda to China
(C) Return Taiwan/Ryukyu to China

(D) Mutual establishment of a 30-year agreement on navy and airbases
(E) Mutual support for Vietnam
(F) Support for an independent Thailand
(G) Indian independence
(H) Mutual support for SE Asia and Burma
(I) Outer Mongolia to come back to China, but maintain autonomy
(J) Sino-American alliance[8]

This list was an intriguing mixture of anticolonial nationalism, attempts to tie the United States into the region, and also to create a sphere of influence where China would de facto become more influential. Throughout this time, and for the entirety of the war, Chiang's attitude toward the United States would swing back and forth between a desire for stronger ties and the sense that the Americans were in some sense trying to weaken China. On March 4, 1943, Chiang wrote that the United States did not want China to have an independent air force because it wanted control of the Pacific after the war. Yet Chiang's monthly reflections for September of the same year stated: "After the war, if we self-strengthen without cease, unify without chaos, and daily advance in politics and the military, then after five years, the US will have to make an alliance with me." In December 1943, he wrote that the communique issued after the November 1943 Cairo Conference ("Sextant") had indeed been a success: the promise to restore Taiwan, the Pescadores, and to create an independent Korea were key to a postwar settlement.[9] A document written by Chiang in 1944 also suggests a rather different vision of what the postwar Asia he wanted might look like:

> It's not an advantage for us if Japan is controlled by the US. A weak but independent Japan is like Belgium and Holland, even France, for Britain, and it can play a protective role in reducing American pressure on our economy. . . . Our peace treaty with Japan should not be too harsh. . . . This will make Japan ashamed and appreciative, and respectful. By returning good for evil, not only do we show the style of a great country, but we also have a leading authority in the world culture and spirit, so that we can stand up to American pressure.[10]

The China of 1937 had been in absolutely no position to dictate terms over its own territory, let alone that of its neighbors. By the middle of the war, even while China's own position remained highly precarious, Chiang was able to project ideas about the role that the country might play in a new Asian order.

Meanwhile, Chiang reflected that the rise in American standing in China exactly coincided with the decline of Britain's, particularly in the aftermath of the disastrous collapse of British authority in Asia in the weeks and months after Pearl Harbor. Churchill became a particular bête noire for Chiang. Churchill was generally contemptuous of China's role in the war, considering it ludicrous that the country should be counted as an ally equivalent in standing to the others. However, Chiang felt that Churchill's own assessments lacked a sense of realism about Britain's diminished power. Chiang's diary entry for March 27, 1943, was typical: he noted that Churchill had talked about the "Big Three" countries that would shape the postwar order, but he "excludes China completely."[11] On September 2, 1943, Chiang reflected after reading Churchill's speech following the Quebec conference ("Quadrant"): "After closing the report, I thought for a long time, for I do admire him." But it was an admiration tempered by a wider reality:

> Remembering our troops' defeat in Burma last year [during the chaotic first Burma campaign in spring 1942], it was a surrender tied up with political issues; it wasted lives and damaged our strength. I remember last year British power was lacking in Southeast Asia, Hong Kong and Singapore, so they surrendered. . . . They wanted other people to sacrifice themselves, and used other people only in the interests of their empire.[12]

As Britain's standing was pummeled by the disaster of its collapse in Asia, one of China's strongest suits—its standing as a plausible anti-imperialist actor—became swiftly evident. One of Chiang's first actions after Pearl Harbor had been to visit India in February 1942, where he met Nehru and Gandhi. The meeting only took place at Chiang's strong insistence, as the British authorities were keen to avoid an anti-imperialist Asian leader meeting the leaders of the Indian independence struggle. Chiang found the encounters frustrating, as he failed in his chosen mission of persuading the Indian National Congress leaders to back the war effort against Japan wholeheartedly in return for eventual independence. However, Chiang's broadcast speech on his departure from India made the symbolic importance of China's role clear. Aside from Chiang, no other non-Western leader could or would be treated as an equal at that point by the British, and Chiang made clear that he intended to press for Indian independence.

Chiang cautioned the Congress leaders that they could not choose to help some Allies and not others, but he reserved his real fire for the British, who he demanded should give power to the Indians without having their hands forced: "I take the position objectively that this would be a wise decision by the British, with no disadvantage to them."[13] In a later speech on March 3, 1942, he repeated his message, pointing out that no country other than China had supplied as many soldiers to the war effort as India.[14]

Chiang spoke further of his conversation with an Indian "friend" (the implication is that it was Nehru), who declared that the fall of Singapore and the Dutch East Indies was not coincidental but rather the product of a wider, unwise European imperialist policy, although the friend did acknowledge that independence might have been even harder to achieve from Germany or Japan than from Britain. Nehru had famously expressed his joy at hearing the news of the Japanese victory in the Russo-Japanese War of 1904–1905; now, Chiang's friend declared: "Before 18 September [1931; that is, the Manchurian crisis], we had hopes of Japan, but afterward, we lost those dreams" and that he no longer regarded the Japanese as part of his "race" but instead as no better than the Germans. Chiang urged his friend to support the Allies in service of independence; the friend replied that India had been deceived after World War I when India had given sterling service to the war effort but had not come any nearer to independence. This was different, Chiang countered; this time, China is with you.[15]

Could Chiang have had this sort of dialogue before Pearl Harbor? It is possible, though unlikely. However, his standing to do so would have been much less clear before 1941. Pearl Harbor and the subsequent alliance meant that China could gain standing both as a formal ally and as a member of the anti-imperialist club, with significant ability to pivot to them both. Using his status as an ally, Chiang was able to put pressure on the Churchill government to enable him to visit India; with his status as a non-Western anti-imperialist, he was able to make a plausible appeal to India's independence leaders. Although he was not successful in persuading Congress to back the war effort, Chiang would continue to be careful to nurture this connection with India. In April 1943, Song Meiling gave a speech in New York that was critical of Gandhi's thought, which she said was narrow and confused. Chiang noted that "the British used her remarks, and this has had a bad effect on our policy toward India. I asked her to be prudent and come back."[16]

The years after Pearl Harbor saw increasing signs of China's new status. John Keswick, political adviser to Lord Mountbatten, former head of the Special Operations Executive (SOE) in China, and the head of Jardine, Matheson, and Co., noted that the signing of the 1943 treaties ending extraterritoriality had started a new era in the relationship between Britain and China. "A MILESTONE IN CHINESE HISTORY," he wrote in capital letters in a note from early 1943. "'Extraterritoriality' is dead. It is time to take stock of our position, for we start a new chapter, and let us do so with an eye on the future."[17]

However, the Chinese entry into the wider war led to difficulties in its relationships with its allies. The breakdown of relations between Chiang and his American chief of staff, General Joseph W. Stilwell, has become well-known and remains one of the most compelling personality clashes of the era, providing an analogy for wider Sino-American misunderstanding during the war and beyond.[18] However, it took place in the context of a wider conflict within Chiang's own mind, reflecting tensions within the Nationalist government as a whole, in which the American presence in China was a risky but necessary force in service of the reduction of the power of British imperialism. Chiang's entries for 1943, a crucial year, show this tension. On June 30, Chiang declared forcefully if inaccurately that "Britain really hates China; and they've banned the reading of [my book] *China's Destiny*." On September 19 Chiang wrote that he was sure that the British were aiming to invade Tibet. The next day, he declared that "the British army is conspiring to join in the China Theatre—I must reject this." A week later, on September 25, he recorded that "British propaganda says that Mountbatten will take charge of Thailand and Vietnam. This means a conspiracy to take [these countries] out of the China Theatre." (This referred to the formation of the South East Asia Command [SEAC] under Mountbatten in summer 1943, which relegated the China Theatre to a secondary role to make way for a concentrated assault in the Pacific.) On October 1 he received a message from Gu Weijun (V. K. Wellington Koo), the Chinese ambassador to London, passing on the message that Mountbatten was postponing any further assault on Burma. "You can see that the British don't want to use their strength in the Far East," Chiang fumed. "Their intentions are selfish in that way."[19] At the end of the week, he observed: "Britain is still not sincere about advancing into Burma, and not only do they prevent our army entering Burma, but are suffocating our economy. They won't be at peace until they've got rid of [us] as troublemakers in East Asia."[20]

Read in close succession, these entries have the effect of making Chiang seem inconsistent, ungrateful, or indeed mildly paranoid. After all, a year later, Chiang would be fighting in Burma with British troops in the second Burma campaign (albeit not with the logistical support that he would have expected.) Yet it is not reasonable to expect him to have shared the viewpoint of an American or British observer. Neither the United States nor Britain was keeping Chiang fully informed of changes in strategy; Chiang had spent much of the early twentieth century as a committed nationalist whose major project was to end the colonial violence and economic injustice attached to the British presence in China; and he felt, with some justification, that Chinese troops had been forced to fight in Burma in 1942 in circumstances that he would not have chosen, and in which neither American nor British commanders had performed at all well. This is not to say that Chiang could not suffer from a rather inflated sense of his own capabilities. After Roosevelt had changed his mind on a full assault on Burma in spring 1943, Chiang wrote in exasperation: "Roosevelt is not a military man and isn't even a politician! Why is it so hard to find someone with talent!"[21]

China's formal status as an Allied power after Pearl Harbor also meant that it was being judged against the standards of much more advanced armies, something of which Chiang became very aware as the war ground on and China's position worsened. At the Fourth Nanyue Military Conference on February 10, 1944, where he had gathered the commanders of the Third, Fourth, Seventh, and Ninth War Zones, Chiang declared:

> Our responsibility to our people and the world is great—unlike the last three Nanyue conferences. At that time, the War of Resistance was just a solo war, but now, our war with our Allies alongside against the invader has become a total war, and the battlefield, a total battlefield. So our military, especially our high-level officers, ought to have a more advanced consciousness and make better efforts.

Chiang added that when it came to making the Chinese military measure up against foreign armies, "I think this is more important than any other victory."[22]

Chiang's speeches showed that he felt the weight of the alliance on his shoulders. At Nanyue, he went on: "On the surface, the foreign military will not say negative things about the psychology and point of view of the Chinese army. But in their psychology and spirit, they do not consider the Chinese army to stand equal. Moreover, they regard us as the same as the old Beiyang army of thirty years ago, or even regard us as the same as the indigenous army of India and other such places." Chiang acknowledged the reasons for this: "In reality, we have no equality with other countries. The basic cause is that our army isn't strong enough."[23] During the depths of the crisis over his attempts to dismiss Stilwell, Chiang wrote bitterly: "Because China is not robust and we cannot stand up to American oppression, they despise us, or they consider my protests a sign that I'm unwilling to cooperate with the US, and I am brushed aside."[24]

The situation would become worse in mid-1944, as the Japanese Ichigo campaign thrust its way into the heartland of central China. The breakdown of the relationship between Chiang and Stilwell meant that China's reputation in the United States became much more negative. Yet the wider changes that had been in place since Pearl Harbor—the faster movement toward China becoming a genuinely sovereign state—were unstoppable. Eventually, it would be the CCP that was able to take fullest advantage of those shifts to reshape domestic policy without interference from the West.

AFTER PEARL HARBOR: THE COLLABORATORS

It was not just those resisting Japan who noted the significance of Pearl Harbor. Wang Jingwei's collaborationist government, based in Nanjing, also understood that the situation had changed. In 1938 Wang and his followers had left the wartime capital at Chongqing and agreed to work with the Japanese. After a lengthy negotiation, Wang was finally given permission to establish his own government at Nanjing in March 1940. In the period leading up to Pearl Harbor, the diaries of Wang's senior minister Zhou Fohai showed a clear understanding of the changing geopolitical situation, even at a time when he began to fear that "the war of resistance faction is right."[25] In December 1940 he noted that "the Italian army has been defeated in North Africa; there's a big shift in power and it makes me worried." Zhou understood the Wang regime's status as an Axis actor, not merely a Chinese one: "We share the same fate as Mussolini; things in the world are not predictable."[26] In a similar vein, he reflected on Rudolf Hess's defection over "different political views": he viewed this action as being comparable with Wang Jingwei defecting from Chongqing. For Zhou, as for Chiang, international alliances and comparisons were important. The year 1941 saw Zhou in turmoil as he tried to interpret the twists and turns of global politics.

Mao had seen Barbarossa as a first major turning point, and so did Zhou. "I heard today that the USSR and Germany are at war," he noted on June 22, 1941. "The war situation has changed greatly and can't be predicted."[27] Zhou, however, believed that Germany would take Moscow within two months. When asked about the prospects for the Nationalist-Communist alliance in China, he reflected that since the USSR no longer had to claim nonaggression with Germany, the CCP would also now be freer to pressure the Soviets to take a harder line against the Nazis' ally Japan.

During the summer of 1941 Zhou brooded on the need for "a permanent Sino-Japanese peace," in the absence of which the two countries would be sowing "the seeds of a hundred years of hatred." Zhou's sons and daughters had already been packed off to Japan to study, "putting in a lot of effort." Yet he also noted that "if you give them [the Japanese] an inch, they'll take a foot." He was becoming steadily less optimistic that Japan would offer China any sort of fair deal: "The peace movement was the product of our misunderstanding."[28]

Nonetheless, throughout much of the summer Zhou remained reasonably certain that Japan would resolve its differences with the United States, and he put his faith in the "wisdom" of Japanese prime minister Konoe Fumimaro, who had formed his third cabinet in July 1941. "I hope that they succeed in settling a US-Japan reconciliation," he wrote, adding with commendable but deluded optimism that "then China and Japan can have equal places, and they can use the strength of the United States to maintain peace and freedom." Zhou did add that if Konoe failed, he would likely fall from office, and that his successor would come in actively into the war with Germany and Italy. In Zhou's post-Barbarossa but pre–Pearl Harbor interpretation of events, Germany and the USSR would be at war, but the United States would stay out. In this scenario, the Sino-Japanese conflict would have to be negotiated in a more limited Asian context, although the United States might act as an honest broker. However, Zhou's hopes were dashed: Konoe's government lasted only until October.

Then came Pearl Harbor. Zhou knew that the situation had changed significantly. However, unlike Chiang, who knew that the alliance with the United States that he had hoped for, and worked toward, had finally arrived, Zhou was not sure how the new order would emerge; he still hoped that the two rival Chinese capitals could do a deal with one another. "I hope Chongqing doesn't declare war on Japan," he noted, "as it will be an obstacle to Chinese unity." He added on December 13: "There's no point speaking to Chongqing now, as they are too excited [about the entry of the United States into the war], but wait till Singapore and Manila have fallen, and we'll have an opportunity to speak to them."[29]

On December 10 Zhou noted: "Japan has already landed in the Philippines and Malaya and acted amazingly fast." Zhou's attitude toward the Japanese fluctuated: on December 11 he wrote that the Wang government needed to get Japan to promise that if Japan won the war, China would not be treated as a colony, but two days later he wrote, "Naturally we want to throw out British and American forces, and of course use our strength to help Japan," though he did add frankly that there was not much they could do to help at that moment. (Nor, at that point, did it appear that the Japanese were in need of much help.) Such fluctuations also mark Chiang's thoughts in his diary; but in his case, instead of blowing hot and cold about the Japanese, it was the Americans who would be praised one day as the only hope for China and as a certain source of downfall on the next.

It was clear also that Zhou and the Wang government were making their judgments on the basis of fast-changing rumors immediately after Pearl Harbor, when information was scarce. Zhou gathered (rightly) that the Japanese were deeply concerned about keeping the USSR neutral, knowing that they could not possibly fight the United States and USSR at once. He also heard that Japan was negotiating both with the USSR and Germany; he found this hard to believe but declared that if it were true, "the world situation will change."[30] By the next day, he thought that Japan, Germany, and Italy had agreed that they would all fight to the end and would not make separate pacts with the Allies.

At the same time, again echoing Chiang's perceptions, Zhou heard about the sequence of British retreats around the region. "If they keep losing," he asked, "won't that be the end for British power in the Far East?" He added: "This will be the day that the yellow man can hold his head up high."[31]

The year after Pearl Harbor showed that Zhou Fohai, and the Wang regime, had a very different mental map from the Nationalists or Communists about how the new order would look. Zhou was still uncertain about whether Japan could win the war or not. In a private discussion with a Japanese interlocutor, Zhou noted the superior production capability of the United States and USSR and observed that "Japan has occupied many places, so they've covered a lot of ground and need to split their forces."[32] However, he was still convinced that a rational agreement between the Chongqing regime and Japan was possible (and that, by extension, the Wang regime in Nanjing could be brought back into the "national" fold). On February 7 he speculated that "if Japan withdraws troops, then Chiang Kai-shek may make peace." By April 5, 1942, when the Burma campaign was well underway, Zhou felt that force, rather than restraint, by Japan might do the trick. "I've heard that Japan will enter Yunnan province from Burma," he asked; "is Chongqing feeling the shock? The Japanese army are keen for complete peace, so Chongqing could get excellent terms." Pointedly, Zhou wrote on July 7: "I told the Japanese: If you want Chongqing to trust you, you have to make us [the Wang regime] trust you first."[33]

Zhou was sticking to what he regarded as the primary task of the regime he served: to create what he viewed as a strong, nationalist China even in the context of collaboration with the Japanese. He consistently maintained the view that various geopolitical outcomes could, somehow, lead to a stable and reunited China: on April 28 he even suggested that a successful Japanese invasion of British India could somehow "resolve" the Sino-Japanese conflict.[34] The Wang Jingwei regime had infinitely less room for maneuver even than the constrained National government in Chongqing. However, its self-declared goals sounded remarkably similar to Chongqing's, even if its path for reaching them was very different indeed.

AFTER PEARL HARBOR: THE VIEW FROM THE BATTLEFIELD

The view of the war from Huangshan, Chiang Kai-shek's house just outside Chongqing, was rather different from the one on the ground. And that ground had changed considerably. After Pearl Harbor, China had to fight in an international context, and part of that context was combat outside China's borders.

The Chinese did not wholly lack overseas military experience in the modern era. During World War I some 96,000 Chinese workers were sent to the Western Front to dig trenches and perform labor not in the direct line of combat. The Chinese government had in fact offered soldiers for the frontline, which the French were willing to accept, but the British declined to accept Chinese as combatants.[35] However, this experience aside, Chinese troops had not been involved in campaigns outside their own territories since the early Qing dynasty.[36] During the 1937–1941 period, Chinese troops were in any case fully involved in defending their own territory. However, after Pearl Harbor China's status as part of a global alliance meant that priorities had changed. Without the globalizing of the war at this point, there would almost certainly have been no Chinese involvement in Burma.

Strictly speaking, there was no reason why China could not have been an ally of the United States and Britain while operating entirely within its own territory. Strategically, that would have made sense: China's greatest contribution was to hold down some 600,000 Japanese troops and prevent them being deployed elsewhere. In the end, no American or British ground combat soldiers fought in wartime China, making it logical that defense of the Chinese homeland would have to come from its own soldiers.

However, Allied commanders as well as Chiang saw the value, in terms of morale and image, in a Chinese involvement in combat outside its own borders. The sudden success of Japan in capturing Burma provided the occasion for the Chinese to deploy troops outside China's borders. Burma was a British colony, but China had traditionally had influence in North Burma, and it also provided a potentially important supply line for southwest China, where the National government was located.[37] An important factor was the assignation by US Army chief of staff General George C. Marshall of Joseph Stilwell as chief of staff to Chiang Kai-shek. The relationship between the two men rapidly deteriorated as Stilwell became keen on the recapture of Burma by bold, and in the opinions of some, reckless, offensives in spring 1942.

Recovery of the direct experience of Chinese combat soldiers during the war years is very difficult.[38] The majority of those fighting were functionally illiterate and did not keep diaries or records of their experiences. However, a certain number of diaries of combatants have survived, mostly from the officer class.[39] One such figure was (the pseudonymous) Luo Gu, who served in the first Burma campaign in spring 1942; this was the first campaign to epitomize the post–Pearl Harbor world in which the Americans, British, and Chinese were fighting, at least in theory, as equal partners. Luo Gu published a diary of his time in combat at the end of the war, in 1945, with an introduction by his fellow officer Li Tao that gives a strong sense of the emotions engendered by the conflict. As Li Tao explains, the prospect of fighting in Burma against the Japanese was inspiring for many: "We were all excited." Also evident, however, was an increasing contempt for one formerly powerful actor in China: "The British troops did not fight, but retreated." Overall, Li declared, they had to brave numerous natural dangers and lost over a thousand men, but "with numerous sacrifices," they retreated in an ordered fashion.[40]

Luo Gu's own diary is likewise a mixture of powerful descriptions of combat experience combined with strong views about the Western allies. One element was the sense of exoticism about service in Burma, a direct result of this first foreign deployment in the post–Pearl Harbor world. It is worth remembering how unique the experience was for soldiers like Luo Gu to be sent on a combat mission in another country whose language and topography were entirely unfamiliar. Burma was on China's southwest border, but few if any Chinese soldiers had had any experience of fighting in the jungles that characterized that part of the country; as Luo noted on May 1, 1942, "jungle covered everything for miles," and temperatures of over 100 degrees Fahrenheit left them constantly dehydrated. Luo's regiment came across two symbols of exoticism, live elephants ("very rarely had our soldiers seen such huge beasts"), which they captured and walked around their camp. The campaign was also marked by constant deaths: over and over again, Luo Gu records the deaths of men killed by the Japanese or by natural hazards such as animals or weather.[41] "Lightning flashed, and rain started to pour. It was hard to walk, and the soldiers' suffering was indescribable."[42]

The wider Chinese discourse of British power being humbled while the United States rose in influence is reflected in Luo Gu's observations. His first entries mention that the American Red Cross had helped the Chinese wounded, while accusing the British of failing to do so: "We did not see any Englishman serving us."[43] Weeks later, after the retreat had been ordered and the company had undertaken a nightmarish trek through the jungle, they reached a British-run refugee station on June 19. A British officer told them that the supplies there were for refugees only, not for soldiers, but Luo's group took them anyway. (On July 4 the same British officer would report them for having stolen some 70 percent of the outpost's supplies.) At a time when they were suffering from malnutrition and malaria, and every day was either "rainy, or very rainy," Luo clearly hardly cared. The first Burma campaign had been a disaster. As General Liao Yaoxiang put it: "Our retreat is greater than that of Cao Cao from Chibi or Napoleon from Moscow."[44] Yet, horrific though the experience was, it was also a turning point in terms of Chinese combat service with other allies. (China's wartime experience remains distinctive in this regard; no subsequent war in which China was involved during the Cold War involved a formal alliance, though People's Liberation Army "volunteers" who served during the Korean War came close.)

The experience of Huang Yaowu during the second Burma campaign in 1944 also suggests a change in language and reference points that came from the post–Pearl Harbor environment. Huang was born in 1928 and joined the army in Guangdong in 1943 at age fifteen. The following year he was flown to India to serve as part of the new Sixth Army, 212th division, in the "student corps" (as a volunteer, albeit at a low rank). After training, the troops were sent to fight in Burma. Their task was to open up the Burma Road; the campaign was simultaneous with Japan's brutal Ichigo campaign, in which Japan was making a final thrust into central China. This campaign would be only the second one in which Chinese troops served outside their own borders with formal allies.

Huang wrote a memoir of his time in Burma that details the sheer difficulty of the task before the Sixth Army. His account of everyday life shows that Chinese soldiers were aware of their allies and shared what had now seemingly become a common feeling at elite and nonelite levels. When American soldiers declared that China was "ting hao" ("A-OK"), they used their thumbs, whereas the British, in contrast, used their little fingers; Huang found this "arrogant." Whether the British intended a slight is not clear, but the memory certainly reflects a wider—and widely perceived—reality: that the British role in China was being eclipsed by that of the United States. Huang was certainly contemptuous of the British performance in the first Burma campaign in 1942: "the British couldn't fight, and we had the responsibility to save them." In contrast, the good performance by the Chinese in 1944 earned them "Roosevelt uniforms"—that is, clothing supplied by the United States.[45]

The British were aware of the shift in perception about their role. The head of the Far Eastern Department in the British Foreign Office, J. C. Sterndale-Bennett, wrote a memorandum at about this time that used a quotation from Sir Eric Teichman (who had had long service in the British consular service) to make the point that, in different ways, Chiang Kai-shek, Zhou Fohai, Luo Gu, and Huang Yaowu had all noted:

> Comparing China's foreign policy in 1943 with her attitude of ten years earlier, nothing is more striking than her dependence on America and acceptance of American leadership. . . . China looks primarily to America, not Britain, to defeat Japan . . . and to build up the great new China after the war is won. On our side, because we are not in a position to do otherwise, we have accepted this condition and have abdicated from the position of leadership which we have occupied in China for the past hundred years.[46]

Luo Gu's account is highly shaped by the narrative of nationalism, as is that of Huang Yaowu. It is hard to imagine that the intra-militarist wars of the 1920s and 1930s, important though they were, could have engendered the sort of ideological nationalism that both expressed. Pearl Harbor allowed two discourses to grow: first, the discourse of combat against an invading enemy, which had been developing since 1937, and second, the idea of China's participation in an international war in which the Chinese were equal actors. These were not the primary emotional colorants of combat experience: military training, exhaustion, and fear were more immediately evident. But they were part of the environment that could only exist after Pearl Harbor. The Chinese troops who made it to India were fed and retrained, mainly at Ramgarh, under the title "X Force." Eventually, the stationing of Chinese troops in India would be significant, not just in terms of strategy when they served during the second Burma campaign but also because their presence was a further confirmation that Chinese troops were now part of a global alliance.

CONCLUSION: THE LEGACY OF PEARL HARBOR FOR CHINA

Chiang's diary entry for March 1, 1943, is a brief note with little detail, in which he suggests that China's political structure should be a "constitutional democracy," with a capitalist economy and a concern for social welfare. This was a long way from a formal proposal and deeply at odds with the reality of economic and social crisis that had gripped much of China by this stage of the war. However, the comment also indicates the way in which, even in rhetoric, the Chinese war effort had become part of a wider political discussion about the postwar world in which China would play a role. The proposals themselves echo Sun Yat-sen's "Three Principles of the People" (nationalism, civic rights, and the people's livelihood), which had been articulated in the 1920s. Yet they also signal an understanding of the expectations of China's Allied partners about what a postwar power should look like. For the United States in particular, the idea of China as a constitutional democracy was powerful, although FDR's idea of what that phrase might mean was a long way from the "tutelage" or "guided" democracy that was the most generous interpretation of what Chiang (never a democrat by instinct) meant by the term. Nonetheless, the fact that Chiang used such language in his personal records showed that he perceived the post–Pearl Harbor alliance, in some sense, as a political project, not just a set of military arrangements.

Pearl Harbor meant that a whole variety of assumptions about the postwar world, and China's place in it, entered the discourse and gained power after December 1941. An idea of Asia began to form in the minds of American and Chinese policymakers in which it was widely expected that there would be a sustained Nationalist Chinese role in the shaping of postwar Asia, not just China. There was also a limited but real discussion on what kind of exemplary state postwar China should be. The Nationalists began to consider ideas of constitutional democracy, albeit with their own party acting as a powerful vanguard, and with a strong interest in social welfare (as Tehyun Ma has shown, Nationalist elites offered high praise to the British Beveridge Plan and the US Social Security Act).[47] In addition, we can see in the wartime self-presentation within Asia of the Chinese Nationalist government, the origins of the grouping of non-European powers whose identity would help define non-Western identity after the Bandung Afro-Asian Conference of 1955, and the emergence of postcolonial identity in the non-European world.

Ironically, considering the hostility of Chiang to the British, China found itself in rather friendly discussions with the postwar Attlee Labour government, which hoped to use a new relationship with China to secure its position against the United States and USSR in Asia. On September 16, 1945, senior Nationalist ministers T. V. Soong and Wang Shijie joined British foreign secretary Ernest Bevin at Chequers, the prime minister's country residence, for lunch and conversation.[48] In practice, the outbreak of the Chinese Civil War in 1946 swiftly put paid to ideas that Nationalist China could play a powerful role in the reshaping of Asia. However, Communist China built on the legacy that its Nationalist predecessor had left it. The CCP is associated with the emergence of a sovereign China that had the capacity to make its own geopolitical decisions and to be an exemplar in its own right to other non-Western nations emerging into independence, but it was the Nationalists who began that process. Without Pearl Harbor, and without the subsequent twist and turns that turned China into a global actor, much of Asia might have remained under Japanese rule for decades, and the rise of today's twenty-first-century Chinese superpower would have remained merely a fantasy in the minds of guerrillas hiding in caves in northwest China.

NOTES

1. Rana Mitter, *Forgotten Ally: China's World War II* (Boston: Houghton Mifflin Harcourt, 2013), 236.

2. Christopher Thorne, *Allies of a Kind* (New York: Oxford University Press, 1978); Erez Manela, "The Fourth Policeman: Franklin Roosevelt's Vision for China's Global Role," in Wu Sihua et al., eds., 開羅宣言的影響與意義 [The Significance and Impact of the Cairo Declaration] (Taipei: Chengchi University Press, 2014).

3. See essays in the *European Journal of East Asian Studies* 11, 2 (2012), "Special Issue on Relief and Rehabilitation in Wartime China."

4. Mao Zedong, "Decision Regarding the International United Front against Fascism," in Stuart Schram, ed., *Mao's Road to Power: Revolutionary Writings, 1912–1949,* vol. 7 (Armonk, NY: M. E. Sharpe, 2005), 764 (hereafter MZD).

5. John W. Garver, *Chinese Soviet Relations, 1937–1945: The Diplomacy of Chinese Nationalism* (New York: Oxford University Press, 1988); Michael H. Hunt, *The Genesis of Chinese Communist Foreign Policy* (New York: Columbia University Press, 1991).

6. "Declaration of the Chinese Communist Party Regarding the War in the Pacific," December 9, 1941), MZD, 844–845.

7. "Estimate of the Situation in the International War," December 12, 1941, MZD, 848.

8. Wang Jianlang, citation of Chiang diary, November 9, 1942, in "Daguo yishi yu daguo zuowei," *Lishi yanjiu* (June 2008), 133.

9. Chiang Kai-shek diary, Hoover Institution Archives, March 4, 1943 (hereafter CKSD).

10. Wang Jianlang, "Xinren de liushi: cong Jiang Jieshi riji kan kangzhanhouqi de ZhongMei guanxi," *Jindaishi yanjiu* (March 2009), 62.

11. CKSD, March 27, 1943.

12. Ibid., September 2, 1943.

13. "Gao Indu guomin shu" [To the Indian people] in *Zongtong Jiang gong sixiang yanlun zongji* [Collection of the thought and speeches of President Chiang Kai-shek], www.chungcheng.org.tw/thought/class06/0019/0008.htm], 292 (hereafter ZT).

14. "Fangwen Indu de ganxiang yu duiyu Taiping zhanju de guancha" [Feelings on visiting India and viewpoint on the Pacific war situation], March 9, 1942), in ZT, 56–57.

15. Ibid., 57–58.

16. CKSD, April 16, 1943.

17. John Keswick files, Jardine Matheson archives collection [unclassified], Cambridge, UK.

18. The classic statement from Stilwell's point of view is Barbara Tuchman, *Stilwell and the American Experience in China* (New York: Macmillan, 1971), with the major response being Hans J. van de Ven, *War and Nationalism in China, 1925–45* (London: Routledge Curzon, 2003).

19. CKSD, June 30, 1943; September 19, 1943; September 25, 1943; October 1, 1943.

20. Ibid., October 3, 1943.

21. Ibid., May 16, 1943.

22. "Di si ci Nanyue junshi huiyi kaihui xunci" [Speech to the Fourth Nanyue Military Conference] February 10, 1944), ZT, 324.

23. Ibid.

24. Wang, citation of Chiang diary, August 29, 1942, "Xinren de liushi," 60.

25. Cai Dejin et al., ed., *Zhou Fohai riji* [Zhou Fohai diary], 2 vols. (Beijing: Beijing Shehui Kexue Chubanshe, 1986).

26. Ibid., December 20, 1941.

27. Ibid., June 22, 1941.

28. Ibid., September 22 and 23, 1941.

29. Ibid., December 10 and 13, 1941.

30. Ibid., December 11, 1941.

31. Ibid., December 20, 1941.

32. Ibid., February 7, 1941.

33. Ibid., February 7, 1942, and April 5, 1942.

34. Ibid., April 28, 1942.

35. Xu Guoqi, *China and the Great War* (Cambridge: Cambridge University Press, 2005).

36. Peter Perdue, *China Marches West* (Cambridge, MA: Harvard University Press, 2005).

37. Van de Ven, *War and Nationalism in China,* chapter 1.

38. Diana Lary, *Warlord Soldiers: Chinese Common Soldiers 1911–1937* (New York: Cambridge University Press, 1985), is one thoughtful study that addresses this problem for a slightly earlier era.

39. Aaron Moore, *Writing War: Soldiers Record the Japanese Empire* (Cambridge MA: Harvard University Press, 2013).

40. Li Tao, in Luo Gu, *Zhanzheng zhi MianYin* [India and Burma in war] (Shanghai, 1945), 2–3.

41. Luo Gu, *MianYin*, 6, 12–13, 18.

42. Ibid., 18.

43. Ibid., 4.

44. July 31, 1942, in ibid., 73.

45. Huang Yaowu, *Wode zhanzheng, 1944–1948* [My war], (Shenyang: Beifang lianhe chubanshe, 2010), 36, 40.

46. DBPO (Documents on British Policy Overseas), series 1, vol. 8: Britain and China, 1945–50), "Memorandum on Present China Situation and on British and American Policies in China," F 4171/186/10, July 7, 1945, sec. 15.

47. Tehyun Ma, "'The Common Aim of the Allied Powers': Social Policy and International Legitimacy in Wartime China, 1940–47," *Journal of Global History* 9, 2 (2014).

48. DBPO, series 1, vol. 2: Conference 1945, London, Washington, Moscow, September 16, 1945, 189).

CHAPTER 6

Worldly Medicine in Wartime China

An Exploration of Pearl Harbor's Unintended Consequences

Nicole Elizabeth Barnes

When Imperial Japanese Army (IJA) pilots dropped their bombs across the Pacific on December 7 and 8, 1941, Chinese immediately celebrated the certain arrival of their first fully committed allies in their battle against Japan. Known in China as the War of Resistance against Japan (*KangRi zhanzheng*), World War II began in Asia two years earlier than in Europe, four and a half years before the Japanese attacks of December 1941 linked the two regional wars. From July 7, 1937, until the Allies declared war on Japan in December 1941, China faced one of the world's most powerful militaries alone.[1] During these lonely years, the Nationalist government lost nearly one-third of its territory and 80 percent of its tax base. In the first few months of the war, the IJA marched very quickly down China's eastern coast and won a string of victories. By December 1937, six months into the war, the Japanese held the old imperial capital Beijing (known at the time as Beiping), the industrial city Tianjin, the Nationalist capital Nanjing, and China's most commercially developed city, Shanghai. General Chiang Kai-shek had committed his best-trained and most loyal troops to the defense of Shanghai and lost nearly three-quarters of them in the protracted battle.[2] It seemed nearly inevitable that China would fall to Japan.

Two things that the Japanese did not count on ultimately saved China: the strength of Chinese resistance, and the strength of the Allies who finally came to China's aid after the Pacific bombings. China's resistance unfolded on two fronts.

Across the North China plain, Communist fighters continually assailed Japanese troops and recruited Chinese villagers to their ranks. They developed the guerrilla tactics of entrenchment in the countryside and stealth attack that later brought them to victory in China's Civil War in 1949. In the southwest the head of the Nationalist Party and officially recognized leader of China, General Chiang Kai-shek, ruled his country from two provisional capitals: Wuhan, which fell to the Japanese in October 1938, and Chongqing, which remained under Chinese control for the duration of the war. It took Japanese bombings in the Pacific to bring the second crucial piece to China's aid: the powerful assistance of new allies. These new allies brought more military aid to China, including advanced weaponry, and eventually forced Japan to surrender with the atomic bombings of Hiroshima and Nagasaki on August 6 and 9, 1945.

The arrival of the Allies opened a new theater of World War II—the Pacific Theater—that tied the Eastern and Western Hemispheres together and brought China from its position as an isolated and lonely resister against an internal invader to that of a central player in the war. China thus became one of the Big Four allies, alongside the United States, the United Kingdom, and the Soviet Union.[3] From this new position, Chinese leaders celebrated their contributions to a global war against fascism in which Germany, Italy, and Japan were all equally recognized as threatening enemies. Because they recognized the coming shift in war alliances, both the Nationalists and the Communists acknowledged news of the attacks with some relief, as seen in both written communiqués and comic magazines.

While military aid from China's new allies had important effects on the outcome of the war, within China the surge in charitable donations from newly allied countries produced a more immediately visible result that saved countless lives and allowed the country to emerge from the eight-year war in a much stronger position. The Japanese invasion had triggered a terrible crisis in China's nascent military and civilian health systems. Japan's conquest of Nanjing placed China's largest military hospital in enemy hands, and its doctors and nurses had to join civilian refugees in a panicked flight to the southwest. The number of wounded soldiers quickly overwhelmed all available field hospitals, and dire shortages of both available supplies and medical workers led to high rates of infection that transformed otherwise treatable battle wounds into death threats. The cash-strapped Nationalist government could not provide adequate funding, so for the first five years of the war both military and civilian health organizations survived thanks to charitable donations from Overseas Chinese, predominantly those in Southeast Asia.[4] The Pacific bombings and resultant Pacific War simultaneously closed off access to funds from these Overseas Chinese communities that now faced their own military crises as the Japanese rapidly expanded their empire across Southeast Asia after debilitating the US Navy fleet. At the same time, however, the Pacific War connected China to new sources of donations and government-sponsored medical aid from the United States and Britain. Coupled with the labor of Chinese health workers and a small number of foreign volunteer workers, this aid fueled a remarkable expansion in health services that kept Chinese soldiers and civilians alive through the deadliest war in world history.

The growth of China's civilian and military medical systems in a time of extreme duress was both unanticipated and unprecedented. In extending the war to the Pacific, leaders of the Imperial Japanese Army intended to seize necessary resources to fuel ongoing warfare and secure victory but instead attracted their most formidable foes to China's side. The stories of the military battles and bombings that ensued are well known, but the story of what happened inside China as a direct result of the Pacific War is seldom recognized as a central factor in China's ultimate victory.

This chapter contends that the Pacific bombing campaign altered the course of history by bringing crucial resources to Chinese health systems and thereby granting China the strength to survive the last few years of the war. It begins by exploring Chinese people's immediate recognition of the bombings as a potentially lifesaving turn of events in political and popular publications. These publications show their intense anger at Japan, which contradicts the notion that Japan would have been able to build a Pan-Asian solidarity movement that included Asia's largest and most populous country. The chapter then considers the impact of the December 1941 Pacific bombing campaign on China's medical system, arguing that the period of greatest advancement occurred in 1942, precisely when increased foreign aid poured into China while Allied soldiers kept IJA soldiers locked down in bloody battles across the Pacific.

PUBLIC RESPONSES

Chinese understood the December 1941 bombings as a welcome catalyst of truly global warfare. More precisely, they interpreted them as the key event that would bring about the long-anticipated aid of Western allies in their deadly battle with the Imperial Japanese Army.[5] Although they sympathized with the plight of their fellow Asians who suffered in the attacks across the Pacific, they celebrated the fact that the bombings shook the slumbering United States out of its isolation and brought the combined power of the US and British militaries to China's aid. This attitude showed quite clearly in the Chinese Communist Party's public and party directives regarding the Pacific War, as well as in popular comics of the era.

On December 8, future chairman and then supreme leader of the Communist Party Mao Zedong first received news of the bombings and proposed that the top party leaders, the Politburo, hold an immediate meeting to develop a public statement. First published in the party's official newspaper, *Liberation Daily* (*Jiefang ribao*), on December 9, 1941, the statement began, "The Japanese fascist government declared war on Britain and the United States and bombed Hawaii, the Philippines, Hong Kong, and Singapore. Its army landed in northern Malaysia."[6] Excluding only Guam and Wake Island from the targeted locales, the statement interpreted the campaign as an attack against American and British colonial territories; therefore, although Asian and Pacific Islanders were the primary victims, the statement focused on the American and British declarations of war against Japan. Despite living in caves in the remote northwest, Communist leaders possessed sophisticated knowledge of world affairs. Future premier Zhou Enlai was stationed in the Nationalist capital Chongqing as the Communist Party liaison, and he likely wired the news to the Communist headquarters in Yan'an.

Specific words mattered. The Politburo deliberated for two straight days of meetings, and Mao edited the statement one last time before making it public. It likened Japan to Italy and Germany with the claim that "this aggressive act by the Japanese fascists is . . . exactly like the acts of aggression of the German and Italian fascists against Europe and the Soviet Union." Tying Japan to Europe's two belligerent, fascist regimes helped to justify the European Allies' declaration of war against Japan. It furthermore demonstrated that China, for many years the sole opponent of fascist Japan, stood in a geopolitical position equivalent to that of the European Allies. Although China's official ally status had not yet been determined, the Communist Party's statement further linked China to the United States and Britain in a "just war of liberation in defense of independence, freedom, and democracy."[7]

When read in the context of internal divisions between the Communists and Nationalists—who had ceased to collaborate after the so-called New Fourth Army Incident of January 1941—this public statement illustrates the renegade Communist Party's attempt to usurp the role of the Nationalist Party and speak for the country. The Communist Party's internal directive showed this even more clearly. Declaring the Pacific War "a just liberation war," it called for the realization of a "military alliance against Japan of China, Britain, the United States, and the other Pacific countries."[8] This was not in fact the Communist Party's decision to make but a declaration that belonged solely to the Nationalist Party, yet making such public statements during the war allowed the Communist Party to rewrite history and strengthen its political legitimacy after it gained political power in October 1949.

Comics provide another means of analyzing Chinese responses to the Pacific bombings, and they show a widespread feeling of relief and jubilee resulting from the assumption that the Americans would easily defeat Japan. In late 1941 the *Huacui* (華萃) *Pictorial*, drawn in Luoyang (Henan Province) and published in Xi'an,

Shaanxi Province, devoted an entire twenty-page issue to comics on the Pearl Harbor attack. The cartoons showed a nuanced understanding of geopolitics; one cartoon depicted the United States prepared to violate its neutrality policy while another showed an outsized American man using a US Navy ship to spank a Japanese child, with the headline "We want revenge."[9] While these cartoons appear to miss the main point about the December attacks that this book highlights—they were not an American story, but rather a Pacific story—they merely depict the most obvious aspects of the Pacific War. In actuality, China benefited not only from the belated arrival of powerful allies in late 1941 that the Communist leaders and popular comics celebrated but, more important, from the IJA's tactical shift to Southeast Asia and the Pacific. Japanese troops' move south produced a two-year respite during which little fighting occurred on Chinese soil.[10] Taken together, the entrance of the Allies into China's war with Japan *and* the lull in military conflict gave China a long-anticipated yet unexpected opportunity to focus on rebuilding society and taking care of people's basic needs, including their medical needs. As the next section shows, this rest period may well have saved China from conquest.

One cartoon makes the same ideological move that the Communist Party Politburo had done by linking Japan to fascist Germany. Under the caption "This is why he is cheeky and impudent," it depicts Adolf Hitler's hand winding a jack-in-the-box labeled "Hitler's puppet," out of which pops Japanese general Tōjō Hideki. The puppet Tōjō holds a knife labeled "Pacific War" and reaches for Uncle Sam, who is walking toward Tōjō armed for battle with a superior weapon (see page 126).[11] The image appears to be an attempt to remove the sting of having been invaded by "younger brother" Japan, the country that, according to the Sinocentric worldview, ought to have remained deferent to China into perpetuity. Like the other images, it relies on a demeaning form of racialization to achieve this end. The cartoonist debases Tōjō by using the animal form of the pronoun "*ta*" (with the ox radical) to refer to him, rather than the human form of the character with the person radical. Tōjō appears in classic racist caricature, with enormous buckteeth and tiny squinty eyes. The caption implies that Hitler's support is the only reason that the Japanese exhibit any bravery on the battlefield, even though that very sponsorship is what renders them less than human, reduced to the status of a beast of burden sent to do the bidding of a fascist dictator.

Another comic also illustrates a Chinese tendency to infantilize and demonize Japanese military men in a manner akin to American racialization during the war.[12] Titled "Mistaken Vision," this cartoon shows a tiny Japanese soldier looking at an enormous American soldier through a periscope. The cartoonist renders this situation humorous by labeling the periscope "made in Germany" and depicting the Japanese man holding it backwards, such that it shows the giant man in miniature. The Japanese soldier exclaims, in his ignorance, "I didn't realize he was so

Anonymous, "Suoyi Ta shangdan fangsi" [This is why he is cheeky and impudent], *Huacui Pictorial* No. 11 (1941): 9.

Anonymous, "Shiguan de cuojue" [Mistaken vision], *Huacui Pictorial* No. 11 (1941): 5.

small" (see page 127).[13] The cartoon pokes fun at Japanese for the supposed small size of their bodies and mental faculties and simultaneously lauds Germany as the source of military equipment and the United States as the land of formidable soldiers. It also urges readers to scoff at Japan for having dragged itself into war with a foe that clearly overpowers it.

Such humor relied on anti-Japanese feeling among Chinese readers, who plausibly gained a sense of relief from the knowledge that Japan had overstepped its bounds and now faced an ally capable of squashing it like a bug. A later cartoon in the same issue mirrors this sentiment. It depicts a miniature Japanese marine arriving in American waters on a reconnaissance mission, only to make the belated realization that the United States is massive, calm, and ready for battle.[14] Although Japanese visions of Pan-Asian solidarity did inspire some Asian nationalists, the intense anti-Japanese feelings of many Chinese during the war belie Japanese claims that imperial expansion could create a "Greater East Asia Co-Prosperity Sphere." Rather, these cartoons show the truth of China's most popular motto during the war: *kangzhan daodi* (抗戰到底), "resist to the end."

The powerful dislike that the Chinese had for their invaders during the war helps to explain why they turned so willingly toward their Caucasian allies after the Pacific bombings. China's extension of open arms to the United States and United Kingdom was not automatic. Both the Nationalist and Communist Parties criticized Western imperialism and resented how much their country had suffered from the unequal treaties that Western nations—including the UK and United States—had imposed on them. Even as members of the Big Four allies, Chiang Kai-shek and Winston Churchill disliked one another quite strongly (although jocular FDR disarmed the generalissimo).[15] Yet the Chinese so resented the Japanese for invading their country that they were willing to collaborate with their erstwhile foes in order to defeat the IJA. While the official communiqués of the Communist Party expressed this willingness in geopolitical terms, popular comics expressed it in emotional terms that resonated with a broad public.

Once this new partnership between China and the Allies was secure, it had a tremendous impact on China's public health and military medicine systems. Although medical advancements did not directly determine the outcome of the war, they certainly rendered China strong enough to endure it. In this way, the December 1941 bombing campaign, designed to ensure victory for the Japanese Empire, in fact spelled its doom. While in the short run the bombings helped the Japanese military expand its empire across Asia, when viewed from a longer perspective it is clear that the bombings across the Pacific began to spell the end for imperial Japan. Through a series of unforeseen circumstances, the Pacific bombings sparked a process that led instead to China's victory.

WORLDLY MEDICINE IN WARTIME CHINA

After the Pacific War began and China joined the Big Four, the international community of health philanthropy that contributed to China's medical needs expanded from its previous focus on Overseas Chinese communities to include non-Chinese communities around the world. Chinese health officials tapped into a new stream of generous funding, particularly from the United States and United Kingdom, that fueled a rapid expansion of the civilian and military health systems. This was particularly the case in 1942, when fighting in China slowed to a crawl while the IJA requisitioned its soldiers for battles in the Pacific. In that single year, China's National Health Administration delivered more than 9 million vaccines and inoculations against smallpox, cholera, and typhoid and expanded the network of health stations across southern China.[16]

This growth also transferred power from grassroots organizations with more inclusive politics and shifted it toward more hierarchical organizations. This had an effect as far away as in the United States. Perhaps most important, Japan's conquests in the early years of the Pacific War furthered China's economic isolation, prompting a search for quinine substitutes that ultimately led to the chemical isolation of artemisinin in the postwar era. These unintended consequences of the December attacks had a sum effect of helping the Chinese populace to survive the onslaught of an invasive war on their own territory and end the eight-year war with a stronger health system than at its start.

The first impact of the Pacific War in China manifested two months prior to the December 1941 bombing campaign. Air raids in the wartime capital of Chongqing entered a two-year hiatus after September 21, 1941, as the Japanese Air Service transferred pilots to begin training and planning for the December raids. Japanese bomber pilots returned to China's wartime capital in early summer 1943, but after August 23 of that year the intensity of the Pacific War forced them out of the Chongqing skies for good. Their departure granted people a break from the harrowing air raids that had left more than 15,000 dead and 20,000 wounded in the most-bombed city in China.[17] The slowing and then cessation of air raids had a dramatic impact on public health, not only because the air raid wounded ceased to fill the sick beds and hallways of all the local clinics and hospitals but also because public health workers no longer had to curtail their routine duties in order to perform emergency air raid relief. Previously, maternal and child health workers tended to fewer deliveries during air raid season, when the bombing victims commanded their labor and medical supplies.[18]

For health officials in the wartime capital, for whom air raids had constituted a more significant obstacle than toe-to-toe fighting on battlefields, this welcome change provided an opportunity to focus on their primary goal of promoting aseptic midwifery. China's high infant and maternal death rates—200 per thousand and 10 per thousand, respectively—had been a focal point of discussion during the August 1937 Conference of Far Eastern Countries on Rural Hygiene, held in Bandung, Indonesia. Attendees noted that China's suspected (though not fully documented) death rate of children under the age of five—a shocking 45 percent—was twice that of rural Yugoslavia, signaling dire circumstances that they blamed on "old style" midwives.[19]

Dr. Yang Chongrui (Marion Yang, 1891–1983), a highly educated, politically astute, and proactive midwifery specialist, agreed with this assessment and did everything in her power to curb maternal and infant deaths. Educated at various missionary schools, including the precursor to China's preeminent Peking Union Medical College (PUMC), where she later taught, Dr. Yang cofounded and then directed both the National Midwifery Board and the First National Midwifery School in Beijing in 1929. She created the standards for training new students and retraining practicing midwives in aseptic practices, and she successfully trained thousands of women over the course of her career.[20] From 1942 to 1945 Yang served as head of the National Health Administration's Division of Maternity and Child Health. The administration had moved to Chongqing during the war, and from its mountain redoubt just outside the city (Geleshan) it continued to manage the nation's health with a skeletal staff and reduced funding.

Inspired by Yang Chongrui as much as by their country's alarming death rates, Chongqing health officials built eight Maternal and Child Health (MCH) clinics by October 1940.[21] The Chongqing Bureau of Public Health (CBPH) planned to hire one female doctor and four midwives for each of the eight clinics, sponsored in part by a per-clinic start-up fund of 9,000 yuan from the central government's Executive Yuan.[22] Once the eight clinics were in full operation, in the single year of 1940 their collective staff performed over 9,000 pre- and postnatal exams, 450 prenatal home visits, over 1,100 births, over 1,100 gynecological exams, and over 1,600 children's health exams.[23] All of these services were supported by the government and provided to the public free of charge. While these numbers may not seem impressive if compared with today's statistics, at the time this level of service put Chongqing at the forefront of modern maternity care in China.

This impressive work might have been even more impressive had the staff not had to face the multiple challenges that air raids posed. During the same year of 1940, two of the eight clinics burned down in raids that employed incendiary bombs, and staff at two others spent most of their time dealing with air raid wounded rather than their usual duties. The remaining four clinics operated out of substandard premises with insufficient equipment—two in temples and two in a school.[24] These challenges demonstrate the limits of government support during a war and help to explain why the best that wartime health officials could do was still woefully inadequate. They also underscore the impact that the cessation of air raids had on Chongqing when the Japanese bomber pilots were ordered to operate in the Pacific.

Once the air raids finally ceased, the CBPH initiated plans for a Maternity Hospital (Chanfuke Yiyuan) in 1942, and finally opened it in 1944. The largest MCH facility in the city, this hospital boasted thirty beds and three departments (Obstetrics, Gynecology, and Pediatrics) and employed two physicians, two midwives, and five nurses. Women sought its services immediately, and it became Chongqing's single most popular site of medical care for women.[25] In a bid to allot more patient beds to this well-used hospital, in May 1945 health officials merged it with the Chongqing Municipal Hospital, where it boasted forty-five beds as the Obstetrics and Gynecology Department.[26] Although even this new hospital did not provide enough MCH services for the city's estimated 766,000 residents, its establishment illustrates the impact that the Pacific War had on increasing available MCH services in unoccupied China. It further demonstrates the dedication of local officials to the cause. City officials had managed to fund the Maternity Hospital during a period of runaway inflation, at the same time as a collection of local magnates had failed to raise sufficient funds for the same goal.[27]

Another impressive form of wartime growth in public health services occurred not in Chongqing but throughout Sichuan Province. From its founding in May 1939 through November 1945, the Sichuan Provincial Health Administration (SPHA) established County Health Centers (CHC) in 131 of Sichuan's 139 counties. Director Chen Zhiqian (1903–2000) returned to his native province to head the new organization, and from its headquarters in the provincial capital Chengdu he courted enough foreign funding to grant himself leeway to defy his superiors' orders. A dedicated advocate of basic health services in rural communities, Dr. Chen bristled at the requirement that his home province's first official health administration limit itself to air aid relief.[28] Instead, he satisfied this requirement but went far beyond its confines. Like officials in the nation's wartime capital, he opened new MCH facilities in Sichuan's provincial capital, and he built a network of rural health services throughout the province. Each of the 131 CHCs employed one to two physicians, two nurses, and three midwives, and Chen worked to distribute them evenly throughout the province so as to deliver health services to people who lived in the most remote areas.[29]

Even more so than health officials in Chongqing, Chen Zhiqian relied quite heavily on foreign charitable donations to fund the work of the SPHA. The Pacific bombings and resultant war changed funding networks to Chen's benefit, since his administration received a large amount of funding from the American Red Cross (ARC), the organization that came to dominate charitable funding for public health in China. Whereas before the Pacific War the American Bureau for

Medical Aid to China (ABMAC) provided 70 percent of outside funding to the Chinese Red Cross, from 1942 onward the American Red Cross provided this same percentage of funding.[30]

Founded in September 1937 by three American-born Chinese in New York City—Dr. Frank Co Tui, Dr. Farn B. Chu, and Mr. Joseph C. Wei—ABMAC had the best qualities of both a large charity and a grassroots organization. With China's first lady Song Meiling as its honorary chair, China's ambassador to the United States Hu Shi as a prominent sponsor, and renowned Chinese-American actress Anna May Wong as a performer at fundraising banquets, ABMAC raised millions of dollars. ABMAC's illustrious connections quickly established its reputation as a reliable charity and attracted contributions from Overseas Chinese organizations in Cuba, Canada, Mexico, Brazil, and Chile. ABMAC also succeeded because it was deeply imbedded in local communities. Its first collection campaigns employed an army of Chinese-American high school and college students who walked the streets of New York collecting pocket change in tin cans. During the Christmas season of 1937—the inaugural year of the war in China, when world leaders turned a blind eye to the Japanese invasion—these streetside collections had yielded $8,000. Within three years, ABMAC had established branches in two hundred locations across the United States. It also ran primarily on volunteer labor, which allowed it to maintain an impressively low overhead cost; throughout the war ABMAC donated nearly $10 million in medical aid and supplies to Chinese health organizations while its operating costs barely exceeded $100,000 (equal to roughly 1 percent of total donations).[31]

Progressive racial politics also distinguished ABMAC among foreign charities. Ethnic Chinese, both nationals and Overseas Chinese, held the most powerful roles while non-Chinese occupied advisory positions. Even in promotional materials that featured Caucasian partners, Chinese appeared in a supervisory and legitimizing role. Another indication of the organization's progressive racial politics distinguished it from the American Red Cross. When ABMAC launched its mobile blood bank in the early 1940s to deliver fresh blood to wounded Chinese soldiers, it established its first collection banks in the United States and accepted African American donors. ABMAC leaders cited the fact that there is no biological difference in the blood of African Americans and European Americans. They did this at a time when the ARC, bowing to US racism, refused African American blood donors, making the collection of blood for the China field an important moment in US race history.[32]

This distinction between ABMAC and the ARC meant that when the ARC began to dominate charitable public health funding in China after the Pacific bombings, tensions arose between local and foreign workers in Chinese health organizations. Major General Zhou Meiyu, who directed the training of military nurses for the Chinese Red Cross Medical Relief Corps and the Emergency Medical Services Training School, reported several instances of such tension in her oral history interviews. Conducted in her postwar home of Taipei, Taiwan, in 1985, the interviews clearly reflect Zhou's memories as refracted through many decades of life experience. Nonetheless, she recalled with apparent clarity a heated disagreement that she had with American military personnel stationed in Guizhou Province in southwest China over food. Chinese suffered from severe food shortages throughout the war due to economic blockade and runaway inflation. Americans stationed in China, in contrast, enjoyed such generous funding that they failed to understand the dire straits of their fellows in arms, whose severe malnutrition compounded their wounds in virtually every case. When Major General Zhou asked a man of similar rank in the US military to help out by offering some of their food to sell on the market, or funds with which to purchase food for her wounded soldiers, the American officer suggested that he could just give "leftovers" from their mess hall to the Chinese. Infuriated by the suggestion that her charges merited nothing better than unwanted, discarded victuals, Zhou argued with the US Army major until he refused to give even that. Zhou recalled that after this argument, the American soldiers habitually tossed uneaten leftovers into the gutters outside their mess halls, wherefrom impoverished locals picked out, washed, and reheated the edible portions. Seeing her compatriots reduced to this animalistic behavior only irritated Zhou more, and she found the American soldiers' wastefulness in the face of obvious want galling. Although Chinese foot soldiers, the majority of whom came from poor rural families, received little to no respect in local society at the time, Zhou insisted that "in their homes, they are precious. Even though they are sick, we still have to treat them as people."[33] Her American peers' inability to comprehend and share her compassion for the malnourished soldiers made a strong, bitter impression that she recalled decades later.

American charitable funding that came to China through official channels contrasted greatly with the behavior of individual US Army soldiers stationed there. Zhou recalled that American donations greatly increased after the Pacific bombing campaign and that the American Red Cross in-kind donations of medical supplies piled up in the local warehouses. She remembered measuring donated quinine pills by the ton.[34] This made the Chinese Red Cross rather unique, since for most other civilian and military health units antimalarial medications remained in short supply throughout the war. The general shortage became dire after the Imperial Japanese Army conquered the Dutch East Indies in March 1942, which placed 90 percent of the world's quinine supply in the exclusive grasp of the Japanese. At the time, quinine was the most effective prophylactic drug to combat malaria, one of the most problematic scourges of soldiers stationed anywhere in Africa, Asia, or the Pacific islands. Since the disease is endemic in China, it was also a major public health threat to civilians.

Within the borders of an increasingly isolated China, the scarcity of quinine prompted research into local medicinal plants that possessed antimalarial properties. The most prominent and celebrated of these was *dichroa febrifuga* (*huang changshan*), reported in a 1943 article in the *China Medical Magazine* (*Zhonghua yixue zazhi*) to be one-fifth as powerful as quinine in treating malaria. This success rate sufficed to inspire continued research into the 1950s and earned the plant the common name "Chinese quinine."[35] The National Health Administration and the Central Political Institute supported research on *changshan*, but other scientists tested different drugs; in 1945 the *Chinese Medical Journal* reported successful treatment of malaria with pills containing the powdered root of cat's claw (*caeselpinia sepiaria*, Chinese: *yunshi*).[36] This research was crucial because producing other quinine substitutes was extremely challenging. For example, atabrine, an antimalarial synthetic drug originally produced in Germany, comprised twenty-three chemical compounds and required forty-six pounds of raw materials—most of which China would have had to import—to produce one pound of the drug.[37]

This laboratory research had long-term effects that remain noticeable today. Researchers did not stop at *changshan* and cat's claw but continued to search for even more effective antimalarial plants, particularly during the Vietnam War (1955–1975) when representatives of North Vietnam's Communist soldiers asked China's Chairman Mao Zedong for help. So much of the fighting occurred in dense, humid jungles that Vietnamese soldiers were succumbing to malaria at very high rates. To help their ally, China's People's Liberation Army (PLA) launched a top-secret laboratory research program, dubbed Project 523, to search for an effective antimalarial drug. By 1971 the research team had discovered an effective means of isolating the active component of the sweet wormwood plant (Latin name *Artemisia annua*, Chinese name *qinghao*), which soon became the most effective malaria drug in the world.[38] In 2015 Tu Youyou won a Nobel Prize for her role in leading this collaborative research team. Originally hailed for its ability to combat malaria in a world where resistance to chloroquine imperiled malaria treatment efforts, artemisinin earned the accolades of the World Health Organization (WHO). Unfortunately, its wide use has led to the rise of certain strains of malaria that are resistant to artemisinin, primarily in Southeast Asia and South America. In January 2011 the WHO launched the Global Plan for Artemisinin Resistance Containment, and it continues to monitor the situation closely. Artemisinin remains the most common drug for malaria patients around the world, and its discovery owes at least in part to the original search for quinine substitutes after Japan's conquest of Indonesia in the spring of 1942.

CONCLUSION

Unexpectedly, the bombs that dropped across the Pacific in December 1941 had many implications for China's health services. These effects extended as far as American race relations, the remotest areas of Sichuan Province in southwestern China, and laboratory research on medicinal plants that could prevent or treat malaria. Medicine and public health may seem an unlikely vantage point from which to examine a war, but the traces of this newly global warfare show up very clearly in relationships of medical exchange and health philanthropy. The story of China's internal medical developments also marks this moment as a Pacific history because it illustrates the depth of connection between mainland Asia and the Pacific islands. More precisely, the attacks across the Pacific enveloped that region in the war and greatly diminished the relationships that Chinese had theretofore enjoyed with their Pacific Asian neighbors, and therefore profoundly altered the structure of Chinese medical aid. Whereas prior to December 1941 China received medical donations from across the Pacific, after the Pacific bombings Chinese health agencies relied almost exclusively on aid from the United States and UK.

China sorely needed every dime of this funding because it suffered so greatly during the war that broke nearly every record. China lost twice as many civilians as died in the European Holocaust. Military deaths were on top of this number, making China's total losses second only to those of the Soviet Union. Given the severity of their suffering, it is not surprising that Chinese people celebrated the news of the Pacific bombings and sensed Japan's imminent defeat. It turns out that Japanese prime minister Konoe Fumimaro (1891–1945) had the same premonition of defeat, though for him it produced despair rather than elation. After ceding office to Tōjō Hideki just two months before the bombing campaign, Konoe had a deep sense of foreboding after the bombings even as his country celebrated. On December 8, 1941, he reportedly said, "It is a terrible thing that has happened. I know that a tragic defeat awaits us at the end. I can feel it. Our luck will not last more than two or three months at best."[39] Konoe's prescient remarks now define a significant chapter in world history.

NOTES

1. The Soviet Union did provide very crucial military aid but did not officially declare war against Japan until Britain and the United States did. See Baijia Zhang, "China's Quest for Foreign Military Aid," in Mark Peattie et al., eds., *The Battle for China: Essays on the Military History of the Sino-Japanese War of 1937–1945* (Stanford, CA: Stanford University Press, 2011), 288–293.

2. S. C. M. Paine, *The Wars for Asia, 1911–1949* (New York: Cambridge University Press, 2012), 133.

3. See Rana Mitter, *Forgotten Ally: China's World War II, 1937–1945* (New York: Houghton Mifflin, 2013), and his chapter in this volume.

4. Chinese Muslims played an important role in this exchange. See John Chen, "Just Like Old Friends": The Significance of Southeast Asia to Modern Chinese Islam," *SOJOURN: Journal of Social Issues in Southeast Asia* 31, 3 (November 2016): 685–742, esp. 707–722.

5. Nationalist Party leader Chiang Kai-shek surmised that Western allies would not stand idly by while Japan conquered the largest part of mainland Asia, but it took much longer than anticipated to receive substantial aid. James C. Hsiung, "The War and After: World Politics in Historical Context," in James C. Hsiung and Steven I. Levine, eds., *China's Bitter Victory: The War with Japan, 1937–1945* (Armonk, NY: M. E. Sharpe, 1992), 300.

6. "Declaration of the Chinese Communist Party Regarding the War in the Pacific," in Stuart R. Schram, ed., *Mao's Road to Power: Revolutionary Writings, 1912–1949, Volume VII: New Democracy, 1939–1941* (Armonk, New York: M. E. Sharpe, 2005), 844.

7. Ibid.

8. "Directive of the Central Committee of the Chinese Communist Party Regarding the Pacific Anti-Japanese United Front," December 9, 1941, in Schram, ed., *Mao's Road to Power*, 846.

9. Anonymous, "Luo zai Zhenzhugang de zhadan fencui Meiguo renmin de huanxiang" [Bombs dropping on Pearl Harbor shatter the American people's fantasies], *Huacui Pictorial* No. 11 (1941), 7; and Anonymous, "Women yao fuchou" [We want revenge], *Huacui Pictorial* No. 11 (1941), 12.

10. Diana Lary, *The Chinese People at War: Human Suffering and Social Transformation, 1937–1945* (New York: Cambridge University Press, 2010), 112.

11. Anonymous, "Suoyi Ta shangdan fangsi" [This is why he is cheeky and impudent], *Huacui Pictorial* No. 11 (1941), 9.

12. John Dower, *War without Mercy: Race and Power in the Pacific War* (New York: Pantheon, 1986).

13. Anonymous, "Shiguan de cuojue" (Mistaken vision), *Huacui Pictorial* No. 11 (1941), 5.

14. Anonymous, "Untitled," *Huacui Pictorial* No. 11 (1941), 14.

15. Mitter, *Forgotten Ally*.

16. For a detailed map of these health stations, see John R. Watt, *Saving Lives in Wartime China: How Medical Reformers Build Modern Healthcare Systems Amid War and Epidemics, 1928–1945* (Leiden, Netherlands: Brill, 2014), 230.

17. Edna Tow, "The Great Bombing of Chongqing and the Anti-Japanese War, 1937–1945," in Mark Peattie, Edward Drea, and Hans Van de Ven, eds., *The Battle for China: Essays on the Military History of the Sino-Japanese War of 1937–1945* (Stanford, CA: Stanford University Press, 2011), 257.

18. Nicole Elizabeth Barnes, *Intimate Communities: Wartime Healthcare and the Birth of Modern China, 1937–1945* (Oakland: University of California Press, 2018).

19. Watt, *Saving Lives in Wartime China*, 68–69.

20. Tina Phillips Johnson, *Childbirth in Republican China: Delivering Modernity* (Lanham, MD: Lexington Books, 2011); Marion Yang files, boxes 76 and 77, China Medical Board, Inc., Rockefeller Archive Center (hereafter RAC), Tarrytown, New York.

21. CBPH Work Report, January–June 1940, Chongqing Municipal Archives (hereafter CMA), Chongqing, China, 66-1-3, 171; CBPH Work Report, 1940, CMA, 66-1-3, "Table of Private and Public Hospitals in Chongqing Proper and in the Suburbs," August 1940; and CBPH Work Report, September 1940–February 1941, CMA, 66-1-3, 198.

22. CBPH Work Report, 1938, CMA, 66-1-2, 189.

23. CBPH Work Report, September 1940–February 1941, CMA, 66-1-3, 200.

24. CBPH Work Report, January–June 1940, CMA, 66-1-3, 172; and CPBH Work Report, September 1940–February 1941, CMA, 66-1-3, 199.

25. For an analysis of the reasons for this, see Nicole Elizabeth Barnes, "Disease in the Capital: Nationalist Health Services and the 'Sick (Wo)man of East Asia' in Wartime Chongqing," *European Journal of East Asian Studies* 11 (December 2012), 283–303.

26. CBPH Work Report, October 1946, Academia Historica Archives, Taipei, Taiwan, 90-183, 1b.

27. A group that included Minister of Finance H. H. Kung, Minister of Education Chen Lifu, and twenty other social benefactors had wanted to raise 900,000 yuan to build a maternity hospital (560,000 yuan for construction and an additional 340,000 yuan for monthly operational costs) but failed where the government succeeded. *The Past Four Years in the Women's Welfare Society of the Wartime Capital* (*Sinian lai zhi peidu funü fuli she*) (Nanjing: China Women's Welfare Society, 1946), 2–3.

28. "Report of Committee on Health and Medical Care," submitted to the Commission on Investigation and Planning of Relief and Rehabilitation of the Executive Yuan, July 1, 1944, Chongqing, folder 156, box 22, CMB, RAC, 1, 3.

29. Nicole Elizabeth Barnes, "Serving the People: Chen Zhiqian and the Sichuan Provincial Health Administration, 1939–1945," in David Luesink, William Schneider, and Zhang Daqing, eds., *China and the Globalization of Biomedicine* (Rochester, NY: University of Rochester Press, 2019.)

30. *Chinese Red Cross* (Nanjing: Executive Yuan Media Bureau, 1947), 10; Shanghai Municipal Library.

31. John R. Watt, *A Friend in Deed: ABMAC and the Republic of China, 1937–1987* (New York: ABMAC, 1992), 2–5; *Medicine on a Mission: A History of the American Bureau for Medical Aid to China, 1937–1954* (New York: ABMAC Headquarters, 1954), Section I, 15.

32. Wayne Soon, "Blood, Soymilk, and Vitality: The Wartime Origins of Blood Banking in China, 1943–1945," *Bulletin of the History of Medicine* 90, 3 (2016), 424–454.

33. Chang Peng-yuan, interviewer, and Lo Jiu-rung, recorder, *Zhou Meiyu xiansheng fangwen jilu* [*The reminiscences of Professor Chow Mei-yu*] (Oral History Series No. 47) (Taipei: Academia Sinica Institute of Modern History, 1993), 62–63.

34. Ibid., 62, 100.

35. Liu Shoushan, ed., *Zhongyao yanjiu wenxian zhaiyao* [Summary of research documents on Chinese medicines, 1820–1961], vol. 1 (Beijing: Kexue chubanshe, 1975), 631, 640–641.

36. *Summary of Research Documents*, 75. On NHA support of *changshan* research, see Jin

Baoshan, "*Zhongyi zhongyao sheshi zhi tuixing qingxing*" [The current situation of improving facilities for Chinese medicine], in *Weishengshu dafu xunwen an* [National Health Administration consultative responses] (Chongqing: Datong Publishing House, 1943), September 30, 1943.

37. Helen Kennedy Stevens and Ruth H Block, "The American Bureau for Medical Aid to China: A Survey of China's Medical and Health Problems and the Progress Made by the Chinese Government in Providing for the Health of the Nation," November 1943, folder 62, box 9, CMB,, RAC, n.p.

38. JC Fu, "Artemisinin and Chinese Medicine as Tu Science," *Endeavour* 41, 3 (September 2017), 127–135.

39. Cited in Paine, *Wars for Asia*, 283.

CHAPTER 7

Pearl Harbor and the Asian Cultural Turn

Ethan Mark

Our story begins in Batavia, capital of the colony known as the Netherlands East Indies, in the autumn of 1931. We now know this place as Jakarta, capital of the independent state of Indonesia. But at the time, the Dutch were still firmly in control of the archipelago—as they had been for more than 300 years. Inspired by anticolonial struggles of the peoples of India, China, the Middle East, and elsewhere, a movement for a free Indonesia had begun just four years earlier, but it was making little headway in the face of stiff Dutch suppression. These were dark times for Indonesian nationalists, made all the darker by the pall cast over the world by the Great Depression, whose effects were by now being felt as much in the Netherlands Indies as they were in Amsterdam or New York. Assessing the moment in a newspaper essay, a young outspoken member of the new Indonesian nationalist movement named Sanusi Pané pondered the way forward for his people. Pané's description of the challenges confronting Indonesians went far beyond the question of how to overcome Dutch colonial domination to the broader question of what shape the future "Indonesia" should take. Strikingly, in so doing, he highlighted a crisis in the very economic, political, and cultural foundations of the Western-led modern world itself.

> In Europe traditional political and economic forms come crashing down, new ideas and ideals arise and collide against one another with a great noise, and are in turn mercilessly ground to dust. There is an intense and bitter struggle over principles, a restless search for new life values, there is a hellish racket, mistrust and envy between peoples, classes, and groups, a desperate

> and chaotic situation reigns in nearly all areas of life. With a stentorian voice, Russia preaches new thoughts and principles and incites all proletarians to a bloody revolution against the hated capitalism, with the aim of establishing a "dictatorship of the masses" upon the rubble of the old society. America lays the foundations for a new civilization with materialist-mystical tendencies and ethical and aesthetic norms that deviate from the old. It exports the products of the Hollywood Olympus in heaps, superficial "talkies" and sentimental "songs," threatening the Asian and European arts with ruin . . .
>
> In this chaotic, shaken-up, forward-driving world, amidst nations and classes laying siege to one another, in this time of declining and rising worldviews, of the triumph of science and technology, the Indonesian *Volk* must find its way towards political freedom and national happiness.[1]

Batavia (or, as nationalists like Pané called it, Jakarta), 1931: In both time and space, not normally a place for a discussion of Pearl Harbor—or for that matter World War II more generally—to conventionally begin. Perhaps unsurprisingly, conventional narratives of Pearl Harbor and its significance generally focus on the experiences and perspectives of the direct protagonists, that is, the United States and Japan. As a function of this focus, the experiences of the peoples in the areas over which the two combatants began their fight at Pearl Harbor, including those of Southeast Asians, are generally reduced to a peripheral and passive role—which is how they were perceived by both most Americans and the Japanese at the time. As such, they do not usually enter the picture until Japan invades them.

The smaller number of histories of the Pacific War experience that do focus on Filipinos, Vietnamese, Malays, Burmese, Indonesians, and other Asian and Pacific peoples in this period, meanwhile, not surprisingly accord them a more active role and emphasize the significance of the war for the larger story with which *they* were generally more concerned: their ongoing struggles for national independence, which began before the war started and came to a head, in most cases, after the war ended. Whether written by Southeast Asians themselves or others, such histories frame Pearl Harbor and the period of Japanese occupations as "preludes to independence," with both the Western colonial powers and the imperial Japanese cast in the role of national hurdles to be overcome, colonial antagonists standing in the way of the inevitable birth of the independent nation. Such narratives are important in highlighting the conflict that began at Pearl Harbor as not simply a war between *nations* as Americans, Japanese, and Europeans tend to see it, but as a war between *empires*. In these accounts, although they also fear the uncertainty of what is to come, Pearl Harbor is initially welcomed by many Southeast Asians, who greet the successive, shockingly swift and decisive defeats of the other Western powers in Asia at Japanese hands that followed as a sign that national independence is at hand. For the same reason many of them also welcome the Japanese and their promises to "liberate" Southeast Asia. But these warm feelings turn quickly to antagonism and resistance when the Japanese quickly turn out to be imperialists just as the others—or even worse.

Missing in both sorts of conventional accounts of Pearl Harbor and the Asian experience of the Asia-Pacific War are the nature and implications of the interwar period highlighted in Pané's essay: war coming to the Pacific in a context of crisis not only in the global imperial order, but also of Western modernity *itself*. As reflected in Pané's startling text, the advent of the Great Depression at the start of the 1930s coming as it did on the heels of the horrors of World War I; the rise of the Soviet Union; revolutionary social, economic, and political unrest in Europe; and anticolonial movements in India, China, and elsewhere, seemed to confirm a growing sense of general disintegration in the Western-dominated modern global economic, social, and cultural order of things: in a word, a *Decline of the West*.[2] As such it also amplified already existing anxieties regarding the dizzying, seemingly ever-increasing pace of industrial development and interconnection under the global regime of liberal capitalism. The argument here is that once we recognize this period as one of profound crisis in Western modernity—above all, paying attention to Japanese self-justification of their move southward in the form of promises to bring about an alternative Asian modernity that might surpass that of the West—we are also compelled to acknowledge that for Southeast Asians and indeed many others in the colonial world dissatisfied with the Western-dominated global status quo, the meaning and experiences of Pearl Harbor and the Japanese victories and occupations in its wake were much more ideologically complex, ambivalent, and significant than conventional narratives would have it.

In recent decades, scholarship on modern Japan has increasingly recognized Japan's aggressive imperialism from the early 1930s through 1945 as a response to this simultaneous double-crisis of empire and modernity—the former in the form of rising Korean and Chinese anticolonial resistance movements in particular, and the latter above all in the form of the Great Depression. The ideological response to this double crisis took the form of a scapegoating of "Western" modernity and the increasing appeal of an Orientalist fantasy of a "return" to "Asian tradition" as its antidote. As Louise Young and other Japan scholars have shown, such visions first acquired broad social support in the context of the Manchurian invasion, which took place in the very same autumn of 1931 in which Sanusi Pané penned the aforementioned essay. In its puppet state of Manchukuo, Japanese spokesmen promised to build a veritable social "paradise" in which domestic tensions of class versus class, regional tensions of ethnicity and rising anticolonial resistance, global tensions of great power rivalry and protectionism, and modern afflictions of materialism, individualism, and associated moral decay and corruption "imported" from the West would be transcended through a combined "return" to the lost Asian values of the past and a leap into a state-of-the-art, socially engineered future. Manchukuo thus promised not only a "living space" but a dream landscape in which the very contradictions of Japan's modernity and its multiple crises—economic, social, political, cultural, and imperial—would be resolved at a stroke.[3]

As scholars such as Harry Harootunian have shown, while inflected locally, such Japanese dreams and discourses of "overcoming modernity" were symptomatic of an interwar ideological condition prompted by a multilayered crisis of liberal industrial capitalist modernity whose global nature, effects, and dynamics have been conventionally out of focus. Simultaneously and interactively in Europe and Japan, the perception of the moment as demanding and potentially promising a radical means of "overcoming modernity" was an expression of, in Harootunian's words, being "overcome by modernity."[4] The social dislocations and stark imbalances (what Harootunian calls the characteristic "unevenness") of industrial capitalist economic development and their quickening pace, the emergence of the increasingly assertive masses into political and social life, the rise of radical challenges to the social status quo from the left and the right, the declining authority of established institutions and mores and an associated sense of moral decline, and the virtual collapse of the global liberal capitalist economy triggered by the Wall Street crash of 1929: all were components of the deepest global crisis witnessed in modern times. Such impulses lay at the basis of the heightened international appeals of both communism and fascism at the time. But many, particularly among the middle classes, were also frightened at the "bloody" extremes of the "solutions" both offered, and yearned for some sort of "third way": a revolutionary way out of the crisis of modernity, the crisis of capitalism, and the inequities of the old order that would not require a frightening revolutionary social upheaval to get there.

Toward occupied Asia, such Japanese dreams were expressed in the form of a Japan-led pan-Asianism, which is perhaps more aptly called "Greater Asianism," given its faith in a culturally "restored" yet technologically modern Asia that might transcend Western modernity. Yet scholarly accounts of this phenomenon, centered as they are on Japanese experience, rarely leave room for nuanced consideration of how *other* Asians might have viewed or responded to the interwar crisis of Western modernity and to Japan's calls for a "Greater Asia"—and how Pearl Harbor and Japan's subsequent occupation of Southeast Asia might have impacted the consciousness of other Asians in this context. The essay by Sanusi Pané, written more than eleven years before Pearl Harbor, confirms that the potential appeal of an ideological "return to Asia" as a response to a perceived crisis of Western modernity was not limited to interwar Japan alone. This in turn bears implications that are broader than Japan alone. They also extend more broadly in a chronological sense too: illuminating a *transwar* Asian history of "Greater Asianism" from the prewar period through the war and into the postwar and postindependence era.

Vividly reflected in the Indonesian perspective of Sanusi Pané, and in contemporaneous Japanese fantasies of Manchukuo alike, is a shared perception of a crisis in the Western-dominated global imperial order. Both reflected a sense of living in a time of unprecedented historical vulnerability in that order, offering a correspondingly historic possibility of overcoming it. Though rarely referred to in narratives of World War II, the depth and seriousness of the crisis was felt broadly across Europe as well as outside of it. By the end of the 1930s, commentators from across the political spectrum not only in Berlin, Tokyo, and Moscow but also in London, Paris, Brussels, and Amsterdam were singing a similar refrain about the passing of the old global order and sharing a similar conviction in the inevitability of a radically new one, for better or for worse. In his prophetically titled 1938 *The Crumbling of Empire: The Disintegration of the World Economy,*[5] the liberal German economist M. J. Bonn remarked,

> Before the [First World] War, Western civilization had a profound impact upon the world. But Western civilization as such was a general concept; it was the only civilization worth having. When the peoples of the East began to strive for equality, they desired to make characteristically Western institutions their own. All of this is changing. The nations of Western Europe no longer represent the only and unchanging form of Western civilization. Democracies confront dictatorships. Capitalism, collectivism, and armed [National] Socialism confront one another. Christianity is no longer dominant; it must do battle with atheism in Russia, racial monotheism in Germany, and apathy in wider portions of the world. Western technology is the only thing that the various cultural, political, and economic forms have in common. Film and radio are universal, however national their producers or broadcasts may be. The manufacturing of cannons, flying machines, ammunition and poison gasses represents the only type of enterprise upon which all nations zealously focus—with the exception of the spiritual island upon which Gandhi would isolate India from the roar and riot of the Western world.

In a glowing review of Bonn's book for the Dutch magazine *De Economist* that appeared late the next year, Dr. Th. L. Thurlings, a conservative young economist and future secretary of the upper chamber of the Dutch parliament for the dominant Catholic Volkspartij (KVP), remarked, "In a compelling manner, Bonn, a German professor in exile now working in London, highlights the dislocation of our present-day society and shows how the Great Powers are slowly but surely disintegrating—partly through their own fault, partly through a kind of destiny that seems to seek to drive mankind to ruin."[6]

It was against this dramatic interwar context of a Euro-American imperial domination that was "slowly but surely disintegrating"—not only economically, but also politically, socially, and *culturally*—that Pané closed his remarkable 1931 essay with a radical question:

> Will we, ignoring the lessons of European history and closing our eyes to the political, economic, and social failures of the West, steer our cultural course toward the Occidental model, thereby taking the risk, upon arrival, of finding that we have been left behind and in the meantime, Europe, having abandoned its previous position, has moved on? Must we forever be satisfied with what has been left behind by others and found worthless, trudging behind in the wake of other nations?

For Pané, the implied answer was a new and revolutionary one: perhaps the "non-Western" identity that had up to now only condemned him and so many others only to an "inferior," alien, "backward" status in a Western-dominated global order, might actually be an *advantage* in finding a way to overcome it. Might an ancient "Asian" identity—if it could be recovered anew, in pure form, isolated from the alien Western contaminants that had corrupted it—hold the key to a transcendence of the problems of the Western modernity? With the Western world and its very civilization in serious trouble, perhaps it was time to "turn back East."

Like most of his Asian contemporaries, however, Pané was also a committed modernist, and he remained an absolute believer in the benefits and inevitability of modern progress. He therefore refused to envision this cultural "return to Asia" simply in terms of going backward, but rather as a necessary condition for moving forward into a successful, humane, socially harmonious, and equitable modernity: a modernity that seemed, in the West, further away than ever. In his writings throughout the prewar era, he consistently maintained that Asia's goal should not be to leave the West and its modernity behind altogether but rather to combine the best of East and West in a transcendently successful combination thereof. In what Pané frequently described as a meeting of the West's Faust and the East's (Bhagavad Gita warrior) Ardjuna, the progressive, dynamic modern ideals of both socialism and liberalism were to be combined with, and tempered by, a resurrected, distinctively Asian national essence.

At the time Sanusi Pané penned his lament, the idea of a Pan-Asian alliance against Western imperialism was not in itself particularly new, its desirability having been entertained in anticolonial nationalist movements and interactions throughout the region for some time—Chinese nationalist leader Sun Yat-Sen is credited with coining the term "Pan-Asianism" in this context in a 1924 speech. But Pané's more radical notion of pursuing what might be called an *alternative Asian modernity*—the transcendence of a fatally flawed Western modernity through a judicious injection of Eastern spirituality, morality, and community—was still quite novel. Outside of Japan, it was an idea that would not attract much of a following, at least not for another ten years or so—not before Pearl Harbor and the series of Japanese victories in its wake suddenly made it seem much more than wishful thinking. For so long as Western global domination remained a fact, however unpopular, few of Pané's anticolonial nationalist compatriots in Indonesia or elsewhere were yet seriously pondering an Asianism centered on the possibility of an "Eastern" route to overcoming Western modernity.

Even in Japan, such rhetoric attracted relatively few adherents before the colonization project in Manchuria got underway—a project just beginning when Pané first wrote these words in November of 1931. And in fact Pané himself had little interest in or knowledge of Japan, about which he had written the year before,

> Japan has secured a significant place among the great powers, but does not appear capable of bringing changes to the world political or economic structure; in fact, where the lighting of new paths and the opening of new perspectives is concerned, it has achieved little. The task of leading a searching mankind, of laying new social foundations in the light of the eternal, falls to India.[7]

If not from Japan, then, from where had Pané's inspiration for a "return to Asia" come? Judging from his association of the West with the character of Goethe's Faust, it seems at least in part from the German Oswald Spengler's *Decline of the West*, a dark rumination on European decline published in the wake of World War I.[8] But more deeply in Pané's particular case, a connection can be identified with the Orientalist doctrines of Theosophy, a mystical religious-philosophical movement that had started in late nineteenth-century British India but had its largest following in the early twentieth century among the reform-minded of the Netherlands Indies. Taking inspiration from Indian philosopher Rabindranath Tagore, among others, the Theosophists looked to the ancient moral and spiritual wisdom of "the East" (as contained in texts such as the Bhagavad Gita) as a means of rejuvenating what they saw as a materially, technologically, and civilizationally superior but morally corrupted modern West. First as a student and then as an instructor, Pané had attended a teacher-training school established in 1918 in Batavia by the Theosophist "Union of Association Between East and West." There, like his Dutch counterparts, he had developed a romance with the mystical Asian past and its therapeutic potential for a morally challenged present. But by the tumultuous late 1920s, Pané, like many other fellow frustrated Indonesian progressives, had lost faith in the Dutch colonial rulers and had come to reject the possibility of a peaceful compromise with a Dutch colonialism that responded to growing Indonesian nationalist activism with increasing reaction and repression. This sentiment, along with the deepening international crisis in the wake of 1929, inspired him to combine the Theosophist's romance of ancient India with a Marxist-inspired assault on the Western-dominated imperialist-capitalist status quo, resulting in a new and militant, interwar variant of "Asianism."

Despite the similarities between Japanese imperialist and Indonesian nationalist rhetoric at this time, it is thus essential to note that they arose quite independently from one another. This is a reflection of the fundamentally *global* nature of the crisis that generated them both. Indeed, before Pearl Harbor, Sanusi Pané and other Indonesian nationalists such as Sukarno and Hatta identified much less with Asia's sole imperial power Japan—whose aggression in Manchuria they condemned—than with fellow anticolonial nationalists in places like India and the Middle East. Whatever the fundamental conflict between Japanese imperial and Asian anticolonial agendas, however, between them stood a common enemy under increasingly global siege—the imperial West—and thus at least the latent potential for a revolutionary joining of forces.

Above all in the Netherlands Indies, this potential was augmented by the exceptional degree of Dutch intransigence in the face of rising Indonesian nationalist sentiments and the suffering of the Great Depression. The Dutch response was only more uncompromising: in 1931 a hard-handed governor general, Bonifacius Cornelis de Jonge, was appointed. In 1933 he banished Sukarno and Hatta to exile on the isolated island of Banda. The Dutch and Dutch interests continued to be favored at every turn, and no talk of Indonesian political autonomy, let alone independence, was entertained. With the arrival of war in Europe, little changed. The conservative Dutch interpretation of the Atlantic Charter issued by the Allies in August 1941, which promised the postwar right of self-determination to all countries participating in the conflict, only added fuel to the fire. When pressed in the Consultative Assembly (Volksraad) by Indonesian member Soetardjo as to whether the Netherlands intended to honor the charter with relation to Indonesia, the Dutch authorities characteristically asserted their commitment to "democratic principles" while at the same time maintaining that the promise of self-determination did not apply within empires.[9]

Against this background, when Japan backed up its powerful rhetorical critique of modern Western civilization and claims to "liberate" Asia with astounding military success at Pearl Harbor and in Southeast Asia in late 1941 and early 1942, Sanusi Pané was among many Indonesian nationalists who became—for a time at least—convinced of the "world-historical" necessity of such a collaboration, whatever its risks.[10] Indonesians lined the roads to welcome Asia's new leaders who also proclaimed themselves Asia's liberators, emphasizing the point by hoisting Indonesian flags alongside their own. As if ordained by the gods, the Dutch colonial military crumbled in the path of superior Japanese firepower and apparently superior Japanese spirit. The surrender came on March 9, 1942—just eight days after the Japanese landed in Java and just three weeks after the unheralded fall of the "impregnable" British stronghold of Singapore. Not just for Japanese, but for Indonesians as well, both past and future seemed suddenly bathed in a new "Asian" light.

Up to now Japan had been perennially viewed not only by Westerners but by most Indonesians—including Sanusi Pané—as little more than a distant, second-class Western copycat. Now it suddenly seemed capable of beating the West at its own game. Indeed, not only could Japan now claim to be the only Asian society modern enough to compete with the West, but the ease and scope of its three-month string of military victories even suggested that Japan might have a better recipe for national strength than its Western competitors. Brimming with newfound confidence, Japanese spokesmen in Java and elsewhere proclaimed that the secret of Japan's modern success lay precisely in its remaining faithful to its indigenous, non-Western traditions amid the modern Western capitalist-imperialist onslaught. Or more precisely, in Japan's retention of its indigenous racial and cultural traditions even as it adopted and mastered Western material civilization and its benefits, finely balancing the two for optimum results. The result would be the pioneering of a genuinely alternative "Asian" route to modern nationhood that could avoid the pitfalls of Western experience—individualism, social division and confrontation, exploitation, bloody revolution—while enjoying its undisputed benefits of scientific progress and material prosperity. Japan's aim in expanding into Asia was not selfish imperialism of the Western variety but rather to create a "Greater Asia" by leading the same sort of rejuvenation among its downtrodden Asian brethren. In order to finish the job against a common Western enemy that remained powerful and determined, however, Asian cooperation and sacrifice were essential.

Dazzled by Japan's military successes and intrigued by the lessons of its experience as a uniquely successful modern non-Western nation-state, many Indonesians were more receptive to Japan's appeals than was later acknowledged. This was above all the case among the Indonesian social group that would rise to postwar national dominance: the ambitious, frustrated, and relatively privileged nationalist middle class, or sub-elite. Whatever the inherent dangers and

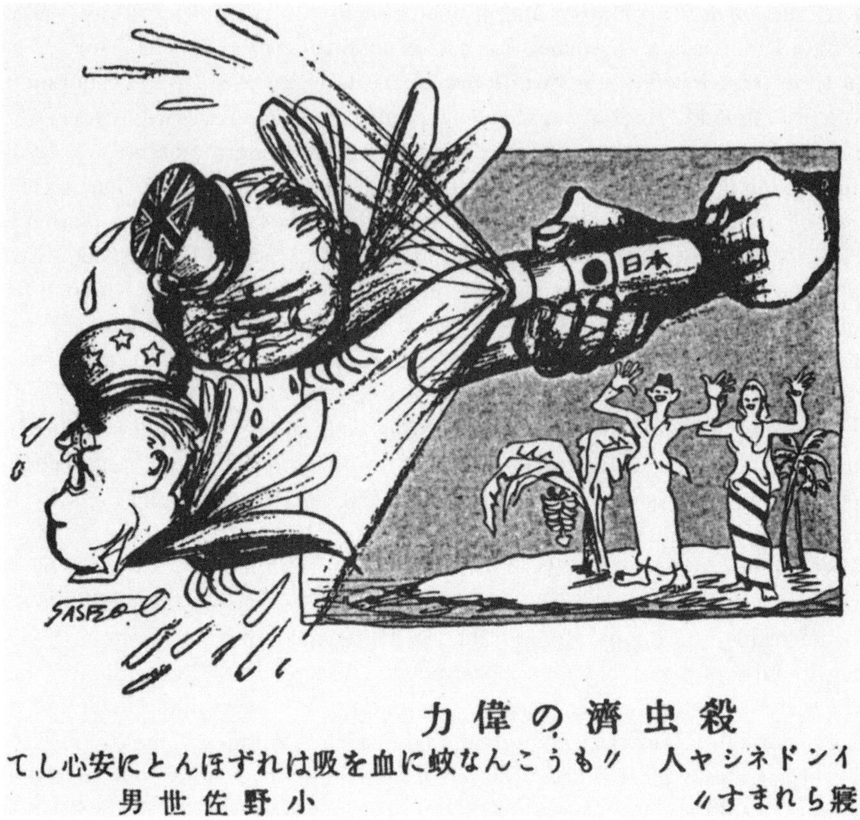

A Japanese propaganda cartoon that appeared in the *Unabara* newspaper for local Japanese consumption in occupied Indonesia depicts Japan as deliverers of "insecticide" against Western imperialist mosquitos personified in the form of Roosevelt and Churchill, as grateful Indonesians look on.

unknowns, many such Indonesian nationalists were drawn to cooperation with the Japanese, whose arrival appeared to represent an opportunity for both personal and national enrichment and empowerment, turning the tables against all the illegitimate forces hitherto arrayed against what they saw as their natural claim to national leadership. These perceived "shared enemies" included the Dutch and the "native" nobility and Overseas Chinese who collaborated with them, along with the colonial policy and ideology of division and inferiority through which "the West" had continued to weaken and ensnare Indonesians as prisoners of the mind, all the while isolating the nationalists physically and mentally from their natural allies—the Indonesian masses.

For the Japanese, the implications of this warm Indonesian reception were spellbinding. Rejected by China, they encountered in Indonesia an anticolonial nationalism that seemed positively eager to embrace an Asianist worldview and to acquire the secrets of a suddenly invincible Japanese national power. Shared Southeast Asian resentment at the Overseas Chinese—who were seen as accomplices to Western imperialism and traitors to the shared cause of Asian liberation—even imparted a retrospective legitimacy to Japan's aggression in China, helping to neutralize or dispel earlier ambivalences and anxieties about it. Reflecting the giddy overconfidence of the moment, the editor of *Unabara*, a Japanese-language newspaper initiated in Jakarta shortly after the Dutch surrender by the conquering Sixteenth Army's Propaganda Squad [*sendenhan*], told the following story of members of a "China pacification unit" [*Shina senbuhan*] that had earlier run into trouble in selling Japan's case to the Chinese—and asserted that Pearl Harbor and the string of "world-historical" victories in its wake had now rewritten the script on Japan's mission in Northeast and Southeast Asia alike.

> [The unit members] argued that Japan and China have the same script and are of the same race [*dōbun dōshu*], they are brothers, and they should proceed with hands joined.
>
> Someone in the audience replied—Alright, but China is the older brother.
>
> It is said the members of the pacification unit had no words to answer this for some time.
>
> How wonderful if they had been able to reply immediately.
>
> It is a problem of history—when you are properly aware of Japan's history, the answer is extremely simple.
>
> Japan has always been leader of the AsiaPacific sphere from ancient times—if you know this history, that is enough.
>
> Japan has always been constructing China—if you know this history, that is enough.
>
> We are now seeing this truth with our own eyes in the Greater East Asia War.[11]

Viewed from Southeast Asia, in the retrospective light of the spectacular "world-historical" string of military triumphs against the hitherto invincible West that began with Pearl Harbor, the Pacific War appeared, in sum, no longer an "ordinary," old-fashioned colonial war of the sort seen in Northeast Asia, but rather represented a sort of virgin, "post-Western" historical territory. For all those in a subordinate position in a Western- and white-dominated world—but above all for Japanese, who could now claim a leadership role for that world on the basis of concrete achievements—the sense of discontinuity and accompanying possibilities of historical transcendence that appeared to open up were both dizzying and empowering. This led to a boom in romantic fantasizing of Japan's occupation of Indonesia as a "reunion" with long-lost Asian brethren.

Remarkably and revealingly, such assertions of cultural and even imagined racial similarities were often accompanied by the suggestion that Indonesians were more "closely related" to Japanese than their (more resistant) East Asian neighbors the Chinese and Koreans. In another editorial, *Unabara*'s editor Shimizu Nobuo observed,

> After landing on Java, what everyone has noticed is that among the native race here, there are a number who look just like Japanese. You've encountered them many times. No matter how much you look at them, theirs could not be anything other than a Japanese face. This is only natural, however. In ancient times, this place was within the sphere of governance of *sumera mikuni*, a region of great culture with Japan at its center.[12]

In memoirs written more than twenty years after the war had ended, Shimizu's former commander in the Java propaganda squad, Lieutenant Colonel Machida Keiji, still comfortably maintained that "a dark skinned Japanese,"

> certainly looked more like a native than a fair-skinned Indonesian. [Indonesian] women in particular generally had light-colored skin, and if you put one somewhere in Japan, no one would realize that she was of a different race. This physical similarity extended also to the Thais and Malays. They didn't have flat faces like the Chinese or the Koreans, but had faces just like the Japanese. Japanese people were surprised at it, but when it came to Javanese, they were just exactly like the Japanese.[13]

Both in propaganda at the time and in later memoirs, the romantic Japanese focus on purported commonalities of race and culture with Indonesians was a common theme among military and civilian spokesmen alike. Such romanticism regarding their Southeast Asia "brethren," which could be seen among Japanese hailing from across the political spectrum, was not only a reflection of relief at the contrast with the China experience.[14] For to the extent that all Japanese spokesmen for the "new Asia" subscribed *both* to the illegitimacy of conventional (Western) imperialism and to an imperial worldview of their own, they all faced a common dilemma: how to define Japan's difference, its means to imperial transcendence? Advertising revolutionary change yet lacking in concrete, revolutionary structural alternatives to Western imperial modernity, Japan's spokesmen for Asia shared a compulsion to define this transcendence in terms of blood, morality, history, and destiny—terms of race and culture. Centuries of global Orientalist discourse, decades of exclusivist Japanese national rhetoric, and the unique achievements of Japan's modern development—confirmed in the miracle of Japan's sweeping military victories over the Western Other—offered a wealth of ammunition for such constructions of difference.

Conventional histories of Southeast Asia, which reflect a retrospective Southeast Asian nationalist tendency to view the Japanese occupation in stark black-and-white terms of oppression and resistance, generally limit their assessment of the impact of Pearl Harbor to its effect on undermining the notion of Western invincibility and thereby stimulating nationalism, rather than fostering local interest in Japan as an Asian model. To the extent that Japan impacted Southeast Asia as a model, such characterizations focus on institutions rather than ideology. As Robert Cribb and Li Narangoa write in their introduction to the edited volume *Imperial Japan and National Identities in Asia*, for example, "For the most part . . . what the Southeast Asians learnt" from the Japanese "were technical skills not worldviews."[15] Certainly in its middle and later stages, Japan's occupation of Indonesia, as elsewhere in Asia, turned out to be a disaster for Indonesians—above all, for working-class Indonesians. The brutal habits and priorities of Japanese imperialism and militarism were imported to Indonesia just as they were to other parts of Asia, and they were heightened by the rapidly deteriorating war situation. By the end of the occupation, in light of the yawning gap between what they had promised and what they delivered, the Japanese would be more despised by many Indonesians than the Dutch had ever been.

It is not surprising, then, that subsequent scholarship on the Indonesian experience of the Japanese occupation has emphasized the fundamental incommensurability of Japanese imperialist and Indonesian nationalist agendas. Certainly in light of the structural role of Indonesia for the Japanese as little more than a supply base for manpower, oil, raw materials, and territory, as well as the ongoing imperial Japanese conviction of the superiority of their own culture over that of the "natives"—a conviction that Pearl Harbor had only strengthened—the notion that the two could ultimately be reconciled was a hope against hope. Yet to a degree unacknowledged in conventional histories of the occupation period, the nation-building appeal of such a "return to Asia" under Japanese auspices was a transnationally shared one. Precisely here lay an ambiguous gray zone of ideological overlap between Japanese imperialists and Indonesian nationalists alike, with deeper and longer-lasting implications than generally recognized—above all, when historically situated in the wake of Japan's earth-shattering victories at Pearl Harbor and beyond. For a time, both for Japanese and Indonesians—especially those of the ambitious nation-building middle classes of both societies—Pearl Harbor and the victories that followed had much deeper and more ambiguous effects than were later remembered, bringing the two sides not only physically and practically but also ideologically "closer" and fostering what I call a transnational Asian cultural turn.

"Regardless of political questions, the relationship between Japan and Indonesia indeed strikes more of a chord and is more in tune with the feelings of the people [than that with the Dutch]," noted an Indonesian nationalist newspaper commentator just three days after the Dutch surrender, "because the extent of the difference between Japan and Indonesia is not as great nor as deep as that between Holland and Indonesia. In their facial appearance and their skin color, in the simplicity of their lives and all their common customs and traditions, the children of Indonesia feel closer to and more similar to the Japanese race than to the races of Europe."[16]

On this subject, even the senior Indonesian administrator Hoesein Djajadiningrat, steeped in Dutch culture and the perks of the old system, informed his Dutch acquaintance Leo Jansen in early June 1942 that "what appealed to him in the Japanese" was their "reduced distance, their smaller size [*gestalte*] and darker skin. The Dutch superiority complex is after all mostly a question of size and skin color. The Japanese is by nature trustworthy for the Indonesian," he concluded, "[although] unfortunately also brutish [*hardhandig*]."[17] Djajadiningrat's administrator colleague Soetardjo Kartohadikoesoemo, author of an ill-fated petition for home rule in 1936, had his own distinctive interpretation of the racial connection. Three hundred years of Dutch rule had made Indonesians "weak in mind and body," and

> our weak condition allowed other races who were more clever, stronger, and more spirited [*lebih bersemangat*] to dominate us. This was also the case with the other races of Asia, with one exception: God who commands Nature placed a drop of Malay blood in a part of Asia now known as Japan. It was apparently already God's wish that this drop of Malay blood would in later days become a catalyst [*lantaran*] for the awakening of the Asian races. According to the wishes of Nature this drop of blood blossomed into a mature people, mature enough to avoid being dominated by others. Now the time has apparently come, that God has chosen that the Japanese should awaken the other peoples of Asia.[18]

In Soetardjo's reasoning, Japan's coming thus represented none other than the reuniting of a common Malay bloodline—a distant branch family returning to reinvigorate the degenerated main line.

In an essay penned around the same time, Islamic nationalist leader Anwar Tjokroaminoto pointed ominously to fascist anti-Semitic purges in Europe as a model for how the "Indonesian race" should take advantage of Japan's advent to reckon with "inhabitants" whose "jewish nature" predisposed them to the corruption of Indonesia's culture and the exploitation of its people. For local readers, the reference to a "shared enemy" perceived to occupy a somewhat comparable socioeconomic position to the Jews in Europe—Indonesia's Overseas Chinese—was unmistakable.

> As Germany once faced the society of Jews, as a result of the Weimar Republic, so Indonesia too has a problem of jewishness. Meaning that there are more than a few among Indonesia's inhabitants who truly possess a jewish nature, whose behavior is jewish behavior. Laws that do not prohibit prostitution, for example, are exploited to run houses of prostitution. As in the jewish period in Germany, [when] these sorts of people produced books of prostitutes, pictures of whores to destroy the spirits of German youth, so there are not a few in Indonesia who secretly or openly do these sorts of things, ruining the spirit and character of Indonesian youth. In the social environment, there are also not a few instances of "man eats man," meaning one sucks the other dry, assuming many forms, such as usury, or pursued by others through other means. People's poverty has been exploited in producing a system of credit [*systeem bon*], until the life of the average Indonesian is a life on credit, even though life on credit is more expensive than life on cash. This jewish-type of person does not fail to take maximum advantage of the peasants' ignorance. For example, when the peasant buys something, the scales are weighted heavy, while the contents are reduced. If the peasant sells something, the scales are lightened, even as the contents are many.

"Just as the German race has risen up in the aim of shining forth all its [true] qualities," concluded Tjokroaminoto, "so the new Indonesia, under Japanese leadership, deeply desires the same sort of change, the cleanest possible filtration [*saringan*]."[19]

For Sanusi Pané too, the dramatic Japanese arrival in the Indies in March 1942—billed and perceived as the harbinger of a world-historical change in the balance of power between East and West—set in motion a profound psychological adjustment. Publicly at least, reservations that Pané had nurtured regarding Japan when it was still at a distance—and while global Western hegemony was still a given—were quickly abandoned in favor of an all-out embrace. In fact, as much as any public figure in Indies society, it was Pané, as cultural commentator of the new Japanese-sponsored *Asia Raya* newspaper, who took an early lead in connecting Japan and Indonesia in past, present, and future, and in promoting Indonesia's cultural Asianization under Japanese stewardship.

In his contribution to *Asia Raya*'s first issue on the emperor's birthday of April

29, 1942, entitled "The Culture of Greater Asia," Pané proposed a virtual grocery list of cultural traditions supposedly shared by Japanese and Indonesians alike. Both honored their ancestors. Both built monuments to dead kings—a phenomenon also found in the West, he admitted, but "without the sense of religion as in the East." Both shared a Buddhist tradition. Japan's warrior code of *bushidō* could be compared to the Bhagavad Gita and the stories of Sri Krishna. While Westerners considered themselves apart from nature, employing science as a weapon to "make Nature their servant" and to "add to their pleasure and their wealth," he wrote, Japanese, Indonesians, and other Easterners aspired to "become one with Nature." Westerners, he argued, were the prisoners of a materialism and greed that had possessed their spirit, their society, and their economy. Now the West was falling into a chasm of confusion [*kekaloetan*] and death [*kebinasaan*]; worse, it sought to take the rest of the world down with it. Crisis followed upon crisis, malaise upon malaise, but the West had been unable to solve these problems because it had neglected to "change the basis of its culture."

Here as elsewhere in Pané's wartime writings, correspondences to his prewar positions were striking, but with two critical distinctions: first, Japan, rather than India, was now being foregrounded as Asian representative, and, more importantly, as Asian success story. Second, in the context of Japanese hegemony, the theme of culture as the answer to the challenge of Western modernity, within the aim of modern nation-building, had been brought into sharp relief, presented with a new conviction and intensity.[20]

When Sukarno returned to Java from a previous Dutch exile some six months into the occupation, his voice also joined the general chorus of support for Indonesian nation-building under Japanese auspices, enhanced by a distinctive rhetorical flair. In his first substantial public writings since his long-awaited return, written for a special glossy magazine published by *Asia Raya* to commemorate six months of "Japanese Protection of Indonesia," Sukarno pulled few punches in a stinging cultural indictment of an Indonesian people whose spirits—under colonialism—had become infected with the self-centered pettiness and passivity typifying a slave mentality, a mentality antithetical to the building of a powerful nation. The Japanese and their accomplishments meanwhile appeared as a vivid counter-referent. Making a parable of a scene he had witnessed in the office of a Japanese administrator in Sumatra shortly after the Dutch surrender, Sukarno referred to an expectant young Indonesian, one of many who appeared in the administrator's office

> to ask for something! To ask that he be released from paying taxes, because he was out of work. Lieutenant Sakaguchi smiled. He regarded this young man, who was "jobless" and yet still a dandy. And then he said something to this

> youngster that made me too feel *ashamed*. This is what he said: "You still have a nice shirt, you still have nice pants, you still have a nice tie, you still have nice shoes. Is it not possible for you to join in making some small sacrifice for your homeland? Look at me! My shirt is in tatters and it's the only one I have. These are also the only trousers I have, and my shoes are no longer in any shape. I have undergone months of shortages, I have *sacrificed* for months—sacrificed *for your homeland*. Can you not sacrifice for your homeland?"[21]

"Although these words of Lieutenant Sakaguchi were spoken in a friendly way," wrote Sukarno, "they struck like dagger into my heart . . . into my soul. The youngster's face turned red from shame, but my face turned a bright red." The implications of Sukarno's juxtaposition of Sakaguchi with his pampered, Westernized Indonesian visitor could not have been less subtle.

While the wartime statements of such spokesmen for Japanese-Indonesian cooperation appeared under Japanese auspices and must certainly be taken with a grain of salt, their enthusiasm thus reflected an interest in the Japanese that was not only practical or opportunistic but also ideological. In newspapers, journals, films, and public rallies, they repeatedly highlighted the appeal of a model of "Asian" nation-building that would successfully combine the best of "East" and "West," harnessing the social and technological benefits of Western modernity, meritocracy, and progress while preserving "old-fashioned," "Asian"-style social harmony, discipline, and self-sacrifice. Indeed, the degree to which the Indonesian nationalist class in particular embraced such notions of an alternative Asian modernity—and sometimes still does—reflected their perceived addressing of a social and cultural problematic that was not limited to wartime Japan alone but was in fact transnational and transwar in scope: how to build a successful, unified modern nation upon the rubble of the colonial past that was more than simply a second-class copy of a Western original—an original now, moreover, *itself* in a deep crisis of legitimacy—while avoiding the cataclysm of a "Western-style" social revolution?

The experience was to leave enduring postwar and postcolonial legacies in Indonesia and more widely across Asia, even after the Japan-centered formulations of "Asia" of the war period had long been roundly discredited and discarded. To acknowledge this is not to suggest, as the returning Dutch colonizers tried to do, that Indonesian nationalists had somehow been duped by the Japanese. Rather, the nature of such impacts needs to be understood in terms of the *longue duree*: the transwar and *transnational* lineage of such "Asian" cultural formulations, whose appeals lay fundamentally in the shared experience of the global crisis of modernity and of Western imperial hegemony in the interwar period.

While Greater Asianism shared with European fascism a combination of anticapitalism, anticommunism, social corporatism, and racial, cultural, and gender essentialism, its distinctive trump cards in the context of Japan's advance into Southeast Asia were its ability not only to claim a natural affinity with Asia's populations based upon shared race, culture, and history but also to associate itself with history's most progressive forces in battle against the hypocritical, antiprogressive (racist, oppressive, exploitative, feudal) imperial regimes of a common Western enemy. It was this mix—and the way that it seemed to address a range of shared dilemmas, offering an idealized means of transcending the dislocations associated with capitalist modernization in non-Western societies in a Western-dominated world—that fueled the appeal of Greater Asia across Japanese-Indonesian and other Asian boundaries in the prewar and wartime eras, particularly among Asia's nation-building classes. The depth of their transnational penetration cannot be separated from the effects of the power with which imperial Japan, from Pearl Harbor to Jakarta, appeared to ride on the crest of an irresistible "world-historical" post-Western—and postcolonial—tide.

By August 1945 all but the most committed of Japanese emperor-centered die-hards were forced to acknowledge Japan's wartime version of Greater Asia as a failure. Yet the transnational questions that "Greater Asia" claimed to address remained as prominent as ever. Shorn of its Japan-centrism and repackaged in national garb or in the transnational form of "Asian Values," the broader appeals of a "return" to an imagined indigenous "Asian" race and culture as offering a harmonious non-Western alternative to the chaos and social tension of capitalist modernity—a discourse that had peaked during the war years but in any event had its roots in a longer historical trajectory of national identity-building—continued to influence and inform the ideological landscape of postwar Asia. The significance of Pearl Harbor, as such, needs to be understood and assessed in the context of a much longer Asia-Pacific history.

NOTES

1. Sanusi Pané, "Java en de 'Buitengewesten'" [Java and the "Hinterlands"]. *Timboel* 5, 19: 1–2 (1931), 1.

2. First published in German as *Der Untergang des Abendlandes* in 1918–1922 and appearing in an English edition in 1926–1928 (New York: Knopf), *The Decline of the West* was the title of an influential, somber two-volume work by philosopher Oswald Spengler.

3. Louise Young, *Japan's Total Empire: Manchuria and the Culture of Wartime Imperialism*, (Berkeley: University of California Press, 1998).

4. Harry D. Harootunian, *Overcome by Modernity: History, Culture, and Community in Interwar Japan* (Princeton, NJ: Princeton University Press, 2000).

5. M. J. Bonn, *The Crumbling of Empire: The Disintegration of the World Economy* (London: Allen and Unwin, 1938).

6. Th. L. Thurlings, review of M. J. Bonn, *The Crumbling of Empire*, in *De Economist* 88, 1 (December 1939), 258.

7. Sanusi Pané, "De Boodschap van India," *Timboel* 4, 8-9, (1930), 112–113.

8. Spengler's work depicted modern Westerners as "Faustian" and Western civilization as entering its final "season." See note 2.

9. Bernard Dahm, *A History of Indonesia in the Twentieth Century* (London: Praeger, 1971), 80.

10. For a more focused discussion of Pané, his experience under the Japanese, and his work as an expression of interwar Asianism as a transnational ideology, see Ethan Mark, "'Asia's' Transwar Lineage: Nationalism, Marxism, and 'Greater Asia' in an Indonesian Inflection," *Journal of Asian Studies* 65, 3 (August 2006), 461–493.

11. "Sekidōhō" editorial section (Shimizu Nobuo), *Unabara*, July 2, 1942, p. 1.

12. Shimizu Nobuo, "Ajia-Taiheiyōken no fukkō" [The rebirth of the Asia-Pacific sphere], *Sekidōhō*, March 27, 1942, p. 1. Emphasis added.

13. Machida Keiji, *Tatakau bunka butai* [The fighting propaganda squad] (Tokyo: Harashobô, 1967), 260–261.

14. For an in-depth study of a former leftist writer and critic of Japanese fascism and imperialism who emerged as one of Japan's most enthusiastic spokesmen for the wartime mission in Indonesia, see Ethan Mark, "The Perils of Co-Prosperity: Takeda Rintarō, Occupied Southeast Asia, and the Seductions of Postcolonial Empire," *American Historical Review* 119, 4 (October 2014), 1184–1206.

15. Robert Cribb and Li Narangoa, eds., *Imperial Japan and National Identities in Asia* (Copenhagen: Nordic Institute for Asian Studies, 2003), 8.

16. Author anonymous, "Nippon Indonesia," *Pemandangan*, March 12, 1942, p. 2.

17. Mr. dr. L. F Jansen, *In Deze Halve Gevangenis: Dagboek van mr dr. L. F. Jansen, Batavia/Djakarta 1942–1945*, edited by G. J. Knapp (Franeker: Uitgeverij Van Wijnen, 1988).

18. Soetardjo Kartohadikoesoemo, text of speech to the Indonesian Sport Federation (Ikatan Sport Indonesia), *Pemandangan*, April 21, 1942, p. 2.

19. Anwar Tjokroaminoto, "Saringan," in *Pemandangan*, April 4, 1942, p. 1. "Jewishness" [*jahoedism*] was not capitalized.

20. For an in-depth discussion and analysis of Sanusi Pané's transwar experience, see Mark, "Asia's Transwar Lineage: Nationalism, Marxism, and 'Greater Asia' in an Indonesian Inflection," 461–493.

21. Sukarno, "'Djiwa Ksatria' dan 'Djiwa Boedak'" [The soul of the warrior and the soul of the slave: The difference between the Herrengeist and Sklavengeist], *Memperingati Enam Boelan Balatentara Dai Nippon Melindoengi Indonesia* [Commemorating six months of Japanese Army protection of Indonesia] (Djakarta: Asia Raya, 1942).

CHAPTER 8

The Philippines and the Politics of Anticipation

Christopher Capozzola

On November 27, 1941, Admiral Harold R. Stark, the US chief of naval operations, sent a message to several recipients noting that "an aggressive move by Japan is expected within the next few days" against "the Philippines" or some other target in Southeast Asia. "This dispatch," he intoned, "is to be considered a war warning." Among those warned was Admiral Thomas C. Hart, commander-in-chief of the US Asiatic Fleet based in Manila, nearly 5,000 miles from the military facilities at Pearl Harbor in Hawai'i. He was not surprised to receive the news, convinced that any Japanese push into Southeast Asia "would not leave us on their flank" and that "consequently . . . they would attack." Nor was Captain John D. Wood, a young officer stationed on Corregidor Island in Manila Bay, who wrote the next day to his wife Mary back in Virginia that "I can't seem to get very excited about this M[obilization] Day business. . . . [We] have been living in this atmosphere too long to get excited now."[1]

Accounts of the Japanese attack on Pearl Harbor regularly observe—if only in passing—that Hawai'i was not the only site targeted on the morning of December 7, 1941. In fact, the Japanese bombing raid on Clark Field, a US army air installation at Fort Stotsenburg, some fifty miles north of Manila, has been described by historians as the "other Pearl Harbor." But that phrase would have made little sense to most people in the Philippines, Hawaii, or elsewhere in the months before the attacks, because on December 7 (or 8), 1941, O'ahu was actually the "other" Clark Field. On the fateful afternoon in Washington when he learned of the Pearl Harbor attacks, Secretary of the Navy Frank Knox revealed his assumptions. "My God! This can't be true," he said. "This must mean the Philippines." Years of anticipation shaped the choices of military officers, Philippine politicians, and ordinary Filipinos. Thus, a Pacific history of the Pearl Harbor attacks must account for the history of the Philippines, not only for the devastation on the morning of December 8, 1941, but for the centrality of Philippine anticipation to the onset of the Pacific War.[2]

This chapter examines the period between the 1934 Tydings-McDuffie Act, a US law that announced and set a timetable for Philippine independence, and the attacks of December 1941. Throughout this seven-year period, observers on both sides of the Pacific believed that the Philippines would be the first target of any Japanese military offensive against the United States. US military war plans built on this assumption, and much postwar analysis has focused on the viability of those proposals, the extent to which they were carried out, and their effectiveness even had they been fully implemented. This chapter considers the politics of anticipation: what did it mean to live in a country that was simultaneously on the verge of political independence and on the edge of war? The politics of anticipation ultimately shaped not only military and civil defense but also definitions of national sovereignty and the bounds of executive power, with long-term consequences for Philippine politics not only in the 1930s but enduring into the 1970s and up to today.[3]

If a Pacific history of Pearl Harbor begins in the Philippines, and examining the Philippines draws our attention to the notion of anticipation, recovering anticipation in turn enables us to decenter surprise as the primary narrative trope for explaining what kind of event Pearl Harbor was. This chapter asks, as well, how Americans (in particular) came to think about Pearl Harbor in the years after the attacks. Wartime US congressional investigations framed Pearl Harbor as a surprise and focused attention on assigning blame for failure to predict the attacks that took the lives of more than 2,000 US civilians and service personnel.

Cold War theorists and early scholars in the fields of international relations and security studies continued to analyze Pearl Harbor as a surprise, even as one of their number, the political analyst Thomas Schelling, acknowledged in 1962 that "rarely has a government been more expectant." A narrative of surprise is thus an artifact of domestic US politics and foreign policy contexts. So what is at stake in the difference? Quite a lot, actually. Describing Pearl Harbor as a surprise is not only historically inaccurate but politically problematic, in that a narrative of surprise suggests a failure of *intelligence* on the part of a peaceful nation, whereas a focus on a politics of anticipation shows Pearl Harbor as a failure of *diplomacy* on the part of two militaristic empires.[4]

What would happen if we thought about the Japanese attacks in the places where in the late 1930s they were feared, and where in the summer of 1941 they were expected to take place? Such a task brings us to Manila.

ANTICIPATING INDEPENDENCE, PREPARING FOR WAR

The story begins with the Tydings-McDuffie Act of 1934, which announced with great flourish that the United States intended to grant independence to the Philippines on the distant future date of July 4, 1946. In the meantime, the law established the Philippine Commonwealth, a notionally distinct state whose citizens "owe[d] allegiance to the United States" during the twelve-year transitional period. The new commonwealth would have a bicameral legislature and a president elected by the Filipino people, but it would also have a high commissioner appointed by the American president. Nor would the US military be far from the scene. The Tydings-McDuffie Act noted that during the twelve years of transition "foreign affairs shall be under the direct supervision and control of the United States" and established that the Philippine Commonwealth "recognizes the right of the United States" to call into service "all military forces organized by the Philippine Government." Thus there were two politics of anticipation at work in the Philippines in this period: after 1934 (at least), the anticipation of independence, and after July 1941 (at least), the dread of a coming war. Disagreement about responsibility for defense became tangled up in both those political contests, long before the threat of Japanese invasion became real.[5]

Speaking for the Philippines was the new president of the commonwealth, the lifelong independence advocate Manuel Quezon, who introduced to the new Commonwealth Congress its first piece of legislation: the National Defense Act of 1935. The proposed law meant to give the soon-to-be-independent country the capacity of self-defense. It would establish a substantial new force—the Army of the Philippines—which would train citizen-soldiers and build up an officer corps. (Prior to this, Filipinos' only opportunities to serve in uniform were in low-ranking service roles in the US Navy or in the Philippine Scouts, a colonial force, both of which had officer ranks restricted to Americans.) Taking cover under the US defense umbrella, there would be only a tiny "mosquito" navy, incapable of defending the archipelago.[6]

The proposed National Defense Act divided Philippine politicians. Some thought it cost too much money. Assemblyman Camilo Osias warned that "we are embarking upon a saturnalia of extravagance" and urged funds be spent on health and education instead. "We are appropriating money for imaginary enemies from outside," he said, dismissing the Japanese without naming them. "The real enemy is here with us." Indeed, the proposed spending of 16 million pesos a year—nearly a third of the commonwealth's budget—was a heavy burden for a nation of 14 million people struggling in the depths of a global depression. But assemblyman (and journalist) Maximo M. Kalaw dismissed Osias's doubts as "nothing but the result of the pacifistic theory which we heard in America when we were students." Perhaps "America can afford to have a little pacifistic philosophy," Kalaw argued, but the Philippines, "under the stormy clouds of Asia, with Manchukuo, China and the restless teeming millions of India and the militarism of Japan,—how can we in fairness here have a doctrine of pacifism?"[7]

The American left also perceived colonialism. Writing in *The Nation* under the pseudonym James S. Allen, American Communist Party leader Sol Auerbach called the National Defense Act "as clever a piece of diplomatic imperialism as has ever been forced upon a colony," because it "provide[d] for . . . the establishment of a conscript army, owing allegiance to the President of the United States, which with the trained reserves will number at least a half-million men by 1946." The Soviet press concurred, calling the law "a mask."[8]

While some found the new plan too militaristic, for others it did not go far enough. Costs would be paid by the new government out of the Philippine treasury, requiring training and equipment to be gathered on the cheap. This was particularly the viewpoint of the US military officials hired as advisors by the Philippine commonwealth government. Overseeing the transition and advising on the new force was the former chief of staff of the US Army, General Douglas MacArthur. Working alongside him was a midcareer US Army major named Dwight Eisenhower.[9]

Debates about what kind of military force the soon-to-be-independent nation needed were always also debates about the authority of Filipinos to decide for themselves the terms of their country's orientation toward national defense and foreign affairs. The commonwealth's new constitution embodied strands of militarism and internationalism that had structured public discussions around the world in the previous decade. Article II, Section 2 of the new constitution announced that "the defense of the State is a prime duty of government." But Article II, Section 3 invoked the 1928 Kellogg-Briand Pact and insisted that "the Philippines renounces war as an instrument of national policy, and adopts the generally accepted principles of international law as a part of the law of the Nation." Questions of sovereignty—whether Americans or Filipinos had the authority to decide the terms of the archipelago's defense—were at least as important as more technical questions about the equipment of the Philippine Army or the size of the Philippine Navy. American diplomat Claude Buss, posted to the Philippines in January 1941, later recalled that "the problems of the Philippines between 1939 and 1941 became problems of international relations. They were no longer problems of colonial policy."[10]

The question of whose responsibility it was to defend the Philippines was therefore complicated and overlapping, inevitably subject to debate and thus inherently susceptible to political manipulation. This, in turn, raised the stakes for President

Manuel Quezon. Global events polarized Philippine politics in the early years of the commonwealth, and the politics of anticipation culminated by 1940 in a de facto dictatorship under Quezon's personal control. Thus, the anticipation of a Japanese attack was already having political consequences across the Pacific long before December 7, 1941.

President Quezon himself fostered political extremism as he attempted to centralize power in the new government's executive branch. By 1937 he had already sponsored draconian sedition and censorship laws, consolidated his personal control over the Philippine constabulary, and expanded its secret service division. Under his leadership, the Philippine legislature authorized the formation of reserve officers' training corps (ROTC) units at universities in 1935; athletic training and military drill appeared in Philippine schools, where civics textbooks taught youth that "in times of war the loyal citizen must take sides with his country, right or wrong, and be ready to make the supreme sacrifice of dying for it." Critics who denounced the National Defense Act as overly militaristic thus feared that the new Philippine Army could easily become the private force of a military dictatorship. President Quezon loudly denied the charges of dictatorship: "I have never violated a single provision of our Constitution!" he thundered. But his responses did not always calm his critics' fears.[11]

Concerns about war with Japan appeared in the Philippine press with increasing regularity—and rising alarm. On July 4, 1939, at a Manila meeting of the left-leaning Congress for Democracy and Collective Security, Antonio Bautista urged a boycott of Japanese goods, decrying, "Every ounce of metallic ore sent to Japan will return in the form of bombs and bullets." Others rejected closer ties and urged immediate American departure as the Philippines' best means of national self-defense. "The American flag may . . . be an invitation to invasion," wrote Vicente Albano Pacis in a Manila paper in October 1939. Americans agreed. In October 1940, New Dealer Hugh Johnson called the defense of the Philippines "a grotesque absurdity" and urged Americans to "get out of this dangerous and extravagant busybody Oriental kibitzing."[12]

In the relatively tranquil 1920s, the only commentators who warned of the Japanese menace were eugenic scientists, manila hemp dealers, naval fetishists, or acolytes of the militaristic governor general Leonard Wood, all of them crying wolf with the deliberate aim of scuttling Filipinos' independence efforts. When such rhetoric was renewed in 1940, plenty of people were predisposed to downplay the threat. In 1940 Manuel Quezon assured an applauding law school reunion banquet at the University of the Philippines that "I give you my word as your President that we have nothing to fear from Japan."[13]

The threat, as Quezon and MacArthur knew, was real. And so the work expanded even as the reassurances continued. Planning for the defense of the

Philippines—and paying for it—prompted political controversy. More and more frequently, Quezon asserted power over the Philippines in the name of national emergency, but it was not always clear that his drastic actions were leading to any defense preparation. In Manila, in response to Quezon's creeping authoritarianism, supporters of democracy founded the Civil Liberties Union in 1938. Quezon tried to crush it.[14]

In August 1940 Quezon forced through passage of an Emergency Powers Act, giving him near-total control of the Philippine government. From Washington, DC, President Franklin D. Roosevelt demanded an explanation from Quezon, who assured Roosevelt that he "would not exercise the powers granted under that Act unless an emergency arose." Distracted by events elsewhere, Roosevelt made do with Quezon's promise, and Quezon retreated to the protection of his bulletproof car. In 1941 the Philippine Supreme Court upheld Quezon's actions; Justice José P. Laurel noted that the Philippines' new "constitutional dictatorship"—which Laurel compared to the "constitutional and benevolent dictatorship in Japan"—was well suited for a world of "totalitarianism gradually supplanting democracy."[15]

When Quezon wasn't seizing power for himself, he was demanding resources from the United States. Quezon reminded Americans that the Tydings-McDuffie Act reserved decision making over the Philippines' military and diplomatic affairs to the US government. He told the Philippine Assembly that "this is as it should be, because so long as we are under the American flag it rests exclusively with the United States, and not with us, to determine whether we shall be at peace or at war." He then cut funds that had been allocated to Philippine air and naval defenses. Some of the leftover money, wisely, funded a campaign to increase domestic production of foodstuffs that the Philippines would otherwise have to import; a great deal of money, though, went to pay for the designs for a new capitol, to be called Quezon City.[16]

By early 1941 war loomed, and as talk turned to air raid shelters, refugee camps, and gas masks, Quezon argued that civilian defense was also a US responsibility. "The protection of the civilian population of the Philippines is as much the primary responsibility of the Government of the United States as is the military defense of the Islands," he told High Commissioner Francis Sayre in April 1941. "Indeed, the protection of the civilian population is, by the very nature of modern warfare, an essential part of military defense." But Sayre claimed that America's hands were tied, since "the United States lacks jurisdiction to take action in such essential 'passive defense' measures as strengthening and increasing the Constabulary and the municipal police forces [or] organizing and training home guard units." Divided authority hampered preparation for an attack many now openly anticipated. It was obvious there were nowhere near enough supplies to feed and clothe the civilian population in wartime, let alone protect them from an attack. Nor was there money to acquire civil defense supplies on the open market in a world already at war, and neither the time nor the means to transport them to the Philippines.[17]

Troop buildups in the Japanese colony of Taiwan and the march of Japanese armies into southern Indochina on July 28, 1941, troubled those who had believed (or were merely hoping) that the Japanese had no interest in the Philippines. "There we were," recalled Claude Buss, "right in the middle of it." Mobilization began immediately, but as the soldiers of the Philippine Army swore oaths to "bear true faith and allegiance to the United States of America," complications over transport, miscommunications in multiple languages, and contests over whether the US Army or the Philippine Army had jurisdiction over the soldiers created obstacles. Two torpedo boats, ordered from Britain, had been delivered by December 1941, but America's small Asiatic Fleet had already been withdrawn from the Philippines. The US Army Air Corps began transferring B-17 bombers and P-40 fighters to Clark Field, an hour north of Manila. The new Far East Air Force arrived in November 1941 without any airplanes, warned by Colonel Harold H. George, their commanding officer, that "Men, you are not a suicide squadron yet, but you are damned close to it."[18]

Overall, equipment was in sorry shape and short supply. So were the troops. The Philippine Scouts reached a peak enlistment of 12,000 men in July 1941; their numbers actually declined in the next few months as experienced scouts took up officer positions in the rapidly expanding Philippine Army, which in turn left the scouts—the best-trained force in the Philippines—in organizational disarray. By December 1941, following MacArthur and Eisenhower's plan, the fledgling Army of the Philippines had trained 130,000 men, some of whom had completed their five-and-one-half months of training without ever firing a rifle. The number of Philippine Army soldiers actually in uniform shot up from 4,168 men in 1940 to 22,532 in December 1941, but the underfunded and undertrained force faced an increasingly strident enemy with little backup from the United States. With the Battle of Britain raging and an undeclared naval war underway in the Atlantic, Roosevelt believed he had no option but to move US ships out of the Pacific to defend shipping in the Atlantic. Questioned on this by MacArthur, Roosevelt essentially admitted that he had no intention of defending the Philippines.[19]

As Douglas MacArthur shuttled back and forth between his apartment at the Manila Hotel and his office down the hall from Manuel Quezon at the Malacañang Palace, he knew there was little that Philippine civilians realistically could do to prepare for war. "This is a relatively poor country and in the disbursement of its scant resources, priorities of expenditure are of the utmost importance." He praised the Civilian Emergency Administration's modest efforts, which included a citywide blackout drill on November 21, 1941, and a practice evacuation the next day. Practically speaking, such measures hardly aided preparation, MacArthur thought, but he applauded the "psychological reaction which resulted from the voluntary submission of the public will to the control and training measures introduced by competent authorities." While MacArthur praised psychological measures to bend the public will, he declined to train Philippine Army recruits for the possibility that they might engage in guerrilla warfare, lest a backup plan sap the combat morale that the general—and War Plan Orange—still believed would steel them to hold off the Imperial Japanese Army long enough for the US Navy to steam into Manila Bay from Pearl Harbor.[20]

The Pacific fleet, devastated by the Pearl Harbor attacks, never arrived in Manila. In the years after the war, politicians, military officers, and historians parceled out blame left and right for the failure to defend the Philippines. The US Navy felt betrayed, first by Republican administrations that cut budgets and dismissed warnings about Japan as money-seeking scare tactics, then by Roosevelt's explicit Atlantic priorities. Filipinos blamed the United States for dragging them into the war, and their own leaders for playing politics with war mobilization. But it's not clear the situation could have worked out much differently: there was simply not enough money, or time, or goodwill. Filipino internationalists' hopes that Japan would make no moves on an independent and neutralized Philippines may have had a chance in the 1920s, but as war-minded leaders crowded out other voices in Tokyo, diplomatic options evaporated. A real defense like the one Manuel Quezon wanted, with a rapid buildup of US soldiers and enormous deliveries of weapons from America, very well might have provoked Japan sooner. And while military planners were right when they warned thirty years earlier that it would be cheaper to defend the Philippines than to reconquer it, massive expenditures to protect an almost-former colony that most Americans were trying to get rid of were politically infeasible. The Philippine Army did the best it could with the money and soldiers it had, and Chief of Staff Basilio Valdes assured MacArthur and Quezon that a meaningful national defense would be in place by the summer of 1942. They did not know they would not have that long. But when the attacks came on Clark Field on the morning of December 8, 1941, there was, as Colonel Richard C. Mallonée recalled, "a grim, thoughtful silence." But no one was surprised.[21]

And so the invasion came, more or less as everyone anticipated it would. Gregoria Espinosa, a civilian nurse with the US Army Nurse Corps at Fort McKinley, recalled that "I was not so excited as I should have been." As air raids began on December 10, hasty defense efforts continued. Santiago Pamplona Dakudao, a doctor who had studied and trained in Japan and then settled to work among the Japanese community in Davao, recalled the first attacks on that city, after which he and his wife hoarded food and medicine, hurriedly planting a fresh crop of rice and corn.

Soon, Philippine authorities rounded up Davao's Japanese. In a wartime diary, Dakudao noted that "Filipino laborers who had grievances against their former Japanese masters took the opportunity to inflict bodily harm on them and looted their houses or stores as the poor Japanese were escaping their misfortune." On December 22, just two weeks after Pearl Harbor, the Japanese Fourteenth Army under General Homma Masaharu landed at Lingayen Gulf in the northernmost part of the Philippines. Although Rear Admiral Kemp Tolley would reflect in hindsight that it was "absolutely a lead pipe cinch" that the invaders would come ashore at Lingayen, the Japanese faced little resistance from green Philippine Army recruits.[22]

In the space of a few weeks, the Japanese Imperial Army invaded, conquered, and occupied the Philippines, wiping away some forty years of US colonialism. On December 26, MacArthur declared Manila an open city, which meant that all US Army Forces in the Far East (USAFFE) soldiers remaining in the city had to evacuate, destroying whatever they could as they departed. Overall, the open city declaration was a meaningless gesture. "The Japanese weren't interested in destroying Manila," recalled Robert Lee Dennison, then serving as a captain in the US Navy's Asiatic Fleet. "They wanted the city, not a bunch of rubble." When they arrived, they faced weak resistance and inflicted little damage, rounding up about 4,000 US and other civilians and interning them for the duration of the war, most at the University of Santo Tomas. In a December 28, 1941, address, President Franklin Roosevelt gave Filipinos his solemn pledge that "their freedom will be redeemed and their independence established and protected," but as Japanese troops entered Manila on January 2, 1942, many Filipinos likely agreed with journalist Maximo M. Kalaw, who recalled that many "felt they had been duped" by the "tone of misinformed optimism" that preceded December 8. After all, they had known it was coming.[23]

SIGNALS AND NOISE

In the press, on Capitol Hill, and even within the ranks of the army and navy, President Franklin Roosevelt, his administration, and senior officers faced blistering attacks for their lack of preparation. Intensive congressional investigations in late 1945 and early 1946 recovered crucial missed signs that when strung together with the benefit of hindsight, made the possibility of a coordinated Japanese attack on Hawaii appear obvious and depicted US defense policies as wholly incompetent. This was not only a history of surprise, it was a politics of surprise, in which Roosevelt's opponents mobilized the devastating attacks to discredit the president's prewar policies and undermine his political authority more generally.[24]

Outside of Washington—and sometimes within it—accounting for Pearl Harbor generated theories of conspiracy, attributing to Roosevelt and his inner circle prior knowledge of the attacks, which FDR allegedly permitted to go forward in order to generate popular support for a war that his political coalitions were unable to deliver. Such conspiracy theories were debunked and denied even by Roosevelt's most bitter opponents. More insidious, however, is the means by which the politics of blame inverted Americans' attention from the politics of anticipation that shaped the Pacific in the late 1930s to a politics of surprise that helped them make sense of a post–December 7 world.[25]

As surprise moved from political headlines to social scientific analysis—most notably in international relations and security studies—it quickly dominated and consistently distorted historical understanding. Tracing how that happened brings us back to the Cold War and to one of its intellectual architects, Roberta Wohlstetter. Working in the late 1950s as a defense analyst at the RAND Corporation, Wohlstetter undertook research for and—over military objections—ultimately published *Pearl Harbor: Warning and Decision* (1962), an influential study of the Pearl Harbor attacks. Wohlstetter told readers she was "concerned almost exclusively with the facts of warning and surprise and their implications for today," meaning, implicitly, nuclear war. In the book's introduction, nuclear strategist and game theorist Thomas C. Schelling echoed Wohlstetter's present-minded mentality when he described Pearl Harbor as "a dramatic failure of a remarkably well-informed government to call the next enemy move in a cold-war crisis." Unlike the congressional investigators of a generation before, Wohlstetter avoided placing blame on individuals, choosing instead to trace the near-impossibility of intelligence systems that could distinguish "signals" from "noise." "Since we cannot rely on strategic warning," she concluded, "our defenses . . . must be designed to function without it." The lesson of Pearl Harbor was that preventing surprise was an impossible enterprise.[26]

Wohlstetter's conclusions have been debated by scholars, but her assumption—that Pearl Harbor was a surprise attack and thereby a problem of intelligence—persists to this day. The influential historian and security studies scholar John Lewis Gaddis, for instance, has likened Pearl Harbor to the September 11, 2001, terrorist attacks: "Both were bolts from the blue on bright mornings. Both achieved total surprise, as the result of a total failure of intelligence." Setting aside surprise helps us see the attacks as the culmination of failures of diplomacy rather than blindnesses of military intelligence. Returning to anticipation also helps us move away from what didn't happen before Pearl Harbor, to what did—what the politics of anticipation actually generated in the years before and after the attacks.[27]

ANTICIPATING EMERGENCY

In the conclusion to her Cold War–era study of the Pearl Harbor attack, Wohlstetter noted that "we have to accept the fact of uncertainty and learn to live with it. No magic, in code or otherwise, will provide certainty. Our plans must work without it." True enough. But in the meantime, what is the political work that uncertainty can do? For John Lewis Gaddis, "surprise attacks tend to sweep away old conceptions of national security and what it takes to achieve it." Indeed they do, but the sweeping begins not in the aftermath but in the anticipation of attack, in response to legitimate concerns for national defense that lend themselves to mobilization by a politics of fear.[28]

This was clear in the Philippines. Independence did, in the end, arrive on July 4, 1946, after three years of Japanese occupation and a massive American reinvasion (or "liberation") that together devastated the country for decades to come. Its politics were also forever changed, as the politics of anticipation and emergency fed into a dynamic of expanding presidential power, amplified by weak controls on executive authority in the constitution of the Philippine republic. Facing political unrest and communist insurgency, President Elpidio Quirino suspended the writ of habeas corpus in October 1950; three years of anticommunist terror followed. Two decades later, on September 21, 1972, President Ferdinand Marcos went a step further, declaring martial law. "I, as your duly-elected President of the Republic, use this power implemented by military authorities to protect the Republic of the Philippines and our democracy," he said, citing constitutional provisions that gave the president authority to declare martial law "in cases of invasion, insurrection or rebellion or imminent danger thereof." During the fourteen-year suspension of democracy, an estimated 6,000 Filipinos were killed by state authorities. At least that many and more have died since 2016 in the violence that has accompanied the purportedly anticrime and antiterror campaigns of President Rodrigo Duterte, a man who openly appeals to the authoritarian traditions embodied by Ferdinand Marcos and Manuel Quezon. The origins of that authoritarianism run deep in the histories of the Philippines and its erstwhile colonial power, the United States. But they took root in a soil of anticipation, fear, and emergency that we forget if we think of Pearl Harbor arriving as a bolt from the blue on a sunny morning in December 1941.[29]

NOTES

1. Stark's message is widely reprinted, most recently in Steve Twomey, *Countdown to Pearl Harbor: The Twelve Days to the Attack* (New York: Simon and Schuster, 2016), 81. Thomas C. Hart, in Twomey, *Countdown to Pearl Harbor*, 84; Charles H. Bogart, ed., "Corregidor, The Last Month of Peace: The Letters of Captain John D. Wood," *Virginia Magazine of History and Biography* 93 (October 1985), 435–455, at 451.

2. Frank Knox, in Louis Morton, *The Fall of the Philippines* (Washington, DC: Office

of the Chief of Military History, Department of the Army, 1953), 78. See also William H. Bartsch, *December 8, 1941: MacArthur's Pearl Harbor* (College Station: Texas A&M University Press, 2003); D. Clayton James, "The Other Pearl Harbor," *MHQ: The Quarterly Journal of Military History* 7 (Winter 1994), 22–29; Richard B. Meixsel, *Clark Field and the U.S. Army Air Corps in the Philippines, 1919–1942* (Quezon City: New Day, 2002), 106–121; Michael Schaller, "The Debacle in the Philippines," in Robert W. Love Jr., ed., *Pearl Harbor Revisited* (New York: St. Martin's Press, 1995), 111–129.

3. On prewar plans, see Edward S. Miller, *War Plan Orange: The U.S. Strategy to Defeat Japan, 1897–1945* (Annapolis, MD: Naval Institute Press, 1991).

4. Thomas Schelling, in Roberta Wohlstetter, *Pearl Harbor: Warning and Decision* (Stanford, CA: Stanford University Press, 1962), vii.

5. Robert Aura Smith, *Philippine Freedom, 1946–1958* (New York: Columbia University Press, 1958), 97; Michael Schaller, *Douglas MacArthur: The Far Eastern General* (New York: Oxford University Press, 1989), 31–32. For analyses of the political status of the Philippine commonwealth from the period, see Bernabe Africa, "The Foreign Relations of the Philippine Commonwealth," *Philippine Social Science Review* 8 (September 1936), 205–215; Ralston Hayden, "The Philippines in Transition from Commonwealth to Independence," *Foreign Affairs* 14 (July 1936), 639–653; Grayson L. Kirk, *Philippine Independence: Motives, Problems, and Prospects* (New York: Farrar and Rinehart, 1936); George A. Malcolm, *The Commonwealth of the Philippines* (New York: D. Appleton-Century, 1936); and Jose Reyes, "What American Policy in the Philippines Would Do to Relieve Potential Sources of International Conflict," *Philippine Social Science Review* 8 (September 1936), 218–222.

6. Commonwealth Act No. 1, December 21, 1935.

7. Maximo M. Kalaw, "Why I Favor the Defense Bill," *Philippine Forum* 1 (February 1936), 73, 74; Camilo Osias, "My Opposition to the National Defense Bill," *Philippine Forum* 1 (January 1936), 30, 32.

8. James S. Allen, "Manuel Quezon—Philippine Dictator," *The Nation* 144 (March 20, 1937), 321; Charles B. McLane, *Soviet Strategies in Southeast Asia: An Exploration of Eastern Policies under Lenin and Stalin* (Princeton, NJ: Princeton University Press, 1966), 222–223.

9. Matthew F. Holland, *Eisenhower between the Wars: The Making of a General and a Statesman* (Westport, CT: Praeger, 2001), esp. 177–205; Carol Morris Petillo, *Douglas MacArthur: The Philippine Years* (Bloomington: Indiana University Press, 1981); Schaller, *MacArthur.*

10. Philippine Constitution (1935), Art. II, Secs. 2, 3; Claude Buss Oral History, typescript (1984), 3, Center for Oral and Public History, California State University, Fullerton, California (hereafter CSUF). See also Oona J. Hathaway and Scott A. Shapiro, *The Internationalists: How a Radical Plan to Outlaw War Remade the World* (New York: Simon and Schuster, 2017); and "Roosevelt Signs Philippines Bill," *New York Times*, March 25, 1934, p. 1.

11. Commonwealth Act No. 111, October 31, 1936; Manuel Abella, "The Issue of P. I. Dictatorship," *Philippines Star Press*, August 28, 1937, p. 12; Allen, "Manuel Quezon"; "Defense Program Upheld by Quezon," *New York Times*, April 4, 1937, p. 7; C. C. Bartolome, "The Need for a National Physical Education Movement in the Philippines Today," *Philippine Social Science Review* 7 (October 1935), 280–281; E. K. Higdon, "Enroll Girls in Philippine Army," *Christian Century* 53 (January 8, 1936), 58–59; E. K. Higdon,

"Filipinos Back Military Regime," *Christian Century* 54 (January 13, 1937), 54; Geronimo Suva, "Physical Education in the Philippines," in *The Social Integration of the Philippines* (Manila: Philippine Commission of Independence, 1924), 67; E. D. Hester, "Outline of Our Recent Political and Trade Relations with the Philippine Commonwealth," *Annals of the American Academy of Political and Social Science* 226 (March 1943), 81; "The March of Events," *Philippine Forum* 2 (January 1937), 13; "President Quezon's Citizenship Code," in Filipino Agricultural Laborers' Association, *FALA Year Book, 1940* (Stockton, CA: FALA, 1940), in Box 15, Papers of Carey McWilliams, Young Research Library, UCLA, Los Angeles (hereafter UCLA).

12. Hugh S. Johnson, "Anchors Away," *Saturday Evening Post* 213 (October 5, 1940), 77, 80; Pacis, quoted in Catherine Porter, *Crisis in the Philippines* (New York: Alfred A. Knopf, 1942), 6; Grant K. Goodman, "'Anti-Communism' in Japanese-Philippine Relations during the 1930s," *Journal of Southeast Asian Studies* 9 (September 1978), 219–233; Robert E. Herzstein, *Henry R. Luce: A Political Portrait of the Man Who Created the American Century* (New York: Charles Scribner's Sons, 1994), 241–244; George A. Malcolm, *American Colonial Careerist: Half a Century of Official Life and Personal Experience in the Philippines and Puerto Rico* (Boston: Christopher, 1957), 71.

13. Hernando J. Abaya, *The CLU Story: 50 Years of Struggle for Civil Liberties* (Quezon City: New Day, 1987), 4; Buss OH, CSUF, 8; Malcolm, *American Colonial Careerist,* 71; Smith, *Philippine Freedom,* 101, 105. For a selection of the most alarmist accounts of US-Japanese relations, see William Henry Chamberlin, *Japan over Asia,* rev. and enl. ed. (Boston: Little, Brown, 1939), 178–187; and George F. Eliot, *The Ramparts We Watch: A Study of the Problems of American National Defense* (New York: Reynal and Hitchcock, 1938), esp. 59–63.

14. Abaya, *CLU Story,* 1–3, 9–23; Buss OH, CSUF, 8; Philippine Army, *Semi-Annual Report of the Chief of Staff of the Philippine Army for the Period, January 1 to June 30, 1939* (Manila: Bureau of Printing, 1940), 7–8; Schaller, *MacArthur,* 39–40. For an example of tension, see Francis Bowes Sayre to Cordell Hull, November 27, 1939, Box 4, Papers of Francis Bowes Sayre, Library of Congress Manuscript Division, Washington, DC (hereafter LCMD).

15. Commonwealth Act No. 600, August 21, 1940; Bernstein, *Philippine Story,* 168; Buss OH, CSUF, 5; Francis Bowes Sayre, *Glad Adventure* (New York: Macmillan, 1957), 210–229; Francis Bowes Sayre to Cordell Hull, December 14, 1940, Box 4, and Francis Bowes Sayre to Harold Ickes, April 9, 1941, Box 5, both in Papers of Francis Bowes Sayre, LCMD. Provisions of the Emergency Powers Act allowing Quezon to seize private business in time of war also frightened the Manila Americans. Gerald E. Wheeler, "The American Minority in the Philippines during the Prewar Commonwealth Period," *Asian Studies* 4 (August 1966), 367–371.

16. Michael D. Pante, "Quezon's City: Corruption and Contradiction in Manila's Prewar Suburbia," *Journal of Southeast Asian Studies* 48 (February 2017), 91–112; Porter, *Crisis in the Philippines,* 111–112; "Quezon's Food Plan Supplies Philippines with War Larder," *Washington Post,* December 21, 1941, p. B2; Schaller, *MacArthur,* 40.

17. Manuel Quezon to Francis Bowes Sayre, April 3, 1941, and Francis Bowes Sayre to Harold Ickes, April 9, 1941, both in Box 5, Papers of Francis Bowes Sayre, LCMD; Buss OH, CSUF, 7; "Instructions Governing Air Raid Warden Service," in Civilian Emergency

Administration, *Rules and Regulations for the Organization and Training of Volunteer Guards and the Air Raid Wardens Service and Air Raid Precautions* (Manila: Bureau of Printing, 1941), 55; Schaller, *MacArthur,* 40.

18. Buss OH, CSUF, 4; "Filipinos Wonder about Bomb Refuge," *Washington Post,* July 29, 1941, pp. 1, 2; Christopher L. Kolakowski, *Last Stand on Bataan: The Defense of the Philippines, December 1941–May 1942* (Jefferson, NC: McFarland, 2016), 3; James William Morley, ed., *The Fateful Choice: Japan's Advance into Southeast Asia, 1939–1941* (New York: Columbia University Press, 1980).

19. Delbert Ausmus Oral History, typescript (1965), 1307, Papers of Delbert Ausmus, UCLA; John Gordon IV, "Among the Best: The Philippine Scouts," *Military Review* 67 (September 1987), 70–71; Ricardo Trota Jose, *The Philippine Army, 1935–1942* (Quezon City: Ateneo de Manila University Press, 1992), 196; Miller, *War Plan Orange,* 61–62; Morton, *Fall of the Philippines,* 27–28; Porter, *Crisis in the Philippines,* 110, 112–113; Schaller, *MacArthur,* 40; Smith, *Philippine Freedom,* 103.

20. Douglas MacArthur to Francis Bowes Sayre, October 10, 1941, Box 5, Papers of Francis Bowes Sayre, LCMD; David W. Hogan Jr., "MacArthur, Stilwell, and Special Operations in the War against Japan," *Parameters* 25 (Spring 1995), 104–115, at 106; Porter, *Crisis in the Philippines,* 119; Carlos Quirino, *Quezon: Paladin of Philippine Freedom* (Manila: Filipiniana Book Guild, 1971), 328–348.

21. Richard C. Mellonée, quoted in Morton, *Fall of the Philippines,* 80.

22. Maria Cynthia B. Barriga, "The Asia-Pacific War in the Davao Settler Zone, December 1941," *Kasarinlan* 30, 1 (2015), 56–90; Michaelangelo Ebro-Dakudao, "A Davao Wartime Diary," *Philippine Quarterly of Culture and Society* 22 (March 1994), 64–72, at 69; Gregoria I. Espinosa, "Filipino Nurses in Bataan and Corregidor," *American Journal of Nursing* 46 (February 1946), 97–98; "Filipino Troops Push Back Japs in Vigan Battle," *Chicago Tribune,* December 18, 1941, p. 4; Maria Luna Lopez, "A Filipino Woman Looks at the War," *Philippine Review* 1 (May 1943), 40–42; Kemp Tolley, "Army Snubs Navy in the Philippines," in John T. Mason Jr., ed., *The Pacific War Remembered: An Oral History Collection* (Annapolis, MD: Naval Institute Press, 1986), 23–30, at 27. See also Victor Buencamino, *Memoirs of Victor Buencamino: A Biography* (Manila: Historical Conservation Society, 1996); Juan Labrador, *A Diary of the Japanese Occupation* (Manila: Santo Tomas University Press, 1989); Antonio Perez de Olaguer, *El Terror Amarillo en Filipinas* (Barcelona: Editorial Juventud, 1947); and Eliseo Quirino, *A Day to Remember* (Manila: Benipayo Press, 1958).

23. Robert Lee Dennison, "The Philippines: Prelude to Departure," in Mason, *Pacific War Remembered,* 31–37, at 35; David DuBois, "Admiral Thomas C. Hart and the Demise of the Asiatic Fleet, 1941–1942," MA thesis, East Tennessee State University, 2014; Maximo M. Kalaw, "Filipino Opposition to the Japanese," *Pacific Affairs* 18 (December 1945), 340–345, at 341; "Messages on Philippines," *New York Times,* December 29, 1941, p. 1; Paul W. Ropp, "Thomas Delamore and the Defense of the Philippines: Heroism, Bureaucracy, and Fate," *Journal of America's Military Past* 27 (Spring-Summer 2000), 89–99, at 93. For a personal account of the bombing, see Labrador, *Diary of the Occupation,* 26–33.

24. Martin V. Melosi, *The Shadow of Pearl Harbor: Political Controversy over the Surprise Attack, 1941–1946* (College Station: Texas A&M University Press, 1977); US Congress, *Report*

of the Joint Committee on the Investigation of the Pearl Harbor Attack, 79th Congress, 2d Sess., 1946. On congressional opposition to Roosevelt's domestic and foreign policies, see Robert Dallek, *Franklin D. Roosevelt and American Foreign Policy, 1932–1945* (New York: Oxford University Press, 1979); and James T. Patterson, *Congressional Conservatism and the New Deal: The Growth of the Conservative Coalition in Congress, 1933–1939* (Lexington: University Press of Kentucky, 1967).

25. Kathryn S. Olmsted, *Real Enemies: Conspiracy Theories and American Democracy, World War I to 9/11* (New York: Oxford University Press, 2009), 45–82.

26. Wohlstetter, *Pearl Harbor*, vii, 1, 400–401.

27. John Lewis Gaddis, *Surprise, Security, and the American Experience* (Cambridge, MA: Harvard University Press, 2004), 35. Wohlstetter's approach—and Schelling's language—was subtly critiqued in the introduction to Gordon W. Prange's *At Dawn We Slept: The Untold Story of Pearl Harbor* (New York: McGraw-Hill, 1981), xv, which notes that Pearl Harbor "cannot be reduced to a scientific formula or factored like a mathematical problem."

28. Gaddis, *Surprise, Security, and the American Experience*, 37; Wohlstetter, *Pearl Harbor*, 401.

29. Proclamation No. 1081, September 21, 1972; Rolando V. del Carmen, "Constitutionalism and the Supreme Court in a Changing Philippine Polity," *Asian Survey* 13 (November 1973), 1050–1061; Nicole Curato, ed., *A Duterte Reader: Critical Essays on Rodrigo Duterte's Early Presidency* (Ithaca, NY: Cornell University Press, 2017). Two crucial attempts to trace the colonial origins of Philippine authoritarianism are Leia Castañeda Anastacio, *The Foundations of the Philippine State: Imperial Rule and the American Constitutional Tradition in the Philippine Islands, 1898–1935* (New York: Cambridge University Press, 2016), esp. 248–257; and Alfred W. McCoy, "Quezon's Commonwealth: The Emergence of Philippine Authoritarianism," in Ruby R. Paredes, ed., *Philippine Colonial Democracy* (New Haven, CT: Yale University Southeast Asian Studies, 1988), 114–156.

CHAPTER 9

Pearl Harbor and Australia's War in the Pacific

Kate Darian-Smith

On February 19, 2017, the seventy-fifth anniversary of the bombing of Darwin was commemorated with a service attended by the Australian prime minister, Malcolm Turnbull, and Governor General Peter Cosgrove at the memorial cenotaph on the city's esplanade. The piercing screech of an air-raid siren was sounded at 9:58 a.m., the exact time of the first Japanese raid in 1942, and military aircraft flew across the sky. Veteran survivor Mervyn Lloyd Ey, age ninety-five years, was among those who gathered to remember and reflect on the enemy attack. He vividly recalled the suddenness of the raid and the ensuing chaos: "The first we saw was a whole heap of bombers coming over, and it wasn't long before [there were] dive bombers and fighters, and there were planes . . . and explosions everywhere."[1] The bombing of Darwin was the first and most devastating attack by an overseas power on the Australian mainland, killing 250 people and wounding hundreds more. The strike, which launched the Japanese air offensive against northern Australia, has grown in prominence within the national memory of Australia's role in World War II and has been increasingly referred to as "Australia's Pearl Harbor."

When the attack on Darwin occurred, Australia had been at war since September 3, 1939, following Great Britain into conflict with Germany. Its army, navy, and air force served with distinction in the European theater: in the defense of Tobruk in North Africa, during the Allied withdrawal from Greece during 1941, and in the Allied victory at the Second Battle of El Alamein in 1942. However, the Japanese raid of Pearl Harbor on December 8, 1941, brought war into the Asia-Pacific and to Australia's "doorstep," with the military and civilian fronts brought into close proximity.[2] Australian troops were recalled home from Europe, and with the extension of government controls the civilian population was geared up for total war. For Australia, unlike its allies Britain and the United States, the key theater during World War II was in the Pacific rather than Europe. This chapter provides an overview of Australia's war after Pearl Harbor, with a focus on Japanese attacks on Darwin and the Australian mainland, experiences on the home front, and the impact of the war in modernizing Australia's society and economy and reshaping its security alliances with the United States and the Asia-Pacific region.

AUSTRALIAN-JAPANESE RELATIONS AND THE BOMBING OF DARWIN

The entry of Japan into World War II, thus opening the Asia-Pacific theater of conflict, only confirmed a deep anxiety in Australia about Japan's military aggression in the region. Japanese militarism built on a cultural fear that had existed since the mid-nineteenth century: that a "white" Australia should be subject to the invasion of Asian hordes from the north.[3] With the federation of the Australian colonies in 1901, the maintenance of a racially restrictive immigration policy directed at non-Europeans—particularly at Asians—was the first legislation passed by the new nation. Indeed, in the aftermath of World War I, Prime Minister Billy Hughes was openly antagonistic toward Japan at the Paris Peace Conference in 1919. He effectively vetoed Japan's aspirations to have a racial equality clause added to the covenant of the League of Nations, arguing that this would undermine the White Australia Policy. The rejection of its claims to be on an equal footing with European empires, and in which Australia's view was supported by the United States, was humiliating for Japan. Historians have argued that this rejection contributed to the development of militaristic nationalism in that country during the interwar decades.[4]

Within Australia, personal and business relations with resident Japanese had existed for a century. These were generally friendly prior to Japan's wartime signing of the Tripartite Pact with Germany and Italy in September 1940.[5] In the interwar period, a prosperous Japanese merchant class was concentrated in Sydney, with small Japanese communities in the remote north, particularly in the pear shell fisheries at Thursday Island in Queensland and at Broome in Western Australia. This latter group had immigrated with the provision that as "people of color" they could work north of the 23rd parallel. Commerce between Australia and Japan grew during the 1920s, and the larger Japanese firms with offices in Australia were connected to global trading networks. During the 1930s Australia sent trade missions to Japan, and in 1935 it established the semi-diplomatic post of trade commissioner in Tokyo. As the decade progressed, however, Australia's policy of preferential trade with Great Britain resulted in a series of trade disputes with Japan; while these were resolved, overall relations between the two nations soured.[6]

In August 1940 an Australian legation was established in Tokyo, with the prominent judge and politician Sir John Latham at its head. Latham was in Melbourne when Pearl Harbor was bombed, but his deputy Keith Officer was visited by a Japanese official from the Ministry of Foreign Affairs who presented a declaration of war and searched the premises, with no success, for communication equipment. The Australian staff were confined to the legation's spacious grounds at Hachisuka House. Officer found this a period of "maddening inactivity," though by the spring of 1942 the house arrest was relaxed and he was allowed to walk around the neighborhood and to play a game of golf. On July 30, 1942, following extensive negotiations between the Allied powers and Japan, the Australians and their colleagues from the United States and Dutch legations were repatriated home.[7]

Throughout 1941, with Australian forces deployed in the Middle East and the Mediterranean theaters, the Australian government was increasingly anxious about the territorial intentions of Japan and what this meant for national security. When news of the Japanese attack on Pearl Harbor reached Australia on the late morning of December 8, the press reportage emphasized that Japan had simultaneously invaded the Philippines, then a US dependency, as well as the east coast of Malaya and Hong Kong, both British colonies. The War Cabinet met to discuss Australian priorities in the Pacific. That evening, Prime Minister John Curtin announced on national radio that Australia faced its "darkest hour": "We are at war with Japan. That has happened because, in the first instance, Japanese naval and air forces launched an unprovoked attack on British and United States territory; because our vital interests are imperilled and because the rights of free people in the whole Pacific are assailed."[8] In his broadcast, Curtin called for more volunteers for the Australian Imperial Force (AIF) and stated that 2,000 women were urgently needed to join the military in its auxiliary services. Across Australia, enlistment offices recorded the highest numbers in months, with 500 men signing up at central Sydney's Martin Place office alone.[9]

As the Japanese troops advanced down the Malayan peninsula, the capacity of the British forces to protect Australia was shown to be painfully inadequate. The vulnerability of Australia was exposed further when on December 10 the British vessels HMS *Prince of Wales* and HMS *Repulse*, both intended to protect Singapore, were sunk. The British naval base at Singapore was the central component of an imperial strategy that dated from the interwar years and was vital to the protection of Australia. The previous prime minister, Robert Menzies, had visited Britain in early 1941 to lobby Winston Churchill on Australia's behalf to send reinforcements to Singapore. Menzies's absence abroad enabled his critics at home to become more vocal and led to his resignation in August. A shift in the balance of power in the federal parliament meant that on October 7 the Australian Labor Party assumed control of the government. Curtin was thus relatively fresh to the office of prime minister when the Pacific War was declared.

In his new year address to the nation, published in the Melbourne *Herald* newspaper on December 27, 1941, and titled "The Task Ahead," Curtin stated: "I make it quite clear that Australia looks to America, free of any pangs as to our traditional links or kinship with the United Kingdom."[10] This rallying cry to the Australian people was widely supported by the domestic press. Abroad, the words displeased Churchill and Franklin Roosevelt, who respectively thought Curtin's comments had undermined the leadership of the British Empire and smacked of panic.[11] The two Allied leaders had spent the Christmas period together in the White House in Washington, where at the Arcadia Conference they confirmed the "Europe first" policy, which gave primacy to the defeat of Nazi Germany. Australian priorities were, of course, very different. Curtin continued to lobby Churchill in early 1942 about the importance of securing the naval base at Singapore. When Curtin insisted that the Sixth and Seventh Divisions of the AIF return home from the Middle East, a clash with Churchill was inevitable. Although Churchill made moves to divert some Australian troops to Burma, he reluctantly capitulated to Curtin's demand.

The inability of Britain to send its promised naval fleet, and the subsequent fall of the "impregnable" fortress of Singapore to the Japanese on February 15, 1942, was greeted with widespread dismay in Australia. This only intensified as reports came through that at Singapore the Japanese had taken more than 80,000 Allied prisoners of war (POWs), including 15,000 men in the Eighth Division of the AIF. The "betrayal" of the British to protect Australia and New Zealand in exchange for the sending of Dominion troops to fight in Europe and the Middle East was felt in both countries, and it has continued to echo in the historiography.[12] At the time, Curtin acknowledged the significance of the Allied surrender: "Just as Dunkirk opened the battle for Britain," he told the people, "Singapore opened the battle for Australia."[13] When Darwin was bombed on February 19, only days later, the fear of an enemy attack on the Australian nation was realized.

Darwin was the largest town in northern Australia. Before World War II it was a multiracial settlement of just under 6,000 indigenous, Asian, and European inhabitants that served as an administrative, commercial, communications, and transport center for a huge and sparsely populated section of the Australian continent. In response to Japan's mounting militarization, from the 1930s Darwin's military port facilities and airfields were developed. Anti-aircraft guns were installed, the Royal Australian Navy (RAN) and the Royal Australian Air Force (RAAF) bases were established, and an antisubmarine boom net—an astounding six kilometers long—was strung across Darwin Harbor.

Following Japan's entry into the war, Darwin's administration was on high alert. In mid-December 1941 plans were laid for the evacuation of European women and children. This was implemented over the next two months, mostly via sea, with the last evacuee ship leaving on February 15, 1942. The Native Affairs Branch also sent many indigenous people away from the town, including relocating some women and children to the southern states. In Darwin the 2,500 remaining civilians became a minority among thousands of Allied troops garrisoned there in recognition of the town's strategic position as a base for the defense of the Netherlands East Indies.

The two successive aerial attacks that occurred on Darwin on the morning of February 19 were orchestrated by Mitsuo Fuchida, the captain in the Imperial Japanese Navy Air Service who was responsible for the bombing of Pearl Harbor. As in Hawai'i, the Japanese strike was unexpected. The first raid occurred mid-morning, with around 188 Japanese aircraft launched from carriers in the Timor Sea. The planes reached Darwin before the onshore warning sirens were sounded. Forty minutes of "noise, fury and destruction" followed. The attack destroyed three Allied warships and six merchant vessels, damaging other ships, the entire wharf area, airfields, army barracks, and an oil store. The greatest loss of life was that of eighty-eight sailors aboard the US Navy destroyer *Peary*, which was sunk. In the center of town, the Post Office and Postmaster's Residence, the Telegraph Office, and the Cable Office were all hit, and nine civilian postal workers, including six women, died. An hour later, just before midday, a second Japanese raid targeted the RAAF base. The hangars and other buildings went up in flames, and most of the aircraft were damaged. With widespread destruction of the town, its wharf and military facilities, and hundreds of people killed and wounded, confusion erupted (see photo on page 178). Many civilians and military personnel fled south to the small inland settlement at Adelaide River, fearing a further Japanese bombing or possible invasion.[14]

As press reports of the bombing were circulated, civilian morale in Australia plummeted. In military and government circles, there were concerns about the slow response to the Japanese attack and the disorder and panic that occurred. Curtin swiftly appointed a royal commission to examine the situation, headed by a Victorian state supreme court judge, Justice Charles Lowe. Lowe and his team arrived in Darwin in early March, where they interviewed over seventy people, sometimes among the rubble of destroyed buildings.[15] The commission's final report covered the bombing in detail, documenting the loss of life and examining how the branches of the Australian forces had cooperated during the attack. It found that approximately 250 people had been killed, with a further 300 to 400 injured. The report's criticism was most strongly directed at the RAAF and the station commander, though there was also concern about desertion (though some

The Bombing of Darwin, 19 February 1942: oil tanks burning after direct hits. Alan William Sloan collection of photographs of the North West and Darwin. BA1410/3/81. (Sourced from the collections of the State Library of Western Australia and reproduced with the permission of the Library Board of Western Australia.)

men straggled back to Darwin several days after the bombing) and the widespread looting of government and private properties. Lowe recommended that united control of the military services and improved communications would minimize losses in any future enemy attack.[16] Although the commission concluded its report on March 27, 1942, its content was so explosive that it was not tabled in the Australian Parliament until October 1945, when the Pacific War was over.

In early 1942, however, the impact of the bombing of Darwin was deeply felt throughout the nation. Other enemy attacks on the Australian mainland soon followed. On March 3, 1942, the Japanese attacked the tiny Western Australian pearling town of Broome, then operating as a major military and civilian transit stop for those fleeing the Japanese advance through the Netherlands East Indies (Indonesia). The Dutch refugees were transported to Australia in various Dutch, Australian, and US aircraft, including large flying boats that were owned by Qan-tas Empire Airways. The Japanese bombing at Broome killed around seventy people, injured many more, and destroyed a total of twenty-four aircraft including sixteen flying boats. Among the casualties were Dutch women and children who were waiting on the flying boats in Broome harbor to be taken ashore.

Over the next eighteen months, up to 100 Japanese air raids on northern Australia occurred, intended to destroy Allied ships, planes, airfields, and other military infrastructure. The town of Darwin was attacked repeatedly on more than sixty separate occasions, although the damage each time was very minor in comparison to the initial attacks. Although total numbers are unknown, it is estimated that as many as 1,000 military and civilian fatalities occurred as a result of Japanese air raids on the Australian continent during World War II, with the majority of lives lost in the first, and heaviest, raids on Darwin on February 19, 1942. For those living in Australia's remote north, this was a tense time. In July 1942 the Japanese launched several attacks on Townsville on the east coast in Queensland, by then the largest Allied airfield in Australia. When a lone Japanese aircraft dropped eight bombs over the sugarcane district of Mossman, shrapnel damaged the family home of the Zuilo family. A metal shard grazed the skull of two-year-old Carmel Zuilo, who was asleep; she survived to dedicate a memorial on the site fifty years later.[17]

Japanese submarines also shelled the New South Wales cities of Sydney and Newcastle between late May and early June 1942. Three midget submarines entered Sydney Harbor in a failed attempt to sink Allied warships, although a converted ferry was struck and twenty-one sailors died.[18] Days later, the harborside suburbs of both Sydney and industrial Newcastle were bombarded, but without casualties. Japanese submarine raids in Australian waters resumed in the first half of 1943 and included the torpedoing of the hospital ship *Centaur* off the Queensland coast north of Brisbane. Almost 300 lives were lost, including those of eleven nurses, and there was anger in Australia that the attack on a clearly marked hospital ship flouted the principles of the Geneva Convention.

It is now well established by historians that the Japanese did not intend to invade Australia during World War II.[19] However, the raids from the sky and sea on the continent, particularly during the crisis months in the first half of 1942, contributed to a belief at the time that an enemy invasion was a real possibility. Evacuation plans were widespread, with many schoolchildren sent away from the coastal cities of Sydney and Melbourne to safe inland locations. There were also efforts to outwit any invading force. In Melbourne, for instance, the names of suburban railway stations were removed so that if the Japanese landed they would become disoriented and lost.

By the second half of 1942, as the Japanese forces were checked by the decisive Allied operations at the Battle of the Coral Sea and the Battle of Midway, the fear among the Australian people of an enemy invasion began to recede. In October 1942 the federal minister for labor and national service, Eddie Ward, alleged that the previous Menzies government had planned to abandon the continent above the Queensland capital of Brisbane to an invading Japanese force. Ward based his claims on wartime strategies that prioritized the protection of key industrial cities in the populous southern half of the continent. The suggestion that a "Brisbane Line" existed created much public discussion, especially in northern Australia, although eventually a royal commission in 1943 cleared Menzies of supporting any such policy.[20]

THE PACIFIC WAR ON THE AUSTRALIAN HOME FRONT

In October 1941 the Curtin government recalled Sir General Thomas Blamey, commander of the AIF, from the Middle East to discuss Japan's intentions in the Pacific. Much to Curtin's annoyance, Blamey blasted the Australian people for showing too much of a "carnival spirit" and failing to take the war seriously.[21] A. P. Elkin, professor of anthropology at the University of Sydney, concurred. Drawing on his own survey of public opinion, Elkin argued in a small book published during 1941 that "a more alert attitude" to wartime dangers was needed.[22] Such concerns about civilian apathy were swiftly displaced when the Japanese bombing of Pearl Harbor opened the Pacific theater, and the Australian government introduced measures that directed and enforced an "All-In" war effort on the home front.[23] Over the Christmas period in 1941, the military situation was seen to be so urgent that the government banned holidays for workers as well as festive advertising.

National planning for civil defense had been discussed as early as April 1939, and in June 1941 a federal Department of Home Security was formed to oversee emergency procedures and coordinate actions across the states. With the declaration of World War II, air raid precautions (ARP) training commenced, and Australians became familiar with the devastation caused by aerial bombings in Europe as newsreels showed the effects of "the blitz" in Britain. However, it was only with the Pacific War that comprehensive civil defense plans were enacted in Australia. Despite the very different military conditions in Europe and the Pacific, British ARP practices were adopted wholesale.

In the early months of 1942 it was evident in Australian towns and cities that the nation was at war. Air raid trenches were dug in public parklands, bomb shelters were erected in private homes, and regular air-raid drills were held at schools and workplaces. Sandbags were piled up against shop windows to minimize damage if bombing occurred. Perhaps the most potent symbol of wartime was the "brown-out" introduced in state capitals, with streetlights turned off at night to protect industry and residents from aerial attack. Black curtains and paper were pasted on the windows of shops and homes, and ARP wardens were charged with ensuring such directives were observed. The dimmed lighting was most stringently applied in Melbourne, with its extensive port and centralized armament and aircraft industries—and continued in a modified form until 1945, even though the danger of enemy attack had long passed.

During the Pacific War, Australians were subjected to the most extensive government control over all aspects of their daily lives in the nation's history. The National Security Act allowed for emergency measures, with regulations set out in the War Book and decisions made by a War Cabinet. From early 1942 the production and supply of goods and services were tightly controlled and the government emphasized the necessity for civil sacrifice and "austerity." Rationing was introduced to meet military requirements and Australia's contracts with the United States and Britain. A weekly coupon system, again adopted from the British model, was applied to the sale of clothing and textiles and to foods including tea, sugar, butter, meat, and eggs. Gasoline continued to be rationed, with a permit required for all interstate travel. Australian civilians were confronted with other shortages, including alcohol, cigarettes, and chocolate—considered by many to be everyday, rather than luxury, items. A plethora of other controls were established: rents were pegged, the frequency of sports matches and race meetings cut, and the opening hours of cinemas and theaters reduced. News services by radio and the printed press, and all other communications, including letters from the military front to loved ones at home, were strictly censored.

The government direction of industry and labor accelerated in early 1942, shifting the economy onto a total war footing and laying the foundations for postwar reconstruction and a long-term economic boom in Australia. To fund the cost of the war, the commonwealth assumed exclusive control of income tax from the states, a power it retained into the peace. Financial powers were thus centralized in the federal treasury, and the wartime administration expanded with the doubling of the federal public service between 1939 and 1946. Wartime requirements assisted the rapid growth of the commonwealth-owned munitions and aircraft industries and manufacturing more broadly in vehicle production, metal and chemical processing, and food and textiles. Increased production was spurred by Australia's involvement in the reciprocal lend-lease scheme with the United States, including major commitments to supply the US military in the Pacific with all foodstuff needs. With higher wages and limited access to goods because of rationing, the Australian population invested heavily in government bonds and war savings schemes.[24]

The control of labor was essential for winning the war. Australia had experienced high unemployment and resulting social distress during the 1930s Great Depression, and when it entered World War II in September 1939 about 10 percent of male trade unionists were still without work. As elsewhere in the Western world, war proved a panacea for unemployment; Australia was approaching full male employment when the Pacific War commenced. By early 1942 the federal government nominated essential industries and "protected" occupations, and its Manpower Directorate oversaw the employment of all men and women over the age of sixteen. Australians were required to carry identity cards and could not change jobs without the directorate's permission. Yet, despite such regulation the Australian workforce had never been so highly mobile in geographical and vocational terms. As workers moved from the county to industrial jobs in the city, they created localized shortages in rural areas. These were met through the supply of nontraditional agricultural labor. This included more than 14,000 Italian POWs sent from the European theater; "enemy aliens" of German and Austrian origin, many who were Jewish refugees, shipped from Britain in 1940; and other male internees, many born in Australia who were classified as being of "enemy" origin. Volunteers in the Australian Women's Land Army also assisted with rural production.[25]

The Pacific War heralded a greater contribution of women to the paid workforce than ever before and is often regarded as a watershed in the history of women's contribution to public and economic life. In World War I, Australian women had not been mobilized into industry like their British counterparts but had directed their energies to voluntary work. With World War II, the monetary value of voluntary activities was acknowledged with the collection of thousands of women's names on a national register. Many women were eager to take on civil defense, and the first recruits when the Women's Auxiliary Australian Air Force (WAAAF) was established in 1941 had such prior experience.[26] Although they did not serve at the military front, during the Pacific war the WAAAF, along with the Australian Women's Army Service and the Women's Royal Australian Naval Service, took on increasingly key roles in military communications and transport.

The industrial conscription of civilian women was a priority for the Manpower Directorate, so as to free men for military service and meet widespread labor shortages. By 1944 women's wartime employment peaked at almost 25 percent of the national workforce. In addition, official restrictions on domestic service as "nonessential" to the war economy significantly altered the traditional occupational profile of female workers in Australia. The recruitment of women into high-profile munitions and aircraft production work made explicit links with wartime patriotism and featured widely in newsreels and other publicity campaigns to demonstrate women's support for the war effort. Although armaments work was monotonous and industrial accidents were common, ample overtime and higher pay made it attractive to working-class women. The war also meant women often took on greater responsibilities and gained new skills, including in white-collar office work and the professions. Some were appointed to designated "male" positions, though these were strictly "for the duration." The Women's Employment

Board was established to decide on remuneration in such cases, although equal pay with men was seldom awarded—thereby assuring the trade unions that the demarcation between male and female wages would be maintained in peacetime.[27]

During World War I the issue of military conscription for overseas service had caused deep rifts across Australian society, with successive referenda in 1916 and 1917 narrowly won for the "no" side.[28] In World War II the AIF maintained its voluntary status, while short-term compulsory military training in the Citizen Military Forces (CMF) was introduced for defense of the home territories. With the Pacific War, the boundaries of Australia were geographically widened to encompass New Guinea and Papua, and the nearby islands. Prime Minister Curtin, who had been jailed for his outspoken anticonscription campaigning during World War I, argued at a special federal Labour Party conference in November 1942 that it was essential for the war effort that the CMF fight alongside the AIF in the southwest Pacific. Despite considerable opposition, a bill enabling this change was passed in parliament in early 1943.

The official rhetoric of wartime focused on the unity of the Australian people in working toward Allied victory but also demonized those of "enemy" origin even though they had been born in Australia or were long-term residents. Around 20,000 people of German and Italian ancestry were registered, placed under surveillance, and in some instances interned. The bombing of Pearl Harbor led to the immediate arrest of all Japanese living in Australia and the seizing of the records of Japanese businesses. Around 4,000 men, women, and children of Japanese origin were placed in camps, joining thousands of German and Italian internees.[29] Following Japan's raids on Darwin and the northern towns, attitudes toward the Japanese hardened, and propaganda in the press became more extreme in the racial stereotyping of Japan and its people. The depth of anti-Japanese sentiment meant that Japanese internees were seldom released from the camps, and at the end of the war the majority were forcibly deported to Japan.[30] Thousands of Japanese POWs who were captured in the Pacific were also detained in Australia. In August 1944, in the largest prison escape of World War II, more than 1,000 Japanese soldiers attempted a suicidal "breakout" of a camp at Cowra in New South Wales by storming the barbed wire fences, and as a result 234 were killed.

The scale of the conflict in World War II, and the proximity of the fighting in the Pacific War, meant that Australian regulations excluding those of non-European origin from enlisting in the military services were ignored. This applied to Australia's indigenous people. In the mid-twentieth century, Aborigines and Torres Strait Islanders were not officially recognized as citizens, and their lives were tightly controlled by state government officials and policies of assimilation, including the removal of children and the segregation of indigenous communities on missions and reserves. Despite this, it is estimated that 5,000 Aboriginal and Torres Strait Is-

Buna, Papua, December 25, 1942: Private George C. "Dick" Whittington being helped along a track through the kunai grass by Raphael Oimbari toward a field hospital at Dobodura. Whittington was with the 2/10th Battalion at the time and had been wounded the previous day in the battle for the Buna airstrip. He recovered from his wounds but died of scrub typhus at Port Moresby, February 12, 1943. Photo by George Silk, 014028. (Australian War Memorial)

lander men and women served in the armed services during World War II and were integrated into regular units, receiving the same levels of pay as other Australians.[31]

In addition, special indigenous forces undertook surveillance work along the northern Australian coastline. From May 1941 the Torres Strait Light Infantry Battalion, consisting of 400 men, patrolled the Torres Strait; a portion of their pay was docked by the Queensland government, which survivors only received in 1982.[32] Immediately following the bombing of Darwin in February 1942, the Northern Territory Special Reconnaissance Unit was established in Arnhem Land. Yolngu men used their traditional knowledge to ensure that any potential

Japanese invasion would be detected. The unit, directed by anthropologist Donald Thomson, was disbanded in April 1943 when the immediate Japanese threat had passed. Those men who served were given basic trade goods and only received back pay in 1992.[33] Other Aboriginal men and women were employed by the Australian military in northern Australia, primarily undertaking construction and service duties.

The wartime experiences of indigenous people in Australia, including their overseas travel and acquisition of new skills, were to be important in a longer history of self-determination and civil rights campaigning for racial equality in the decades following World War II. The war also increased Australian knowledge of the indigenous people of the Pacific region, especially the Australian territories in Papua and New Guinea. When Japan's efforts to gain control of Port Moresby by sea were thwarted by the US Navy at Midway Atoll in June 1942, they landed on the northern coast of Papua, intending to take Port Moresby by crossing the rugged Owen Stanley Ranges along the Kokoda Track. After months of fighting in difficult terrain, Australian forces succeeded in turning the Japanese back and were assisted by the local Papuan people. One of the most iconic and enduring images from the Pacific theater was taken by war photographer George Silk near Buna on Christmas Day 1942: it depicted a wounded Australia soldier being assisted by a Papuan. Silk later recalled the "tenderness" of the scene (see photo on page 184).[34]

THE AMERICAN "INVASION" OF AUSTRALIA

During World War II, Australia was a major staging location for Allied troops en route to fighting in the Asia-Pacific theater. This included military personnel from Britain and the British Commonwealth, the Netherlands East Indies, and overwhelmingly from the United States. Between December 1941 and the withdrawal of the last of the US units in 1947, almost 1 million Americans spent time in Australia. Their presence was numerically highest in 1942 and 1943, declining sharply in the last two years of the war. The Americans were stationed throughout the continent, from the state capital cities of Melbourne, Sydney, Brisbane, and Perth to smaller regional towns, most notably in northern Australia. While many US soldiers had transitory experiences of Australia, others spent months and even years in the country and formed strong personal connections with local people. Overall, the cultural impact of the American troops was significant for a small British colonial nation of around 5 million people.[35]

The Pacific War also strengthened the trade and security ties between Australia and the United States, setting out the basis of today's bilateral relationship. The war built upon a history of the reciprocal exchange of goods, ideas, and people between Australia and the United States that dated back to the nineteenth century. This grew in the 1920s and 1930s, when several major US businesses, including General Motors, Ford, Kraft, and Goodyear, established plants in Australia. In the interwar decades, too, Australians were very avid consumers of Hollywood movies, and the resultant equation of US culture with a moral "raciness" had led some intellectuals to express concerns at the Americanization of Australian life.[36] But with war in the Pacific, the United States assumed a new role as the military savior of the Australian nation.

Thousands of US troops began disembarking in Australia beginning in December 1941, though it was only in March 1942 that the Australian press discussed their presence. On arrival, they were issued with a *Pocket Guide to Australia* that explained the local political system, history, and essentials such as customs and slang. The overriding message was that on "The Other Side of the World" in the Pacific, the Allies shared a military and moral purpose: "The Australians have much in common with us—they're a pioneer people; they believe in personal freedom; they love sports. . . . But there are a lot of differences too: their ways of living and thinking on all sorts of things—like tea, central heating, the best way to spend Sunday, or saluting officers."[37]

The Australian government emphasized the strategic nature of the "Pacific Partnership."[38] In March 1942 Curtin sent the minister of external affairs, H. V. Evatt, to the United States to shore up its military support. Coinciding with the visit, a prerecorded message from the prime minister was broadcast on American and Canadian radio stations. In his address to the "Men and Women of the United States," Curtin gave a lesson on the geography of the Pacific Rim, warning that "Australia is the last bastion between the West Coast of America and the Japanese. If Australia goes, the Americas are wide open."[39]

When US General Douglas MacArthur arrived in Melbourne on March 21, 1942, he was greeted by a cheering throng of thousands and was to continue to impress the Australian public with his showmanship. The Allied war in the Pacific was to be fought under US command from a southern base in Australia, with MacArthur appointed supreme commander of the South-West Pacific Area (SWPA). This vast region covered Australia, Papua, and New Guinea, the western part of the Solomon Islands, the Philippines, Borneo, the Netherlands East Indies, and East Timor. Blamey, Australia's head of the army, became one of MacArthur's three immediate subordinates—and the only Australian—with oversight of the Allied Land Forces. However, it was Curtin who worked closely with MacArthur on military strategy through the prime minister's War Conference, and both men shared the view that more Allied resources should be devoted to the Pacific theater. While the Australian government relinquished its national sovereignty through this arrangement, Australia was in a weak position to provide any alternative given the extent of the Japanese threat. The relationship between Australia and the United States can be seen more fruitfully as one of mutual dependence. While they were initially in agreement, relations between Curtin and MacArthur became more strained later in the war.[40]

SWPA headquarters were first established in Melbourne, and by May 1942 there were 30,000 US troops camped throughout the city. Australians needed no encouragement to welcome the GIs, whether through events organized by the hospitality bureau or less formally as visitors in their own homes. They were quick to embrace US popular culture from the latest jazz music to "foreign" foods like hot dogs and hamburgers. Civilians also appreciated the generosity of US servicemen, who had access to cigarettes, chocolate, beer, and other luxury items through PX (postal exchange) canteens. By mid-1942 MacArthur had moved his base to Brisbane to be closer to the military front. In January 1943 Melbourne was to host a second wave of Americans, when 15,000 men of the First Marine Division arrived for rest and recuperation after fighting at Guadalcanal in the Solomon Islands. Suffering from malaria and in ill health, they were to remain in Melbourne and surrounding rural towns for eight months, finding a "home away from home" with Australian families and sweethearts. When the First Marine Division Association was formed by veterans after World War II had ended, the Australian folksong "Waltzing Matilda" was adopted as its battle hymn; it is still played on ceremonial occasions.[41]

The presence of large numbers of American troops, and their inevitable mingling with Australian women, was to coincide with and generate government and community anxieties about changing gender roles, especially the increased economic and social freedom of women and public expressions of sexual intimacy. These were heightened by the general uncertainty and panic in Australia following the Japanese attack on Pearl Harbor, and the "war fever" and emotional excitement that gripped young people. With Australian men away on military service, the arrival of the GIs evened up the ratio between the sexes. Cross-national comparisons arose, with stereotypes of the "forward" nature of American masculinity and, over time, a depiction of the US forces as "over-paid" and "over-sexed." Such tensions were exacerbated when, in June 1942, a US private unexpectedly confessed to the sensational serial murders of three civilian women in Melbourne; he was swiftly court-martialed and hung. Throughout the war, occasional brawls, undoubtedly fueled by alcohol, broke out between the GIs and Australian men, such as the infamous Battle of Brisbane in November 1942. The military authorities on both sides were keen to minimize the publicity given to such incidents. By 1944 Australian troops were increasingly resentful that MacArthur had assigned them to marginal "mop up" operations in the Pacific Islands.

With thousands of soldiers in Australian cities and towns beginning in 1942, prostitution increased, as did intimate friendships. US military authorities were focused on containing the spread of sexually transmitted diseases, which prior to the availability of penicillin required lengthy hospitalization. These concerns resulted in state intervention in private lives, with intimate behaviors placed under scrutiny from the police. Midnight curfews were introduced to monitor the interactions between American soldiers and civilians, and wartime legislation targeted young women and meant they could be forcibly detained and subjected to medical testing if their morality was seen as "questionable."[42] The social and psychological disruptions of wartime, and the sexual interactions that developed between the American soldiers and Australian women, were reflected in the artistic and literary production of the time. Nonetheless, many Australian families formed lasting relationships with American servicemen. The War Brides Act (1945) enabled 15,000 Australian wives and fiancées of American servicemen, and their children, to travel to the United States after the war.

The US military presence also highlighted Australian concerns about race. Among the servicemen and support units stationed in Australia were some 9,000 African Americans, who were in segregated units in the US Army. At the insistence of the Curtin government, which even in extraordinary circumstances remained wedded to "White Australia," African Americans were primarily stationed in the more remote parts of the continent, away from the populous southern cities of Sydney and Melbourne. Nonetheless, there were significant encounters between African American servicemen and the white Australian population, including cross-racial romance and marriage.[43] Recent scholarship has explored how Aboriginal women formed relationships with African American and other Allied servicemen designated as "colored" during World War II, situating this within the broader transnational context of social and political struggle and change. Across the Pacific theater more widely, including in the white British dominions of Australia and New Zealand, thousands of children whose fathers were in the American military and whose mothers were local indigenous women were born as a result of World War II.[44]

CONCLUSION

The Pacific War came to an end on August 15, 1945, following the dropping of the atomic bombs on Hiroshima and Nagasaki; it had been several months since the surrender of Germany to the Allies on May 7. In Australia, the news was met with wild jubilation and relief. Curtin, the great wartime Labour Party leader, had suffered ill health and died in July; it was said that his tireless work on behalf of the nation had spurred on his death. Ben Chifley assumed the role of prime minister and moved to implement an ambitious plan for postwar reconstruction that was to lead to the development of the modern welfare state.

The experience of World War II transformed Australia's society and economy and shifted its security alliances within the Asia-Pacific region. One million men and women had served in the military—a high participation rate from a country of just over 7 million people. Many more civilians had contributed to war industries such as munitions and to the growth of primary and secondary production. Around 34,000 Australians were killed as a result of the fighting, and over 30,000 were taken prisoner. Of these, 22,000 POWs were held by the Japanese, working on such grueling projects as the building of the Burma-Thai Railway; one-third of them died in captivity. The suffering of Australian POWs has been a particularly potent memory of the Pacific War, and Australia conducted roughly 300 trials of Japanese war criminals in the immediate postwar years.[45] It also sent 16,000 men to Japan under the British Commonwealth Occupation Force, where they played a part in the rebuilding of its former enemy and led to the development of trade between the two nations in the postwar decades. Trade also expanded with the United States following the war, and security ties in the region with America were formalized through the signing of the ANZUS Treaty in 1951.

Australia's comprehensive program of postwar social and economic reconstruction looked to the future rather than the past. The north was ripe for development, and by the 1950s scrap iron from wartime fortifications was sold to Japanese buyers. In March 1955 Paul Hasluck, the federal minister for external territories in the Menzies government, unveiled a memorial plaque at the new Northern Territory Legislative Council buildings in Darwin—erected on the site of the old post office, which was destroyed by the Japanese in 1942. Hasluck used the occasion for political purposes, describing the bombing of Darwin as "the anniversary of national shame" and criticizing Curtin's wartime leadership.[46]

While there have been evolving interpretations of the significance of the Japanese raids on Darwin, by the twenty-first century these have become associated—more so than any other site in Australia—with the Australian-American alliance. The memorial to the USS *Peary*, in which eighty-eight American sailors died, has become a pilgrimage for members of the US Navy and was visited by US president Barack Obama in a fleeting visit to Darwin in 2011.[47] Even more recently, Darwin has actively sought to position itself as the national site of World War II tourism. An immersive interactive exhibition titled "The Defence of Darwin Experience" has opened at the Darwin Military Museum, there are multiple tours to war heritage sites, and a new tourist facility at Stokes Wharf tells the story of the bombing through virtual reality technology. These all point to the ways that, as time has passed and survivors like Mervyn Ey become scarce, commemorations of "Australia's Pearl Harbor" have become more central to the national remembrance of the Pacific War and its place in the making of modern Australia.

NOTES

1. Neda Vanovac and Xavier La Canna, "Bombing of Darwin Veterans Commemorate the Time World War II Came to Australian Soil," *ABC News*, February 20, 2017, http://www.abc.net.au/news/2017-02-19/bombing-of-darwin-remembered-75-years-on/8282024.

2. See Kate Darian-Smith, "World War 2 and Post-war Reconstruction 1939–49," in Alison Bashford and Stuart Macintyre, eds., *The Cambridge History of Australia*, vol. 2 (Cambridge: Cambridge University Press, 2013), 88–111. For a military history, see Jeffrey Grey, *A Military History of Australia*, 3rd ed. (Cambridge: Cambridge University Press, 2008).

3. David Walker, *Anxious Nation: Australia and the Rise of Asia 1850–1939* (St. Lucia, Queensland: University of Queensland Press, 1999); see also David Walker and Agnieszka Sobocinska, eds., *Australia's Asia: From Yellow Peril to Asia Century* (Crawley, Western Australia: UWA Publishing, 2012).

4. See Naoko Shimazu, *Japan, Race and Equality: The Racial Equality Proposal of 1919* (London: Routledge, 1998); and Neville Meaney, *A History of Australian Defence and Foreign Policy 1901–1923,* vol. 2 (Sydney: Sydney University Press, 2009).

5. Pam Oliver, "World Wars and the Anticipation of Conflict: The Impact on Long-Established Japanese-Australian Relations, 1905–43," in Peter J. Dean, ed., *Australia 1942: In the Shadow of War* (Melbourne: Cambridge University Press, 2013), 33–52.

6. Paul Jones, "'Trading in a "Fool's Paradise'? White Australia and the Trade Diversion Dispute of 1936," in Paul Jones and Vera Mackie, eds., *Relationships: Japan and Australia 1870s–1950s* (Melbourne: University of Melbourne History Monograph, 2001), 133–162.

7. Alan Fewster, *Trusty and Well Beloved: A Life of Keith Officer, Australia's First Diplomat* (Melbourne: Melbourne University Publishing, 2009), 211–226.

8. John Curtin Prime Ministerial Library, Records of the Commonwealth of Australia, Digest of Decisions and Announcements and Important Speeches by the Prime Minister, No. 10, December 1–16, 1941, pp. 19–22, JCPML00110/15; http://john.curtin.edu.au/diary/primeminister/fulltext/fulltext%20prime%20minister_1941_4.html, accessed February 10, 2017.

9. *Sydney Morning Herald*, December 10, 1941, p. 1.

10. *Herald* (Melbourne), December 27, 1941, p. 10.

11. Troy Bramston, "Curtin's New Year Message Put a Case for Australia First," *The Australian*, December 21, 2016, p. 15.

12. See David Horner, *High Command: Australia and Allied Strategy 1939–1945* (Sydney: Allen and Unwin, 1982); David Day, *The Great Betrayal: Britain, Australia and the Onset of the Pacific War, 1929–42* (Melbourne: Oxford University Press, 1992); Augustine Meaher, *The Road to Singapore: The Myth of British Betrayal* (Melbourne: Australian Scholarly Publishing, 2010).

13. *Army News* (Darwin), February 19, 1942, p. 1.

14. Alan Powell, *The Shadow's Edge: Australia's Northern War*, 3rd ed. (Darwin: Charles Darwin University, 2007); Douglas Lockwood, *Australia's Pearl Harbor: Darwin 1942* (Melbourne: Cassell, 1966); Douglas Lockwood, *Australia under Attack: The Bombing of Darwin 1942* (Sydney: New Holland, 2013); Peter Grose, *An Awkward Truth: The Bombing of Darwin, February 1942* (Sydney: Allen and Unwin, 2009).

15. Timothy Hall, *Darwin 1942: Australia's Darkest Hour* (London: Routledge, 2015), 199–200.

16. "Commission of inquiry concerning the circumstances connected with the attack made by Japanese aircraft at Darwin on 19th February, 1942," National Archives of Australia, A431, 1949/687.

17. "The Miallo Japanese Bombing Site," *Queensland WWII Historic Places*, http://www.ww2places.qld.gov.au/places/?id=946, accessed July 20, 2017.

18. Two of the midget submarines were detected and attacked at the time, and the Japanese crew scuttled their submarines and committed suicide. The wreck of the third submarine was recovered off the coast north of Sydney in 2006.

19. Pam Oliver, *Raids on Australia: 1942 and Japan's Plans for Australia* (Melbourne: Australian Scholarly Publishing, 2010); Peter Stanley, *Invading Australia: Japan and the Battle for Australia, 1942* (Melbourne: Viking, 2008).

20. Paul Hasluck, *The Government and the People 1942–1945* (Canberra: Australian War Memorial, 1970), 711–717.

21. David Horner, "Australia in 1942: A Pivotal Year," in Dean, *Australia 1942*, 11–30.

22. A. P. Elkin, *Our Opinions and the National Effort* (Sydney: Australasian Medical Publishing, 1941). See John Pomeroy, "A. P. Elkin: Public Morale and Propaganda," in Geoffrey Grey, Doug Munro, and Christine Winter, eds., *Scholars at War: Australasian Social Scientists, 1939–1945* (Canberra: ANU Press, 2012), 35–54.

23. Key works on the home front, and which have informed this chapter, include the two volumes of the official history: Paul Hasluck, *The Government and the People 1939–1941* (Canberra: Australian War Memorial, 1952); Hasluck, *Government and the People 1942–1945*; Michael McKernan, *All In! Australia during the Second World War* (Melbourne: Thomas Nelson, 1983); Kate Darian-Smith, *On the Home Front: Melbourne in Wartime 1939–45*, 2nd ed. (Melbourne: Melbourne University Press, 2009); and Joan Beaumont, ed., *Australia's War 1939–45* (Sydney: Allen and Unwin, 1996).

24. See Marnie Hay-Muir and Roy Hay, "The Economy at War," in Beaumont, *Australia's War*, 107–135; E. Ronald Walker, *The Australian Economy in War and Reconstruction* (New York: Oxford University Press, 1947); and Stuart Macintyre, *Australia's Boldest Experiment: War and Reconstruction in the 1940s* (Sydney: NewSouth Books, 2015).

25. Sue Hardisty, ed., *Thanks Girls and Goodbye! The Story of the Australian Women's Land Army 1942–45* (Melbourne: Viking O'Neil, 1990).

26. Joyce A. Thomson, *The WAAAF in Wartime Australia* (Carlton: Melbourne University Press, 1991).

27. Darian-Smith, *On the Home Front*, 50–82.

28. For recent work on the conscription debates, see Robin Archer, Joy Damousi,

Murray Goot, and Sean Scalmer, eds., *The Conscription Conflict and the Great War* (Clayton: Monash University Publishing, 2016).

29. Margaret Bevege, *Behind Barbed Wire: Internment in Australia during World War II* (Brisbane: University Queensland Press, 1993); Klaus Neumann, *In the Interest of National Security: Civilian Internment in Australia during World War II* (Canberra: National Library of Australia, 2006).

30. Yuriko Nagata, *Unwanted Aliens: Japanese Internment in Australia* (St Lucia: University of Queensland Press, 1996).

31. Noah Riseman, *In Defence of Country: Life Stories of Aboriginal and Torres Strait Islander Servicemen and Women* (Acton, ACT: ANU Press, 2016), 3.

32. Robert Hall, *The Black Diggers: Aborigines and Torres Strait Islanders in the Second World War*, 2nd ed. (Canberra: Aboriginal Studies Press, 1997), chapter 3; Robert Hall, *Fighters from the Fringe: Aborigines and Torres Strait Islanders Recall the Second World War* (Canberra: Aboriginal Studies Press, 1995) 135–153, 173–191; Elizabeth Osborne, *Torres Strait Islander Women and the Pacific War* (Canberra: Aboriginal Studies Press, 1997), 103–122.

33. Noah Riseman, *Defending Whose Country? Indigenous Soldiers in the Pacific War* (Lincoln: University of Nebraska Press, 2012), chapters 1 and 2; Donald Thomson and Nicolas Peterson, *Donald Thomson in Arnhem Land*, rev. ed. (Melbourne: Miegunyah Press, 2005).

34. Neil McDonald, "George Silk (1916–2004)," *Quadrant* 48, 12 (December 2004), 58.

35. Key works on the United States in Australia are Daniel E. Potts and Annette Potts, *Yanks Down Under 1941–45: The American Impact on Australia* (Oxford: Oxford University Press, 1985); Anthony Barker and Lisa Jackson, *Fleeting Attraction: A Social History of American Servicemen in Western Australia during the Second World War* (Nedlands, WA: University of Western Australia Press, 1996); John McKerrow, *The American Occupation of Australia, 1941–45: A Marriage of Necessity* (Newcastle, UK: Cambridge Scholars Publishing, 2013); and Kate Darian-Smith, "The Home Front and the American Presence in 1942," in Dean, *Australia 1942,* 70–88.

36. Philip Bell and Roger Bell, eds., *Americanization and Australia* (Sydney: UNSW Press, 1998); Philip Bell and Roger Bell, *Implicated: The United States in Australia* (New York: Oxford University Press, 1993).

37. United States Army, *A Pocket Guide to Australia* (Washington, DC: War and Navy Departments, 1942).

38. Australians were instructed about the United States in the popular text by George H. Johnston, *Pacific Partner* (New York: World Book Company, 1944).

39. Broadcast by Prime Minister Curtin over a Network of United Sates, Canadian and South American Stations, 14 March 1942, Australian Archives (NSW), ABC Broadcast Series SP300/1, Box 7.

40. Horner, *High Command.*

41. Kate Darian-Smith, "Pacific Partners: Gendered Memories of the US Marines in Melbourne, 1943," in Corinna Peniston-Bird and Emma Vickers, eds., *Gender in the Second World War* (London: Palgrave, 2017), 135–150.

42. Darian-Smith, *On the Home Front*, chapters 6 and 7; Kay Saunders, *War on the Homefront: State Intervention in Queensland 1938–1948* (St. Lucia: University of Queensland Press, 1993).

43. Sean Brawley and Chris Dixon, "Jim Crow Down Under? African Encounters with White Australia, 1942–1945," *Pacific Historical Review* 71 (2002), 607–632.

44. Karen Hughes, "Mobilising Across Colour Lines: Intimate Encounters between Aboriginal Women and African American and other Allied Servicemen on the World War II Home Front," *Aboriginal History* 4 (2017), 47–70: see also Judith Bennett and Angela Wanhalla, eds., *Mothers' Darlings of the South Pacific: The Children of Indigenous Women and U.S. Servicemen, World War II* (Honolulu: University of Hawaii Press, 2016).

45. Hank Nelson, *P.O.W. Prisoners of War: Australians under Nippon* (Sydney: ABC Books, 1985).

46. *Canberra Times*, March 26, 1955, p. 2; *The Argus*, March 26, 1955, p. 5.

47. Laura James, "Reading Darwin as a Landscape of War," in Keir Reeves, Geoffrey R. Bird, Laura James, Birger Stichelbaut, and Jean Bourgeois, eds., *Battlefield Events: Landscape, Commemoration and Heritage* (London: Routledge, 2015), 171–172.

CHAPTER 10

Tolerance, Reconciliation, and the Alliance of Hope

Pearl Harbor Narratives in Japan

Yujin Yaguchi

Despite the international criticism of "Japanese amnesia" about World War II, certain incidents from the war continue to attract considerable attention in Japan. The attack on Pearl Harbor is one of them, having drawn extensive media coverage at the moments of the fiftieth, sixtieth, and seventieth anniversaries. Pearl Harbor also became front-page news in December 2016 when Japanese prime minister Shinzo Abe made an official visit to the site and met with US president Barack Obama. This chapter discusses the ways in which the attack has been narrated and memorialized in Japan. Specifically, it argues that Pearl Harbor has enabled Japan to have a kind of historical framework that embraces a continuing postwar alliance with the United States, at the expense of a more dynamic and expansive historical memory that would foreground the imperial complicity of the two nations in Asia and the Pacific.

On December 28, 2016, Abe visited Pearl Harbor and the USS *Arizona* Memorial and stood together with President Obama. Although previous prime ministers of Japan had visited the area before, including Abe's grandfather Shinsuke Kishi, he was the first to officially go to the battleship memorial and commemorate the surprise Japanese attack. He and the president were greeted by, among others, Admiral Harry Harris from US Pacific Command, the son of an American naval officer and a Japanese mother, and a small group of aging "Pearl Harbor survivors" who experienced the attack more than seventy-five years earlier.

Abe's visit came almost six months after Obama's visit to Hiroshima, where the United States dropped an atomic bomb on August 6, 1945. The Pearl Harbor visit also came at a moment when the Japanese government was feeling somewhat uncertain about Donald Trump, who was to assume presidency in a month, and his view of Japan. Abe saw a chance to use his unprecedented visit to the USS *Arizona* Memorial to reinforce Japan's relationship with the United States while also solidifying his political base back home by showing his ability to overcome the memory of the painful history that put the two nations at war.

This chapter explores the meaning of Pearl Harbor in contemporary Japan by looking at Abe's visit as well as the recent media coverage of the Pearl Harbor attack. The chapter identifies three significant features that characterize many of the accounts of the attack on Pearl Harbor that have appeared in the Japanese media. First, it argues that a focus on Pearl Harbor enables many in Japan to imagine a specific chronological narrative of the war, one that allows a far simpler understanding than the actual historical reality. Second, it shows that this media portrayal of Pearl Harbor allows the Japanese to view the war Japan fought and lost as a tragic, and yet ultimately triumphant, story of the two nations rather than as a story of global conflict among nations with imperial ambitions. Finally, it points out that the focus on Pearl Harbor as a site of international tension and reconciliation effectively suppresses the understanding and appreciation of local history of Hawai‘i, the very site where the attack took place. In sum, the way the Japanese media has shaped the story of the attack and its meaning suggests that Pearl Harbor is integral to the Japanese embrace of the ongoing postwar alliance with the United States. That narrative, however, comes at the expense of a more dynamic and expansive historical memory of the imperial rivalry of these two nations in Asia and the Pacific.

Japan is often accused by its neighboring nations of "whitewashing" its history. Controversy over the contents of school textbooks has triggered international debates, as both the Chinese and Korean governments have harshly criticized Japanese government's "censorship" over how history is taught in secondary schools. Incidents and issues such as the Nanjing Massacre and Korean comfort women in particular have generated intense and at times acrimonious debates among these nations as well as within Japan.

A cursory look at history textbooks and education may suggest that the attack on Pearl Harbor is also at risk of being suppressed in Japan. Discussion of the Japanese attack on Pearl Harbor in high school history textbooks is generally limited to one or two lines. For example, one of the most widely circulated textbooks explains the attack as follows: "As the Japan-US negotiation stalled from early 1941, on December 8 of that year, the Japanese military made a surprise attack on the

US Naval base in Pearl Harbor and landed its force on the Malay Peninsula and declared war against the United States and the United Kingdom and entered in the Pacific War."[1]

The description of World War II extends for a little more than five pages (in a book that is about 8 inches by 6 inches and printed in an easily readable font) in which important events in Europe (such as the Normandy landing, Yalta Conference, and Potsdam Declaration) as well as a couple examples of Japanese invasions in Asia are noted. The description of battles against the United States are limited to brief references to the loss in the Battle of Midway, the US landing on Okinawa, and the fact that "the United States dropped the new weapon of the atomic bombs in Hiroshima on August 6th and Nagasaki on the 9th, completely destroying the two cities."[2]

Because the standard Japanese history curriculum tries to cover the entire human history from the birth of human beings to the twenty-first century, the description of World War II is inevitably limited to a list of major events, with few specifics or a clear overarching framework. In learning about Pearl Harbor, students have no chance to delve into the specifics of the attack or the context within which it took place. They memorize the term *shinjuwan* (Pearl Harbor) and are tested on their knowledge of the term, but few learn much about the attack itself. Few are aware that thousands of military personnel were killed, and hardly any know there were civilian deaths, in line with the overall emphasis of Japanese history education that tends to foreground the deaths of Japanese civilians in Tokyo, Okinawa, Hiroshima, and Nagasaki rather than the casualties caused by the Japanese military.

However, despite the vague and fragmented knowledge, Pearl Harbor remains a significant component of the popular discourse of twentieth-century history in Japan. Although the surprise attack is certainly not an "icon" of twentieth-century history, as Emily Rosenberg claims it to be for the United States, it does repeatedly appear in the media as a seminal event that has impacted the course of Japanese history to this day.[3]

Charting this media coverage helps to explain Japanese understandings of the meaning of the attack. While quantitative evidence tells us little about the content of the portrayals, it can allow us to trace the level of attention devoted to the event. Significantly, database research on newspaper articles published in Japan since 1991—the fiftieth anniversary of the attack—shows that the number of times *shinjuwan* appeared in Japanese newspapers has not decreased over time. The graph on page 197 shows the number of times *shinjuwan* appeared in Japan's three major daily newspapers—*Asahi*, *Mainichi*, and *Yomiuri*—which currently have a combined circulation of about 18 million copies in a nation of 120 million people.[4] The most frequent appearance of the term *shinjuwan* was in 1991; subsequent

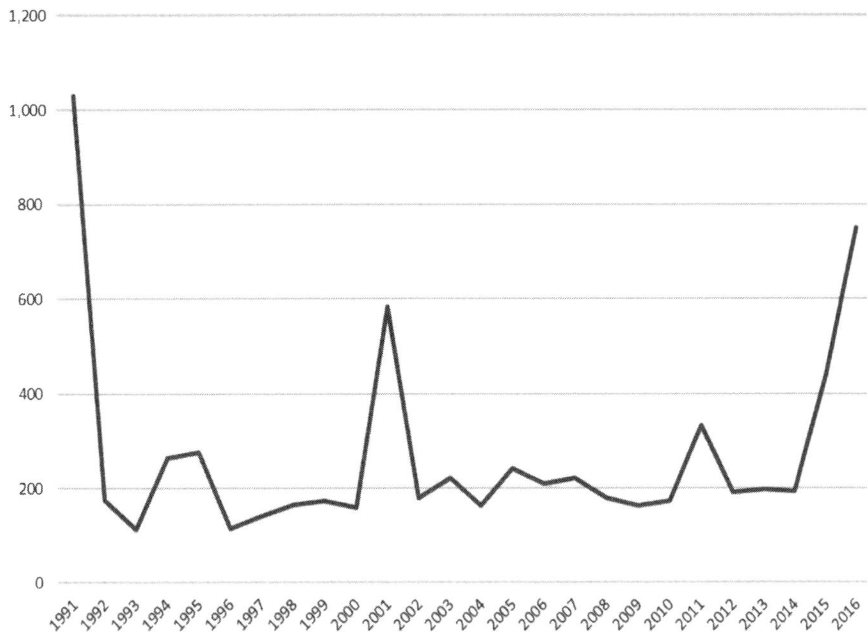

Pearl Harbor in Three Major Papers

years show some fluctuations, with significant spikes in 1991, 2001, 2011, and 2015, as well as in 2016. These spikes suggest "anniversary reporting" to commemorate the fiftieth, sixtieth, and seventieth anniversaries of the attack, as well as the seventieth anniversary of the end of the Asia-Pacific War. The large volume of reporting in 2016 is due to President Obama's visit to Hiroshima in May and Prime Minister Abe's visit to Pearl Harbor in December, as mentioned at the start of this chapter. In other years the combined number of reports has varied slightly, hovering around 200, but it shows no pattern of any progressive decline.

Of course, *shinjuwan* can be mentioned in contexts other than the attack. For example, the spike in 2001 is not only because of the seventieth anniversary but also because of the *Ehime Maru* incident, in which the USS *Greenville*, a submarine based in Pearl Harbor, struck and sank the Japanese fishery training ship *Ehime Maru* off the coast of O'ahu, killing four high school students and five teachers. In order to minimize references to Pearl Harbor in other contexts, overall statistics can be compared to database research limited to the dates between December 1 and 8, as references to *shinjuwan* during that week almost certainly would be referring to the attack (see graph on page 198). Again, by far the largest number was in 1991, the year of the fiftieth anniversary. The rest show a similar pattern of spikes, with no sign of decrease. If anything, mention of Pearl Harbor seems to be on the uptick.

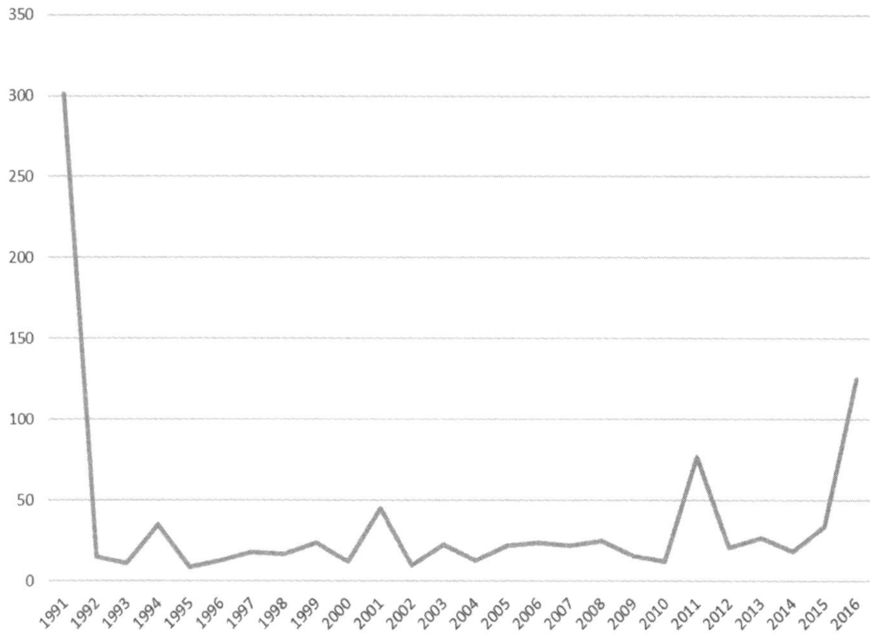

Pearl Harbor, December 1–8

As far as media reports are concerned, then, references to *shinjuwan* seem to have increased over the past seventy years. Indeed, a further search of article titles in the anniversary years before 1991 shows only few, and mostly short, articles on Pearl Harbor appearing in 1951, 1961, 1971, and 1981. The *shinjuwan*-related articles in newspapers begin to increase in the 1990s.

Despite the impression that Japan suffers from historical amnesia, media coverage about Pearl Harbor suggests the opposite. In fact, amid the memory landscape of the past twenty-five years or so in Japan, debates over how World War II should be remembered have become far more intense, generating a range of opinions and positions domestically and internationally over certain historical incidents. Discussions of Pearl Harbor seem to have increased in this environment, as Japan continues to grapple with how to remember World War II, exemplified in international debates over such issues as the Korean comfort women and the politicization of Yasukuni Shrine.

Given such data, the question at hand is not why Japan forgets or ignores its attack on Pearl Harbor—for it doesn't—but about how Japanese representations and memories of Pearl Harbor reflect and serve contemporary Japanese society. How, simply put, is Pearl Harbor narrated and remembered in Japan?

First, Pearl Harbor is popularly treated as a historic marker for the beginning of the war. Often the phrase *kaisen no hi* (literally, "the day when the war started") is used to refer to December 8.[5] Media reports thus suggest that December 8 was when the war that brought so much devastation to Japan began. This obviously is inaccurate, as Japan had been engaged in continuous military conflict with China since at least 1937—or, some would argue, since 1931.[6] The tension with the United States and the eventual confrontation that resulted derived from Japan's ongoing military engagements in Asia. But Pearl Harbor is frequently treated in these articles as the incident that pulled Japan into a "real" war, that is, a fight against the United States.

Pearl Harbor thus serves as a bookend for the chronological framework of the war that ends with a loss in 1945. While Japan annually commemorates the ending of the Asia-Pacific War by a series of ceremonies on August 15, the day when the Japanese emperor announced to his people the nation's acceptance of defeat, it does not officially remember the beginning of the war. The date of the attack on Pearl Harbor, repeatedly characterized in the media as *kaisen no hi* (often without specifying which war it was), is the closest that the nation comes to marking the war's start.

This chronological framework strengthens a strong tendency to connect the attack on Pearl Harbor with the atomic bombs the United States dropped over Hiroshima and Nagasaki: the latter symbolize the end of the war in Japan, just as much as Pearl Harbor symbolizes the beginning. This connection was seen most clearly in the coverage from 1995, when Japan marked the fiftieth anniversary of the end of the war. Out of the 275 articles on Pearl Harbor that were published in the three major newspapers that year, almost 39 percent (106) made references to the atomic bombs, helping to explain why people in Japan connect the two events today (Table 10.1). This association of the attack on Pearl Harbor with America's use of atomic bombs is consistent over time. In 1991, the fiftieth anniversary of the attack and the year with the most extensive coverage of Pearl Harbor, 15 percent (156) of the 1,030 articles published referred to the atomic bombs. In the sixtieth (2001) and seventieth (2011) anniversary years, this figure was 8 percent (47 out of 583) and 17 percent (56 out of 332) respectively. In 2015—the seventieth anniversary of the bombing, rather than of the Pearl Harbor attack—out of 440 articles on Pearl Harbor that appeared in those papers, almost 20 percent (86) contained references to the atomic bombs. Finally, in 2016, 26 percent (196 out of 751) of the texts on Pearl Harbor discussed the atomic bombs. This increase was likely due to the many references to Pearl Harbor made in conjunction with Obama's visit to Hiroshima in May of that year. Moreover, Prime Minister Abe's visit to Pearl Harbor at the end of December further invited discussions that connected the events, as the visit to the USS *Arizona* Memorial was regarded as a return for Obama's visit to the city.[7]

Pearl Harbor and Atomic Bombs

Year	*Atomic Bomb References*	*Pearl Harbor Articles*	*Percentage*
1991	156	1030	15
1995	106	275	39
2001	47	583	8
2011	56	332	17
2015	86	440	20
2016	196	751	26

Memories of the attack on Pearl Harbor and the use of atomic bombs on Hiroshima and Nagasaki are intertwined in Japan; they appear as the beginning and concluding chapters of the war. In other words, public memory of the Japanese perpetration of violence against Americans in Pearl Harbor is tightly linked in Japan with the even more horrific violence caused by the United States in Hiroshima and Nagasaki. The killing of more than 2,000 American servicemen and a smaller number of civilians, executed without any official declaration of war, is overshadowed by what many Japanese deem the unconscionable killing of thousands of civilians by Americans in Japan. Accordingly, to many in Japan, the attack on Pearl Harbor was wrong not so much because it killed Americans or started the war against the United States but because it led to a horrible conclusion of the war. True, Americans are not necessarily faulted for dropping the atomic bombs in this context; few, if any, articles compare the casualties between Pearl Harbor and the atomic bombs. That, however, is because the latter is treated in Japan as unique and unprecedented and thus as an event that should never be put into any comparative framework. But if it does not draw parallels, this association does deemphasize the violence at Pearl Harbor, as evidenced by the lack of knowledge in Japan about the actual content of the attack. Japan's attack on Pearl Harbor is to be regretted not because the attack killed Americans but because it led to the tragic loss of lives and total destruction of the society in Japan.[8]

Memorializing Pearl Harbor in this way, as the symbolic beginning of the devastating war Japan fought against the United States, has the effect of dissociating the attack from Japanese colonialism and its invasions of territory throughout Asia, as well as from the sufferings of people in Asia before and after December 8, 1941. When Prime Minister Abe spoke at Pearl Harbor in December 2016, he followed the typical chronological sensibility of most Japanese and framed the attack on Pearl Harbor as the beginning of the "horrors of war" between the two nations. At the same time, he further extended this chronology to claim that the tragedy of war eventually produced a propitious ending for Japan by putting the nation under the aegis of the US-led world order.[9]

The Japanese attack on Pearl Harbor, Abe noted, was no doubt a low point in the two nations' history, a time when many lives were sacrificed. As he stood by the harbor with President Obama, the prime minister told the US president and the people of both nations that he could "almost discern the voices" of the crewmen who perished there more than seventy-five years ago. December 7, 1941, in Hawai'i, he said, was the day when the "futures and dreams" of young servicemen were destroyed. However, while he offered his "everlasting condolences to the souls of those who lost their lives here, as well as to the spirits of all the brave men and women whose lives were taken by a war that commenced in this very place, and also to the souls of the countless innocent people who became victims of the war," he offered no direct apology. Nor did he ever clearly specify who initiated this attack. Instead he quickly moved to Pearl Harbor's meaning in today's Japan by acknowledging the "goodwill and assistance" of the "good people" of the United States who had made it possible for Japan to make a rapid recovery after the war. Despite the defeat, he noted, the "Japanese people managed to survive and make their way toward the future thanks to the sweaters and milk sent by the American people." It was "the United States," he insisted, "that opened up the path for Japan to return to the international community once more after the war." Abe's speech turned the tragic beginning at Pearl Harbor into the triumph of a new world order led by the United States and followed by Japan. He happily acquiesced to this order by claiming that "under the leadership of the United States, Japan, as a member of the free world, was able to enjoy peace and prosperity."

In this relatively short speech, Abe used the word *tolerance* seven times and *reconciliation* five times. He praised, for example, the "spirit of tolerance embraced by the American people" and extended his "heartfelt gratitude to the United States and to the world for the tolerance extended to Japan." He insisted that Pearl Harbor represented the "power of reconciliation" that in turn enabled the "alliance of hope."

Abe's speech, given in front of prominent Japanese and American flags with the USS *Arizona* Memorial in the background, characterized the Japanese attack on Pearl Harbor as a nadir from which the two nations managed to emerge and eventually reconcile with one another, thanks primarily to the great spirit of tolerance shown by Americans. Indeed, after his speech (which had been shared with the US side in advance), Obama echoed Abe's statement by noting that the "most bitter of adversaries can become the strongest of allies."[10]

Abe's speech framed Pearl Harbor as a seminal challenge in the US-Japan relationship that was eventually overcome thanks mostly to the tolerance and generosity of the United States. By doing so, it deftly abstracted Pearl Harbor from the nexus of the contemporary global power dynamics and reduced it to an incident between the two nations. Historically, the Japanese plan to attack Pearl

Harbor had stemmed from the impasse over Japan's desire to expand its empire in Asia and America's strong opposition to the Japanese aggression. Yet Abe's speech failed to acknowledge the Japanese invasions in Asia that began before the attacks of December 7/8, 1941, and continued on that day, or the deaths and sufferings of the peoples in those places.

The left-leaning *Asahi Shimbun* criticized this vision by noting in its editorial that the speech "hardly touches on" the question of "how to look back and historically position the past war that generated tremendous sacrifice on the nations of not only the United States and Japan but also of Asia Pacific region."[11] A German newspaper sarcastically suggested Abe go visit the Nanjing Massacre memorial next. Moreover, both the Chinese and Korean governments criticized Abe for failing to squarely face the past. A Chinese Foreign Ministry spokeswoman called it a "show" and asked, "Can a so-called victim-consolation trip to Pearl Harbor completely wipe away World War II history? I am afraid it's just wishful thinking on his part."[12]

Yet this binary is precisely the perspective Pearl Harbor offers to many in Japan today. Pearl Harbor *is* about Japan's bilateral relationship with the United States. *Yomiuri*, the largest newspaper in Japan, claimed that Abe's visit to Pearl Harbor made it possible to remove any lingering desire for revenge that may have existed between the two nations and praised Abe's presence there as further reinforcing the nations' bond. It exhorted the two governments to use this already strong Japan-US alliance to continue securing and strengthening the global order.[13] The memory of Pearl Harbor, in other words, is a means through which a strong relationship between the two nations can be ensured today. In this version, Pearl Harbor is severed from the larger stage of international politics of the time and defined instead as a site of two-way conflict and reconciliation between the United States and Japan. Pearl Harbor's link to Japanese colonialism in Asia and the Pacific is suppressed, if not erased, from this perspective. Pearl Harbor is a convenient historical marker that enables the Japanese to understand the postwar peace under the protection of the US-Japan alliance by providing a sense of linear progression from the surprise attack to the atomic bombs to the occupation and to the postwar recovery and embracing of their ties with the United States.

Finally, in the Japanese discourse of Pearl Harbor, what is almost entirely missing is the recognition of Hawai'i as the actual place where it happened. Whereas Abe's speech stirred some debates over its lack of attention to Asia, no voice was raised in the media regarding its total disregard for the people and environment of Hawai'i.

As Jonathan Kamakawiwo'ole Osorio has written, American discussions of the attack on Pearl Harbor generally fail to recognize the meaning of the area to the local residents, especially to Native Hawai'ians. They fail to understand that Pearl

Harbor is to Native Hawai'ians a "visual and kinetic reminder" of loss of their land. The discussions also fail to see that numerous contemporary narratives about Pearl Harbor trigger a sense of "helplessness" among Native Hawai'ians as they confront this overwhelming evidence of the colonial power of the United States.[14]

The Japanese media follow this American pattern. There is a remarkable lack of concern in Japan about the meaning of the Pearl Harbor attack for the local society and to its people. True, media accounts do feature Japanese Americans or Nikkei residents of Hawai'i, particularly those who participated in World War II as members of the US military and returned home to become leaders of the local society. Prime Minister Abe also met with a group of Nikkei residents before his visit to Pearl Harbor and praised their hard work at becoming contributing members of the local society and thanked them for being "a bridge" between the two countries.[15] But there is no attempt to see Pearl Harbor within the context of Native Hawai'ian history and society. This is particularly striking, as there has been a surge of interest in Native Hawai'ian culture and environment in Japan in recent years. Hawai'i is one of the most popular destinations for Japanese tourists, and part of the draw of the islands today (especially among those who visit the islands frequently) is the Native Hawai'ian life, from hula to language to nature. Each year, hundreds of Japanese books, magazines articles, and television programs feature Native Hawai'ian culture and traditions. Yet Pearl Harbor is never associated with Native Hawai'ians or Hawai'ian culture.[16]

Instead, Pearl Harbor is treated as a point where the two nations and their peoples encountered, fought, and now have reconciled with each other, thanks to the "tolerance" of Americans. In these narratives, Pearl Harbor is an abstraction severed from the local reality, even though it may encompass stories of tragic deaths and the suffering of US military personnel and Japanese Americans. Abe's acknowledgment in his speech extended to "sailors and marines hailing from California and New York, Michigan and Texas, and various other places, serving to uphold their noble duty of protecting the homeland they loved, [who] lost their lives amidst searing flames that day," but his remarks and other media accounts failed to remember the people of Hawai'i and their homeland, or *'aina*.

That Pearl Harbor once had a different name, Pu'uloa, and cultural significance for Native Hawai'ians long before it was taken over by the United States was completely forgotten. The reason why Pearl Harbor became a key military site was never questioned. The question why Hawai'i is part of the United States today was never asked. Neither was there any recognition of what life was like in Hawai'i after December 7, 1941. The days and years immediately after the attack, when people in Hawai'i lived through the longest imposition of martial law in the history of the United States, were obviously not acknowledged.[17] These are far from surprising, given that this was a speech intended to strengthen the political and military alliance of the United States and Japan rather than to reflect upon and critique the colonialist policies of the two nations. Pearl Harbor in this way is reduced to a temporal and geographical point that connects the United States and Japan while at the same time disconnecting it from the long, rich, and layered history of the Hawaiʻian Islands.

In his speech at Pearl Harbor, Abe quoted a passage from Ambrose Bierce's poem "To E. S. Salomon," in which the poet celebrated how "the brave respect the brave." The prime minister made the reference to praise the US military for erecting a stone marker for a Japanese pilot who crashed and died at Kaneohe Marine Corp Base when his engine failed on his return from attacking Pearl Harbor on December 7. Americans showed "respect" to this Japanese pilot and commemorated "the bravery of the dead" even as they had just suffered greatly by Japan's surprise attack. For Abe, this exemplified "the spirit of American tolerance" that would be shown in full once the war was over.

His speech, however, failed to note that Bierce, in this poem, was celebrating reconciliation between Northern and Southern soldiers following the Civil War at the expense of memories of slavery and despite the ongoing suppression and deprivation of African American lives and rights in the South. Just as Bierce's poem was crafted to solidify an alliance of the whites between the North and the South, Abe's speech celebrated the "alliance of hope" between the two powers in the Pacific while relegating other integral actors—the nations and peoples of Asia and the Hawaiʻian Islands—to the margins of historical memory.

This disregard for Hawaiʻi's local culture and tradition in the Japanese commemoration of Pearl Harbor effectively conceals the history of US military interventions and colonialism in the Pacific as well. The media accounts, as well as Abe's speech, make it seem as if Hawaiʻi has always been a part of the United States. This amnesia ultimately makes it impossible to understand the fundamental cause of the Japanese attack—that Japan attacked because Hawaiʻi was an *American* territory and because Pearl Harbor was an *American* military base that was busy preparing for war against Japan. In embracing the tolerance of the United States and celebrating an alliance of hope, there is little recognition in Japan that this kind of binational intimacy comes at the expense of suppressing the history of the American empire in the Pacific as well as Japanese settler colonialism in the islands. The colonialism and imperialism that shroud the history and culture of many islands in the Pacific, including Hawaiʻi, are entirely hidden in this story of hopeful alliance between the two nations.

For Franklin D. Roosevelt and many other Americans, December 7, 1941, was the "date which will live in infamy" and thus must never be forgotten. "Remember

Pearl Harbor" became a national slogan, repeated in songs, films, and other media so much that even after the war subsequent generations of Americans continued to use the phrase, as when valuable properties were bought up by Japanese corporations in the 1980s or when passenger planes were forced to crash into World Trade Center buildings and the Pentagon in 2001. Remembering Pearl Harbor in the United States has, over more than seven decades, been accompanied by a mixture of feelings of humiliation, sadness, anger, vengeance, belligerence, and a strong sense of nationalism. The memorials and museums around Pearl Harbor today keep these emotions alive among their visitors. Contemporary incidents, such as terrorism and American military engagements in Iraq and Afghanistan and elsewhere, continue to strengthen the cultural significance of Pearl Harbor in the United States as a symbol for the importance of protecting American values at all cost.[18]

Pearl Harbor in Japan today has different significance. It stands as the beginning, as Hiroshima and Nagasaki serve as the end, of the long and bloody military battles Japan fought and lost. Pearl Harbor thus symbolizes the beginning of the end. Yet it also stands for a renewed beginning made possible by the tolerance shown by the United States after the war. That new beginning, in turn, has changed Pearl Harbor into a stage for reconciliation and for creating a new alliance between two former enemies. According to Prime Minister Abe, Pearl Harbor has become a place where Japan can find its hope and standing in the world under the wing of American hegemony. This may be a useful geopolitical narrative for both nations today. However, like many other forms of popular historical memory, this perspective on Pearl Harbor suppresses both the complexity of global history and the intricacy of local history.

NOTES

1. Tsugitaka Sato et al., *Sekai-she B* (Tokyo: Yamakawa Shuppan, 2011), 332.
2. Ibid.
3. Emily Rosenberg, *A Date Which Will Live* (Durham, NC: Duke University Press, 2003).
4. Newspapers have had an extensive network in Japan and thus a significant social significance over the course of the twentieth century. However, the subscription figure has recently begun to drop. Until recently, the three had a combined circulation of well over 20 million (*Yomiuri Shimbun* alone used to claim it had more than 10 million subscribers).
5. "Enikki no kioku, kurikaesanu. Kyou kaisen no hi" [The memory noted in a picture diary should not be repeated—today is the day when the war started], *Asahi Shimbun*, December 8, 2015, p. 38; "Kaisen no kioku" [Memory of the day when the war started], *Yomiuri Shimbun*, December 8, 2016, p. 30.
6. The textbook quoted here notes the start of World War II as September 1939, when Germany invaded Poland.

7. At the time of Obama's visit there was quite a bit of discussion in the United States to link the two as well. Donald Trump, for example, accused Obama of not mentioning Pearl Harbor during his speech in Hiroshima. "Trump Blasts Obama for not Mentioning Pearl Harbor during Hiroshima Visit," *Japan Times*, May 29, 1996, https://www.japantimes.co.jp/news/2016/05/29/national/trump-blasts-obama-for-not-mentioning-pearl-harbor-during-hiroshima-visit/, accessed August 16, 2016.

8. "Shinjuwan kogeki, Nichibei kaisen 70 nen" [Pearl Harbor Attack: 70th anniversary of Japan-US opening of the war], *Mainichi Shimbun*, December 8, 2011, p. 1.

9. "The Power of Reconciliation: Address by Prime Minister Shinzo Abe Tuesday," December 26, 2016, http://japan.kantei.go.jp/97_abe/statement/201612/1220678_11021.html, accessed August 16, 2017.

10. "Remarks by President Obama and Prime Minister Abe of Japan at Pearl Harbor," December 27, 2016, https://obamawhitehouse.archives.gov/the-press-office/2016/12/28/remarks-president-obama-and-prime-minister-abe-japan-pearl-harbor, accessed August 16, 2016.

11. "Shinjuwan homon, sengo wa owaranai" [Visiting Pearl Harbor—the Post War has not ended], *Asahi Shimbun*, December 29, 2016, p. 12.

12. Von Finn Mayer-Kuckuk, "Als Nächstes nach Nanjing Der japanische Premier Abe gedenkt der Opfer von Pearl Harbor. Doch der Auftritt hat einen Haken: Seine Geste ist nicht stark genug," *Frankfurter Rundschau*, December 28, 2016, http://www.fr.de/politik/meinung/kommentare/kommentar-als-naechstes-nach-nanjing-a-734337, accessed August 27, 2017; An Baijie, "Abe's Visit to Pearl Harbor a Political 'Show,'" *China Daily*, December 28, 2016, http://usa.chinadaily.com.cn/china/2016-12/28/content_27794337.htm, accessed August 31, 2017.

13. "Heiwa he no kimochi wo aratani, Nichibei renkei de kokusai chitusjo wo dou mamoruka" [Renewed thoughts on peace—How to protect world order by Japan-US Alliance], *Yomiuri Shimbun*, August 15, 2017, p. 3.

14. Jonathan Kamakawio'ole Osorio, "Memorializing Pu'uloa and Remembering Pearl Harbor," in Setsu Shigematsu and Keith L. Camacho, eds., *Militarized Currents: Toward a Decolonized Future in Asia and the Pacific* (Minneapolis: University of Minnesota Press, 2010), 5.

15. "Abe shusho, Shinjuwan irei" [Prime Minister Abe in Pearl Harbor to console], *Mainichi Shimbun*, December 29, 2016, p. 28; "Nikkeijin no yakuwari" [Role of Nikkei], *Asahi Shimbun*, December 27, 2016.

16. Yujin Yaguchi, "Longing for Paradise through 'Authentic' Hula Performance in Contemporary Japan," *Japanese Studies* 35, 3 (December 2015), 303–315.

17. For life under martial law see, for example, Beth L. Bailey and David R. Farber, *The First Strange Place: Race and Sex in World War II Hawaii* (Baltimore, MD: Johns Hopkins University Press, 1994).

18. Geoffrey M. White, *Memorializing Pearl Harbor: Unfinished Histories and the Work of Remembrance* (Durham, NC: Duke University Press, 2016).

Contributors

Beth Bailey is Foundation Distinguished Professor; founding director of the Center for Military, War, and Society Studies; and a member of the Department of History at the University of Kansas. Her military history publications include *Understanding the U.S. Wars in Iraq and Afghanistan* (coedited with Richard Immerman), *America's Army: Making the All-Volunteer Force,* and *The First Strange Place: Race and Sex in World War II Hawaii* (coauthored with David Farber).

Nicole Elizabeth Barnes is Andrew W. Mellon Assistant Professor in the Departments of History and Gender, Sexuality, and Feminist Studies at Duke University, where she is also affiliated with the Duke Global Health Institute. She is the author of *Intimate Communities: Wartime Healthcare and the Birth of Modern China, 1937–1945* (Berkeley: University of California Press, 2018).

Christopher Capozzola is a professor of history at the Massachusetts Institute of Technology. He is the author of *Uncle Sam Wants You: World War I and the Making of the Modern American Citizen.* His current work, a history of Filipinos in the US armed forces from the 1890s to the present, will be published in 2020.

Kate Darian-Smith is the executive dean and pro vice chancellor of the College of Arts, Law, and Education at the University of Tasmania. Her publications on Australia in World War II include *On the Home Front: Melbourne in Wartime: 1939–1945*, the relevant chapter in *Cambridge History of Australia*, and numerous chapters and articles on Australian-US relations and the commemoration of the war.

David Farber is the Roy A. Roberts Distinguished Professor at the University of Kansas. His many books include *The First Strange Place: Race and Sex in World War II Hawaii* (coauthored with Beth Bailey), *What They Think of Us: International Perceptions of the United States since 9/11*, *Taken Hostage: The Iran Hostage Crisis and America's First Encounter with Radical Islam*, and *The Age of Great Dreams: America in the 1960s.*

Daniel Immerwahr is an associate professor of history at Northwestern University. His first book, *Thinking Small*, offers a critical account of the US pursuit of grassroots development and won the Organization of American Historians' Merle Curti Award. His second book, *How to Hide an Empire*, is a narrative history of US overseas territory.

Ethan Mark is a university lecturer in modern Japanese history at Leiden University. His publications include "The Perils of Co-Prosperity: Takeda Rintarō, Occupied Southeast Asia, and the Seductions of Postcolonial Empire" (*American Historical Review*, 2014), "'Asia's' Transwar Lineage: Nationalism, Marxism, and 'Greater Asia' in an Indonesian Inflection" (*Journal of Asian Studies*, 2006), and an annotated English translation of Yoshimi Yoshiaki's *Grassroots Fascism: The War Experience of the Japanese People* (2015).

Rana Mitter is a professor of the history and politics of modern China at Oxford University. His book *Forgotten Ally: China's World War II, 1937–1945* won the 2014 Royal United Services Institute's Duke of Westminster Medal for Military Literature and was named a 2013 Book of the Year in six newspapers and a 2014 Choice Outstanding Academic Title. He is a fellow of the British Academy.

Yujin Yaguchi is a professor of American studies at the Graduate School of Arts and Sciences of the University of Tokyo. He has researched tourism and memory at the USS *Arizona* Memorial. He coedited *Shinjuwan wo Kataru, Rekishi, Kioku, Kyōiku (Narrating Pearl Harbor: History, Memory, and Education)*, published by University of Tokyo Press.

Samuel Hideo Yamashita is the Henry E. Sheffield Professor of History at Pomona College. He has written extensively about early modern and modern Japanese intellectual and cultural history. His *Daily Life in Wartime Japan, 1940–1945*, a book based on Yamashita's trove of nearly 200 wartime diaries and three dozen memoirs, was published in the University Press of Kansas's Modern War Studies series in December 2015.

Jeremy A. Yellen is a historian of modern Japan and an assistant professor of Japanese studies at the Chinese University of Hong Kong. His research focuses primarily on wartime-era Japanese diplomatic, political, and transnational history. He is the author of *The Greater East Asia Co-Prosperity Sphere: When Total Empire Met Total War* (Cornell University Press, 2019).

Index